ALSO BY DAVID BELLOS

Is That a Fish in Your Ear?: Translation and the Meaning of Everything

Romain Gary: A Tall Story

Jacques Tati: His Life and Art

Georges Perec: A Life in Words

Balzac Criticism in France, 1850–1900: The Making of a Reputation

EDITOR AND TRANSLATOR

Essays on Seventeenth-Century French Literature, by Leo Spitzer

THE NOVEL
OF THE CENTURY

THE NOVEL
OF THE CENTURY

The Extraordinary Adventure
of *Les Misérables*

DAVID BELLOS

Farrar, Straus and Giroux   New York

Farrar, Straus and Giroux
18 West 18th Street, New York 10011

Copyright © 2017 by David Bellos
All rights reserved
Printed in the United States of America
Originally published in 2017 by Particular Books, an imprint of
Penguin Books, Great Britain
Published in the United States by Farrar, Straus and Giroux
First American edition, 2017

Library of Congress Cataloging-in-Publication Data
Names: Bellos, David, author.
Title: The novel of the century : the extraordinary adventure of Les
    Misérables / David Bellos.
Description: New York : Farrar, Straus and Giroux, 2017. | Includes
    bibliographical references and index.
Identifiers: LCCN 2016049133 | ISBN 9780374223236 (hardback) |
    ISBN 9780374716295 (ebook)
Subjects: LCSH: Hugo, Victor, 1802–1885. Misérables. |
    BISAC: LITERARY CRITICISM / European / French. |
    BIOGRAPHY & AUTOBIOGRAPHY / Literary.
Classification: LCC PQ2286 .B45 2017 | DDC 843/.7—dc23
LC record available at https://lccn.loc.gov/2016049133

Our books may be purchased in bulk for promotional, educational, or business
use. Please contact your local bookseller or the Macmillan Corporate and
Premium Sales Department at 1-800-221-7945, extension 5442, or by e-mail at
MacmillanSpecialMarkets@macmillan.com.

www.fsgbooks.com
www.twitter.com/fsgbooks • www.facebook.com/fsgbooks

1   3   5   7   9   10   8   6   4   2

For my students

Contents

Contents

Author's Note: On Reading
Les Misérables

A lot of people come across the stories of Fantine, Cosette, the Thénardiers, Valjean, Javert, Marius and Gavroche in some form or another when they are young. I don't know why, but I wasn't part of the crowd and I didn't encounter *Les Misérables* until much later on, in circumstances that aren't very creditable in the life of a professor of French. I was actually looking for a light but long book to take with me on a hike, to read by lamplight in the tent, and a one-volume edition of Hugo's novel printed on Bible paper sitting unread on my shelf struck me as having the highest reading-to-weight ratio in the universe. I slipped it into a little bag and took it along. The camping trip on a long-distance trail in the Alps turned out to be a disaster. It rained and it snowed, I caught a cold and then gave up. We trudged down a mountain path and found a hotel, where I wrapped myself in warm blankets and in *Les Misérables*.

I was entranced. I stayed ill rather longer than necessary in order to follow this moving, challenging and immensely engaging tale to the end. I had never before read a work so extraordinarily diverse yet so tightly wound round its central thread. *Les Misérables* may be a monster in size, but there's nothing baggy about it. I don't think I'm allowed to urge you to take sick leave to repeat the experience that I had, nor do I dare suggest you abandon your holiday plans to make time to consume a 1,500-page novel in one gulp. But I doubt you'll regret it if you do.

Fortunately, there is a more practical way to enjoy Hugo's novel within a busy life. *Les Misérables* consists of five 'parts', divided respectively into 8, 8, 8, 15 and 9 'books', making 48 in all. Each 'book' consists of a number of chapters, varying from none at all (Part V, Book 4, conventionally designated V.4, counts as a chapter all on its own) to 22 (III.8, the longest 'book', which ends with the dramatic denouement of the ambush at 50–52, Boulevard de l'Hôpital). The divisions weren't made until the final preparation of the manuscript for printing in the winter of 1861–2, and Hugo never let on, or perhaps never consciously registered, what the underlying numerical design of his book was. But the fact is that *Les Misérables* is made of exactly 365 chapters. You can therefore read one chapter a day – most of them are quite short – and complete Hugo's vast novel of love and revolution in the time that it takes planet Earth to complete its revolution around the sun.

'Everything in a work of art is an act of the will,' Hugo wrote in an introduction to his own son's translation of Shakespeare into French.[1] What makes *Les Misérables* such an amazing work of art is that despite its length, its complexity and its vast scope, every detail and every dimension – even if not made explicit – was designed, calculated and decided by the author.

ℊ

Nineteenth-century France was a turbulent and frequently violent place, but it was also uncommonly generous to the rest of the world. From the Revolution of 1789 to the dawn of the twentieth century it gave away many treasures for free – the Rights of Man, decimal currency, knowledge of hieroglyphics, photography, cinema, the Statue of Liberty, pasteurized milk . . . the list could go on and on. Its painters and composers set new standards that we still admire, and its writers still dominate our ideas of what poetry and fiction can be. But among all the gifts France has given to Hollywood, Broadway and the common reader wherever she may be, *Les Misérables* stands out as the greatest by far. This reconstruction of how this extraordinary novel arose, how it was published, what it means and what it has become is my way of saying thank you to France.

Translations and References

There are many translations into English of Victor Hugo's novel, done in different countries at different times. In this book, quotations from *Les Misérables* are taken from the most recent translation, by Christine Donougher, published by Penguin in 2013, with occasional adaptations of my own, which are signalled when they arise.

References are expressed in alternating Roman and Arabic numerals referring to Part, Book, and Chapter number, so the rough place of a quotation can be found in any complete edition. The page number following takes you directly to Christine Donougher's English translation.

Translations of other sources quoted are my own, unless otherwise indicated in footnotes or in the works cited at the end of this book.

France After Waterloo

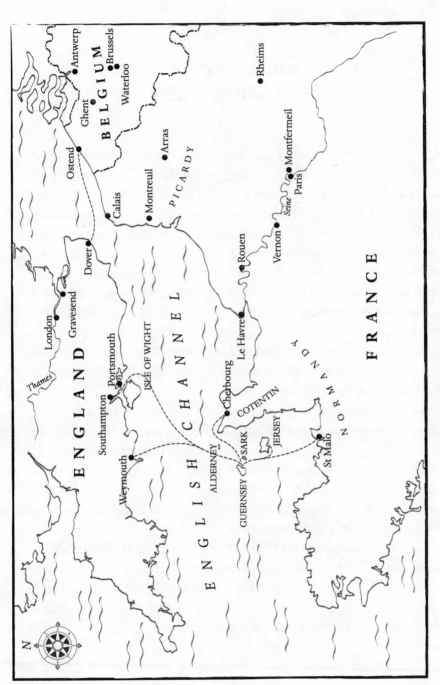

The Journey of *Les Misérables*

Introduction: The Journey of Les Misérables

The *Commodore Clipper*, a 14,000-ton roll-on roll-off ferry, leaves Portsmouth early in the morning, glides through the naval dock-yards at walking pace, gathers speed as the Isle of Wight passes on the starboard side and reaches twenty-two knots in the open waters of the English Channel. The swell can toss small boats up and down, but the ferry's stabilizers deceive you into thinking the sea is made of rippled gelatine. Before long, the westernmost tip of the Cotentin peninsula comes into view; then the ship clears Cap de la Hague to port, heads for the low bar of Sark and, after skirting round Herm and picking its way among jagged rocks breaking the surface of a blue-green sea, enters the harbour of St Peter Port, on the island of Guernsey. The countryside around it is lush and green. The first daffodils bloom before January is out.

Victor Hugo landed here at around ten in the morning of 31 October 1855, after a shorter but rougher crossing in wind and rain on a 300-ton paddle steamer from St Helier, in Jersey. But even the tiny *Courier* was too big to dock at St Peter Port in those days. The poet and his party had to clamber down ladders into small boats to be rowed ashore. Dock hands took care of the baggage, including the all-important manuscript trunk.[1]

Anyone landing in much greater comfort and safety on the *Commodore Clipper* nowadays sees much the same quaint townscape as Hugo did. It's only a short walk from the new harbour to the steps up to High Street, and from there the same lane takes you to Hauteville Street, lined with three-storey town houses built in the earlier part of the nineteenth century. Halfway up is a large, plain, double-fronted mansion now marked by a tricolour flag and a nameplate declaring it to be the property of the City of Paris and the *Maison de Victor Hugo*. That's because Hauteville House, at St Peter Port, Guernsey, is the unlikely location where the most extraordinary novel ever written in French was made.

How did a tiny feudal outpost of the British Crown come to serve as the workbench for a vast panorama of nineteenth-century France? There's barely a word that refers to the Channel Islands in all of *Les Misérables*, yet it is hard to imagine how it could have been brought to completion without the sanctuary provided by Hauteville House. The story of the long-drawn-out composition of this very long book is almost as dramatic as the story it tells.

Victor Hugo didn't land on Guernsey in 1855 in search of a comfortable writer's retreat, but because he had nowhere else to go. Despite his celebrity status on the European stage, he was a migrant and a refugee – in the language of the day, a *proscrit*. *Les Misérables* is a novel of the poor, the downtrodden and the outcast. It was expanded on Guernsey from a draft into a masterpiece by a man who was an outcast himself.

From the day of its publication on 4 April 1862, *Les Misérables* has remained at the forefront of bestseller lists the world over. It has been read in French and in hundreds of translations by millions of people in any country you care to name. It was turned into a play within weeks and has been adapted for radio and the cinema screen over the last century and a half more than any other literary work. But the unique adventure of *Les Misérables* as a global cultural resource did not come about by chance. From his roof terrace with its wonderful view of Sark and the sea, Victor Hugo always intended his great work to speak far beyond the borders of France, and beyond the pages of a book. Most plans to conquer the whole world with a story go awry. *Les Misérables* is a wonderful exception.

But the popularity of the story and the characters Hugo created and their frequent reuse in mass-market entertainments have had a depressing effect on attitudes towards his book. Judging *Les Misérables* by the sometimes inept adaptations of it in comic strips, cartoons and stage musicals, serious readers have often turned up their noses at a work they assume to fall below the level of great art. It's not a scientific survey, but I think it's significant that a higher proportion of baristas and office staff than literature professors I've met have read *Les Misérables* from end to end. However, the modern division of 'literary' and 'popular' fiction had hardly been invented when Hugo wrote it. 'I do not know whether it will be read by all,' he told the publisher of the Italian translation, 'but I wrote it for everyone.' It did not occur to him that a masterpiece could not be a blockbuster too, and he saw no reason why 'everyone' should not be served the same fare as literary connoisseurs. To have done anything less would have been contrary to the moral and political aims of his book.

g

Les Misérables is divided into five parts. Part I, 'Fantine', focuses on an abandoned single mother who loses her job and falls into prostitution, a brush with the law and an early death. Part II, 'Cosette', foregrounds Fantine's daughter, who is cruelly exploited by foster-parents and then rescued by the novel's hero, who brings her up to become a young lady. Part III, 'Marius', features a middle-class student who joins a group of political idealists and fights with them in a failed attempt to overthrow the monarchy. Part IV, 'The Idyll of Rue Plumet and the Epic of Rue Saint-Denis', alternates between the love affair of Cosette and Marius that blossoms in the garden of a house in Rue Plumet and the students' barricade in a small street off Rue Saint-Denis, in the heart of old Paris. Part V is entitled 'Jean Valjean' after the ex-convict whose life-story from the age of forty-five to his death twenty years later is the narrative backbone of the novel.

Valjean's life before 1815 is told in a few paragraphs. A sturdy, uneducated peasant from Faverolles (a village in Brie, to the east of Paris), he is sentenced to hard labour in his mid-twenties for stealing a loaf of bread. He emerges from prison after nineteen years inside, and the novel really begins with his release a few weeks after the Battle of Waterloo. Rejected by innkeepers in a small town on his route north from Toulon because he is an ex-convict, Valjean is offered hospitality by the local bishop, Monseigneur Myriel. He is overwhelmed by the unexpected kindness of the priest and resolves to become a better man. Valjean uses the bishop's charitable gift to go into business under the assumed name of M. Madeleine at Montreuil-sur-Mer, a small town on the Channel coast. He makes a fortune, earns respect and is pressed into accepting the position of mayor. That is where he encounters Fantine.

Fantine's back-story is more extended. A child of the streets from Montreuil-sur-Mer, she goes to Paris to find work and then becomes the lover of a heartless student, Tholomyès, with whom she has a child. In 1817, he abandons her without a penny. She returns to her hometown because she has heard there are jobs to be had, leaving her child to be fostered by the Thénardiers, innkeepers she comes across at the village of Montfermeil. (All the place names are real and can be found on a map of France.) Fantine has a few months of relative comfort in her factory job but she is sacked when her supervisor discovers she has an illegitimate child. She tries to survive on sewing but when piecework rates sink, she has no choice but to go on the streets. One winter's night, she is accosted by a middle-class lout called Bamatabois. She fights back and is arrested by the local police chief, Javert. Mayor Madeleine (that is to say, Jean Valjean) intervenes to save her from a prison sentence. When he learns that her plight is the indirect result of his own factory's policy, he promises to look after her child.

At Montreuil, Javert, who had formerly worked as a prison guard, suspects he has seen the mayor before and is even more suspicious when Madeleine displays formidable strength in rescuing a local carter, Fauchelevent, from under his overturned waggon. These suspicions as to the true identity of the taciturn factory boss are swept away when a vagrant, arrested for stealing an apple-tree branch, is identified as the missing ex-convict Valjean. Madeleine now faces a terrible choice: to let the vagrant take the rap, or to give himself up. After a night of soul-searching, he bursts into the courthouse in Arras and declares his true identity. He is sent back to the hard-labour jail in Toulon for life.

He makes a daring escape and recovers the savings he had put in a buried chest. He persuades the Thénardiers to let him take Cosette away from their brutal care and settles in a quiet corner of Paris, where he brings her up as his daughter (she never learns his real name and calls him 'father'). He lives modestly, but in emulation of the good bishop who had transformed his moral perspective, he never fails to give alms to the poor. Rumours about the existence of a 'rich pauper' in the area reach the ears of the newly appointed chief detective – none other than Javert, promoted from his previous position at Montreuil-sur-Mer. Javert sets a trap and nearly catches Valjean, who escapes the dragnet by climbing over a high wall and hoisting up Cosette after him.

Valjean and Cosette don't know where they are in the dark, but suddenly a man recognizes them: it is Fauchelevent, now working as a gardener in the Convent of the Perpetual Adoration. He is the only man tolerated in this all-female cloister, but out of gratitude for the former mayor who had saved his life he takes on Valjean as assistant gardener, claiming him as his younger brother, Ultime. Cosette is admitted to the convent school, where she is given a regular education. The pair live on in their impenetrable sanctuary for five years and leave it only when Cosette has turned from a girl into a beautiful young woman.

Valjean then rents a well-hidden house in Rue Plumet. On walks in the Luxembourg Gardens, Cosette is noticed by a handsome student, Marius Pontmercy. Marius's back-story is more elaborate and told at greater length. He is the son of a soldier in Napoleon's army who while lying wounded after the Battle of Waterloo was saved but also robbed by a camp-follower called Thénardier. His mother had died when he was an infant, and his father, constantly absent on military campaigns abroad, had had no choice but to let him be cared for by his maternal grandfather, Gillenormand, an aged eccentric who insists on dressing, speaking and behaving as if the French Revolution never happened. He hands on to Marius his own reactionary and royalist views, but when the young man discovers who his father really was, he becomes a passionate admirer of Napoleon Bonaparte. Marius picks a fight with his grandfather and storms out of the house to live on his own. He is befriended by a group of student activists who call themselves 'The Friends of the ABC' – but he also falls head over heels in love with the girl he has seen in the park.

The Thénardiers, meanwhile, have lost their inn and moved to Paris, where they live in the same squalid lodging house where Valjean and Cosette had lived years before, and where Marius now also resides. They use their daughters, Azelma and Éponine, to operate a scam: they hand letters written under false identities to well-off people in the streets, hoping to elicit charitable gifts.[2] Valjean falls for one such approach, and agrees to visit the allegedly starving family under one of its many pseudonyms. He takes Cosette along with him so she can experience the practice of giving alms to the needy. The paupers' neighbour, who is none other than Marius, sees his beloved in the room next door through a gap in the wall. After her departure, he also hears the Thénardiers plotting to rob the white-haired gentleman because they reckon he is a millionaire. Marius is in a bind: he has to save Cosette's father from an ambush, but he also realizes that the crook in the next room is the man who saved his own father's life. When Valjean returns to complete his charitable gift, he is tied to a chair and tortured by Thénardier and his sinister gang. Marius has alerted the police to the planned ambush and lets off a warning shot. In the ensuing arrest of the criminals, Valjean, who remains Javert's most wanted prey, escapes yet again.

Marius doesn't know who the beautiful young woman he so desires really is or how to find her again. However, Thénardier's daughter Éponine has a crush on him as well as contacts in the underworld. She leads Marius to the house in Rue Plumet where Cosette lives. A touching teenage romance ensues, through late-night meetings in the lush and secluded garden of the house.

Meanwhile, unrest is brewing among the working people of Paris. Riots erupt after the funeral of a well-known republican general. However, Marius realizes that his grandfather will never allow him to marry Cosette; worse still, Cosette reports that her father plans to move to England to keep her safe in case the looming strife turns into a violent revolution. In lovelorn despair, Marius throws in his lot with his student friends and goes to get himself killed on a barricade. Valjean intercepts the correspondence between the two lovers and decides that, however much it pains him to lose his adopted daughter, he has a duty to save the life of the man she loves. He sets off to bring Marius back from the barricade.

At the doomed barricade – the last one standing, with no wider support – the students' leader makes an impassioned speech about their cause, and then government troops begin their assault. Javert, who has infiltrated the revolutionary group as a police spy, is unmasked and condemned to death. The task of execution is entrusted to Valjean, but instead of shooting his persistent pursuer, he lets him go free. The policeman can't understand the generosity of a man he can only see as criminal scum. With his world turned upside down, he throws himself into the Seine.

Marius is badly wounded in the battle of the barricade, and there is no easy escape from the army and the police who now control the city. Valjean puts Marius over his shoulder and clambers down a manhole into a sewer. The terrifying trudge through the putrid tunnels beneath the city is the most dramatic and biblical episode in Valjean's long story of redemption.

Marius recovers from his injuries. His grandfather accepts him back into the family home and gives his blessing to his marrying Cosette. She brings her husband a handsome dowry provided by her 'father' from the money he had saved from his business career and kept safe in a hole in the ground for ten years.

Valjean's story is almost over. His last trial is to decide whether to reveal his true identity to Marius or to live as an anonymous hanger-on in what is now a respectable middle-class home. He chooses to reveal who he really is and to withdraw into a monkish existence in a small apartment on his own. Within a couple of years, his health fails, and he fades away. The novel ends in 1835 with his burial in the cemetery of Père Lachaise. The epitaph on his gravestone has now been erased by wind and rain.

§

The overall shape of the story of *Les Misérables* fits a pattern familiar from novels of all ages, but especially of its own period. *Madame Bovary* (1857), for example, also tells a life-story from near the beginning to the end. *Great Expectations* (1861) spends more time on the early years of Pip's life and less on its later decades, but it's designed in the same general way, on a thread of chronology wound round a central character. *Crime and Punishment* (1866), on the other hand, doesn't tell us much about Raskolnikov's childhood and upbringing, but it follows him through from his crime to his redemption in Siberia decades later. As a 'life-story novel', *Les Misérables* is a characteristic work of its time.

It also has in common with other novels of the period – *War and Peace* appeared between 1863 and 1868, *Moby-Dick* in 1851 – the fact that its main story could have been told in a much, much shorter book. But none of these great works aim to tell a story and nothing more, and Hugo aimed to do almost everything it was possible to do in novel form. Like Tolstoy, he includes essays on the meaning of historical events (though none so disappointing as the last chapter of *War and Peace*); like Dostoevsky, he shares with us the drama of the soul; like Dickens, he wants to show us all of what it meant to be poor. The summary of the story of *Les Misérables* is like a path through a forest – but the forest is as much the subject of the novel as the path.

The path is nonetheless the way forward. It leads from a (small) crime and (disproportionate) punishment to conversion and then adherence to a demanding concept of righteous conduct. Valjean is not a complicated, mixed, self-critical or tragic hero to put alongside Raskolnikov or Ivan Karamazov – in a sense, he is not a 'novelistic' character at all. He is not a saint, either, but a model of a new man.

Valjean does not represent directly any particular political or religious position. What he models is the potential that the poorest and most wretched have to become worthy citizens. His repeated victories over physical, moral and emotional obstacles make him a hero, of course, but they also assert, against the attitudes prevalent at the time, that moral progress is possible for all, in every social sphere.

After his conversion Valjean is a generous and charitable man, and his epic struggle is to abide by the commandment to be kind even when tempted by anger, resentment, jealousy and revenge. Through the character of Jean Valjean *Les Misérables* gives stunning reality to an ideal we might otherwise dismiss as naive.

That's why Hugo's novel remains as meaningful today as when it came out 150 years ago. It is a work of reconciliation – between the classes, but also between the conflicting currents that turn our own lives into storms. It is not a reassuring tale of the triumph of good over evil, but a demonstration of how hard it is to be good.

PART ONE
Crimes and Punishments

1.

Victor Hugo Opens His Eyes

Victor-Marie Hugo was born in 1802 in the garrison town of Besançon, where his father was stationed. At that time France was under the rule of Napoleon Bonaparte, a Corsican soldier whose meteoric career had brought him to be commander in chief and, from 1799, the inspirational leader of a nation turned upside down by the Revolution of 1789 and now asserting itself on the European stage.

Hugo's father and uncle were both soldiers in Napoleon's armies and rose to high rank in the campaigns that brought almost all of continental Europe under French rule for a time. Napoleon was crowned emperor at Notre-Dame Cathedral in 1804 and won more great victories after that. The invasion of Russia in 1812 was the turning point. Unable to hold Moscow through the winter, the Great Army began a retreat that turned into a rout. The first French Empire came to its end on 18 June 1815, at the Battle of Waterloo. Napoleon was banished to St Helena, and a Bourbon monarch, Louis XVIII, was restored to the French throne.

Hugo was an intellectually precocious thirteen-year-old when Napoleon fell. He had a great gift for Latin and a prodigious talent for writing fixed-meter verse in French. His father's fortunes shrivelled on the fall of the Napoleonic world, and Hugo left school soon after to earn a living by his pen, which was not an easy thing to do. But his years of scraping by on odd jobs and small commissions did not last long. He was soon recognized as a 'sublime child' for the verses he wrote; he won prizes and acquired royal patronage too. He wrote a breathless short novel about a slave revolt in Haiti culled from secondary sources and also dashed off a seafaring yarn before he ever smelled salt water. Hugo soon became a leading figure in a group of writers and artists of his own generation who called themselves 'Romantics', and set about conquering the theatre, the highest rung on the narrow ladder of literary fame. He was already a Parisian celebrity when his tragedy *Hernani* was performed in 1830, and its unconventional treatment of the strict rules of classical French theatre caused a great stir. He then turned his hand to historical fiction, a genre made fashionable throughout Europe by Walter Scott. *Notre-Dame de Paris* (also known as *The Hunchback of Notre Dame*) appeared in 1831 and was an immense success. Its publication came just a year before the death of the German poet Goethe, the undisputed eminence of European literature for the preceding half-century. Victor Hugo was ready and willing to take on his mantle of European genius-in-chief.

Hugo's poetry and plays of the 1830s confirmed his prominent position and he was elected to a seat in the Académie française, making him one of France's forty 'immortals' at the early age of thirty-nine. His standing was such that in 1845 he was appointed to the Chambre des pairs, the Upper House of the French parliament, making him a *pair de France* or 'lord of the realm'. A splendid career crowned by a spectacular honour for a man still so young. How much higher could he go?

He didn't. Between his maiden speech as a peer and his wet and windy landing on Guernsey in 1855 came ten turbulent years that turned him from a pillar of the establishment into an exile, from a brilliant careerist into a stand-alone protester, from a man of the middle into a spokesman for progressive causes. The social and political transformation of Victor Hugo accompanied and affected profoundly the story of transformation that became *Les Misérables*.

Hugo lost a great deal from the political changes that took place in France between 1848 and 1852, and though he ceased for a while to be a wealthy man, he never became poor in the way Valjean, Fantine, Cosette and the Thénardiers were. In that respect the central thread of *Les Misérables* is not drawn out of the life of Victor Hugo. On the other hand, he knew quite a lot about the material conditions of people far less fortunate than he was. Some of that knowledge he gleaned from reading books, surveys and reports, but he learned it most of all from what he saw.

ℐ

Near the peak of his glory in January 1841, when he lived in a spectacular apartment in Place Royale chock full of antique bric-a-brac (the square is now called Place des Vosges, and the apartment is another *Maison de Victor Hugo*), he went to a dinner party where an army general held forth on the pointlessness of pursuing the conquest of Algeria (first undertaken in 1830, as a punitive raid). Hugo was walking down Rue Taitbout in search of a cab to take him home on that wintry night when a well-dressed young man in the street picked up a handful of snow and shoved it down the back of a girl in a low-cut dress. She screamed out loud and then fell upon the middle-class lout. He hit back, and the noise of the scuffle alerted the police. They ran up and took not the man but the girl into custody. 'Come along with us, you'll get six months for that.'

This story comes from *Choses vues* ('Things Seen'), a precious rag-bag of reportage, memoir, gossip and (literally) things seen to which Hugo kept adding all his life. Unlike other pieces, this report is in the third person, referring to the author not as 'I' but as 'V. H.'. It turns out that it was actually written by Hugo's wife Adèle and put in the wrong folder in the ocean of manuscripts that Hugo left on his death. When was it written? Perhaps shortly after the event, but more probably in 1861 or 1862, when Adèle was drafting a memoir of her life with Hugo, published a few months after *Les Misérables*. Hugo cooperated in the endeavour and allowed his wife to scavenge his memory over dinners on Guernsey. At Hauteville House, as at most other times, Victor Hugo was not averse to talking about himself.

In the text Adèle wrote down, V. H. accompanies the girl to the police station, hesitates to say who he is at first, then decides to identify himself as a member of the Académie française in the hope that pulling rank would stop an injustice being done. He asked the police to release the girl because the offence committed had not been committed by her. V. H. signed a statement, and the girl was let off. She couldn't stop saying how grateful she was. '"How good the gentleman is! My God, how good he is!" These unfortunate women are astonished and grateful not only when you take pity on them; they are just as grateful when you are just.'[1]

Except for telling the story to Adèle – perhaps twenty years later, or perhaps that very night – Hugo never boasted about his generous intervention. What he did do was to attach this episode to the life of Jean Valjean, who saves Fantine from a spell in jail after an identical assault on a snowy night in Montreuil.[2]

There were plenty of poor people to be seen on the streets of Paris, and no shortage of petty thieves either. But Hugo tried to see through the scenes that he encountered and make out the social and political meanings they had. Here's one that he wrote up on a sheet of paper that he put away in 'Things Seen'. It is going too far to call it the inspiration for the story of Valjean, but it certainly belongs to the material from which *Les Misérables* was made:

Yesterday . . . I was on my way to the Chambre des pairs. It was a fine day but very cold despite the noonday sun. In Rue de Tournon I saw a man being led away by two soldiers. He was fair-haired, pale, thin and drawn; about thirty, coarse canvas trousers, bare and bruised feet in clogs with bloody linens wrapped around his ankles in lieu of stockings; a short blouse with mud stains on the back, showing that he usually slept on the streets; no hat and hair standing on end. He had a loaf under his arm. People around said he'd stolen the loaf and that was why he was being taken away . . .

A coach was standing outside the barracks door. It was a covered coach with a coat of arms and a ducal crown on its lanterns . . . The windows were raised, but you could see the interior upholstered in buttoned yellow silk. The man staring at the coach drew my own eyes towards it. Inside was a dazzlingly beautiful woman with a fresh white complexion, wearing a pink hat and a black velvet dress, laughing and playing with a charming sixteen-month-old baby swaddled in ribbons and lace and furs.

The woman did not see the fearsome man who was looking at her.

It made me think.

That man was no longer a man in my eyes but the spectre of *la misère*, of poverty, the misshapen and lugubrious apparition in broad daylight, in broad sunlight, of a revolution that is still deep in the shadows, but is on its way. Previously, the poor could rub shoulders with the rich, such a ghost could meet such brilliance; but each did not look at the other. They went on their way. Things could go on like that for a long time. But once this man realizes that this woman exists while the woman does not notice that the man is there, a catastrophe is inevitable.[3]

The loaf stolen by the man who looked at the Duchess, like the one stolen by Valjean in *Les Misérables*, was not the stick loaf we now think of as 'French bread'. The white-flour baguette was not invented until 1838, and it remained a high-priced specialty for decades after that. The standard loaf of the poor in nineteenth-century France was an oval weighing four and a half pounds, with a thick black crust and heavy grey meal inside. Not the sort of thing you would want to eat nowadays.

Hugo was probably not alone in fearing that injustice as well as the mental gulf between rich and poor would lead to a social catastrophe. Unlike many of his contemporaries, however, he adhered to no particular plan for averting it – he wasn't a Fourierist or a Saint-Simonian or a socialist, nor even a convinced republican yet. He also had no idea how soon the catastrophe would come.

31 August 1847
A pieceworker brings his master, a shoemaker, a job for which the contract price is three francs. The master finds the work shoddy and won't give the man more than fifty *sous*.[4] The pieceworker refuses to accept it. A row ensues. The master throws the worker out. He

comes back with some fellows and breaks the cobbler's windows with stones. A crowd gathers. A riot . . . The whole of Paris is in chaos.

I do not like these symptoms. When there's poison in the blood even a small pimple can set off the malady. A mere graze can lead to an amputated limb.[5]

In the 1840s, France was a constitutional monarchy with a legislative body elected by male taxpayers alone. Because there was no tax on incomes, gains, inheritances or consumption, taxes were levied exclusively on property, and every voter was therefore an owner of a building or of land. The charge of a government responsible to an assembly representing the well-off defined in this way was to maintain order among those less privileged than the voters it served. That's to say, improving the lives of the ragged masses was of interest only if it helped to head off civil strife. The Paris poor were an edgy crowd, always on the brink of disturbing the peace. What caused the common people to be disorderly so often? Were they idle by nature? Irremediably bad? Was poverty the cause of their frightening behaviour, or was their behaviour the reason they stayed poor?

Despite a long history of political and military conflict between them, England and France were constantly borrowing ideas from each other. The *Encyclopédie* of Diderot and d'Alembert, for example, the great monument of Enlightenment thought, began as an imitation of Chambers's *Cyclopaedia*. Its article on 'poverty', however, strikes modern readers as something less than enlightened, for it begins by berating the poor for their own plight. But it turns this conventional attitude around by then attacking monarchs for creating the conditions that turn the poor into such lamentable folk:

Few souls are strong enough not to be laid low and eventually debased by poverty. Common folk are unbelievably stupid. I do not know what magical illusion makes them blind to their current poverty and to the even greater poverty that awaits them in old age.

8

Poverty is the mother of great crimes; sovereigns are responsible for making people *misérable* and it is they who will be judged in this world and the next for the crimes that poverty commits.

A more substantial contribution to the European debate on the 'problem of the poor' comes from the writings of an English cleric, Robert Malthus. And he was even less sympathetic to the lower classes than the French contributor to the *Encyclopédie*.

Malthus's *Essay on the Principle of Population*, first published in 1798 but read for many decades after that, claims that, absent the benefits of education and refinement, human beings are naturally idle and can be roused to productive labour only by a pressing need. Its second premise is that the uneducated and unrefined always take the easiest path. Given the opportunity, poor people steal what they need instead of working to acquire it. In Malthus's dim view of human nature, the poor constitute a different species. Few of his contemporaries yet dared imagine that the overall size of the cake to be shared out could be increased or that poverty itself might be relieved by agricultural, industrial and technological improvements that had barely begun. For that reason, even people who were not convinced by Malthus's grim analysis of the unequal race between population and the land's capacity to feed it took it for granted that crime and poverty were two sides of the same coin. The 'lower classes' were most often seen as 'dangerous classes' in England and in France.

But there were other forces at work. Support for the 'lame and the halt' had long been the responsibility of the church. Malthus and the *Encyclopédie* both expressed in their different ways profound scepticism, if not outright hostility, to the alleviation of the suffering of the poor by religious institutions. In England, however, there was a separate tradition with no equivalent in France. Laws dating from the reign of Elizabeth I obliged parish councils to give 'outdoor relief' to the sick, the disabled, abandoned children and the old. These 'Poor Laws' did not apply to the ill-paid, ill-clad, ill-fed and ill-housed but only to people we might now call victims of life events. Towards the end of the eighteenth century, a change arose in the way the laws were applied. The new rule required parish councils to give relief to labourers whose earnings fell below the poverty line and to unemployed men, including those who were fit for work. This administrative tweak had immense long-term effect on social policy, and it also changed the way the word 'poor' was understood. It came to refer to people who for whatever reason did not have enough to live on – the modern meaning of the word 'poor' (*misérable* in French), replacing the older sense of 'victim of misfortune'. The gradual but fundamental shift in meaning from 'laid low by ill fortune' to 'short of money' ran into a wall of resistance from entrenched economic, moral and political positions, and it took a century and more for them to be overcome. *Les Misérables* was a key element in the history of that long-drawn-out change.

The French Revolution established new political rights for all its citizens, but it did not have much to say about the economic origins of poverty. Article 21 of the Declaration of the Rights of Man, for example, reiterates the traditional distinction between the needy (orphans, the disabled, the sick and the aged) and everybody else: 'Society owes subsistence to citizens in misfortune, either by providing them with work, or by giving means of existence to those who are not fit to work'.[6] Had the article been put into practice it would simply have brought France into line with the Poor Laws of England as they had been for two centuries already, by providing income support to the destitute with no opportunity to work ('citizens in misfortune') and leaving the able-bodied and the unemployed to fend for themselves. But this was just a paper reform. In revolutionary France the state had no institutions or resources to provide alms to those who had no prospect of supporting themselves. As under the old regime, in towns large and small there were beggars on the corner of every street.

The ever more visible gap between needs and resources was filled to some extent by private charitable institutions, many of them acting on behalf of or in association with the church, and also by individual philanthropists. In *Les Misérables*, Bishop Myriel is an exemplar of private charity of that kind. He donates 90 per cent of his stipend to a range of philanthropic institutions, not all of which are specifically religious ones, some giving care to unmarried mothers ('Societies for Maternal Charity'), others giving education to 'girls in need' or looking after foundlings, orphans and hospital patients.[7] These charities are chosen by Hugo on Myriel's behalf, so to speak, because Fantine's life might have been less harsh and less short had she been helped by any of them. However, many potential donors to charitable enterprises were held back by a worry that the ideas of Malthus made sharper and more pressing: how can an association or a benevolent individual provide assistance to people in need without giving a free ride to the idle and the bad? Even those who rejected Malthus's prediction of an ever-rising tide of scum needed guidance to allow them to distinguish 'honest poor folk' from the dangerous and inherently criminal underclass that could so quickly turn into a mob.

People face the same issue nowadays under a different guise. With a choice of over a thousand international organizations seeking to help poor countries (and the poor people who live there) by supporting development programmes, health programmes, environmental programmes, educational programmes, how do we make our charitable donations do only good and not exacerbate the problems they were meant to abate?

One answer among many was provided 200 years ago by Joseph-Marie de Gérando in a widely read 'how-to' book, *Le Visiteur du pauvre* (*The Visitor of the Poor*). The main solution he offered to members of the moneyed middle class was to put prejudice and distaste aside and to call on all the people in the same street who appeared to need help. Men and women of means should get to know 'poor people' as individuals and make their own judgement as to what kind of poor people they were. Paternalistic, condescending and also slightly sinister, a 'visitor of the poor' in de Gérando's construction would become a benefactor of the honest and a corrector of the undeserving. But there is one important thing to be said in defence of *Le Visiteur du pauvre*: those who followed its recommendations would at least become less ignorant, and presumably less fearful, of the other side. It is a small step, but a step nonetheless, towards the social reconciliation that Hugo called for forty years later in *Les Misérables*.

'Poor visiting' is given a key role in the main narrative of Hugo's novel. Valjean goes to pray in the church of Saint-Sulpice and is approached by a waif with a letter that begs him to visit her starving family. He agrees to do so. Éponine rushes back to the Gorbeau tenement to announce the imminent arrival of a 'millionaire'. Valjean goes back to Rue Plumet to collect goods and also Cosette, for he wants her to accompany him to learn what it is to be a visitor of the poor. At this first interview, Valjean willingly hands over warm clothes, woollen stockings and blankets. When he is asked for money, however, he holds back. He's as wary as any other bourgeois of his age of being the victim of benefit fraud.[8] It turns out that the wisdom of de Gérando and all the cunning of Jean Valjean were not sufficient to pierce the Thénardiers' scam. On his next visit to the tenement Valjean is ambushed by a whole gang.

If private charity was no real solution to the 'problem of poverty' in France, the Poor Laws of England also seemed powerless to thin the ranks of the ragged to be seen on the streets. Indeed, although England was at that time ahead of France in industrial development and material wealth, it was even further in front in the number of really poor people it had. On a brief visit to London, the political philosopher Alexis de Tocqueville observed that, despite its galloping prosperity, it was the European capital of poverty too. How did that come about? The fault lay in the system, he wrote – in the entitlement to support fostered by Poor Laws inherited from an earlier age. Tocqueville stepped into a dispute over a reform of these ancient practices and took the side of those who wanted to do away with them altogether. Like many others he was convinced that abolition of 'outdoor relief' for the able-bodied would cause the number of poor people to fall.[9] The out-turn of the political debate was not simple abolition, however, but a new kind of Poor Law that drove a wedge between people who didn't have enough money to live on – the poor, in the modern sense of the word – and *paupers*, who were to be removed from public sight. Income support for the underpaid was indeed abolished, but so was direct payment to the 'victims of misfortune', who were now to be cared for in institutions called poor houses, or workhouses. These were designed to be as unpleasant as possible. The rationale behind the considerable expense of constructing them was to provide a standard of living lower than any that could be had from work: the workhouse should never tempt the able-bodied to abandon toil, however pitiful the wages of honest labour came to be. So horrible and humiliating were they that some indigents, like Mrs Higden in Dickens's *Our Mutual Friend*, preferred to die on the road rather than enter the doors of a poor house for their last days.[10]

Charles Dickens, who had spent his teenage years putting shoeblack into pots in a rat-infested warehouse at Hungerford Stairs, was outraged by the new law. He blasted back at it in his story of a boy brought up in the workhouse. *Oliver Twist* appeared in 1837, came out in French translation in 1841 and has never been out of print in either language since then.[11]

The workhouse is an instance of the cross-Channel traffic that makes the stories of England and France so similar and yet not the same. The idea came from the *dépôts de mendicité* ('beggars' repositories'), prison-like dormitories set up by Napoleon in 1808 to put beggars, vagrants, lunatics and the disabled out of public sight. The scheme may have had a cosmetic effect in town centres, but it made no impact on the number of indigents and beggars in France. It was also open to abuse, as documented by Stendhal in his novel *Red and Black*: the unscrupulous M. Valenod, who runs the *dépôt de mendicité* at Verrières, makes a fortune from spending less to feed the inmates than he receives in fees from the state. Similar scandals in real life led to a gradual abandonment of the nationwide network of *dépôts* in France. There were hardly any left by the 1840s – when workhouses had spread to almost every English town.

But *Oliver Twist* takes for granted the transition from poverty to a life of crime. Oliver leaves the workhouse and joins a band of junior thieves working for Fagin, who resells what the boys steal. Oliver is mentored in scarf-snatching by Jack Dawkins, the 'Artful Dodger', a wisecracking Cockney who wears a (filched) top hat. Dickens's happy scamp came to play a key role in the later history of the reception of *Les Misérables*. In 1960, Lionel Bart, a musical prodigy from London's East End, devised a stage musical based on *Oliver Twist*. When *Oliver!* had another run in London in 1977, the French composer Alain Boublil went to see it. 'As soon as the Artful Dodger came on stage,' he recalled, 'Gavroche came to mind. It was like a blow to the solar plexus. I started seeing all the characters of *Les Misérables* – Valjean, Javert, Gavroche, Cosette, Marius and Éponine – in my mind's eye . . .'[12] Dickens's warm-hearted vision of good and evil among the riffraff on London's streets turned out to be the first prompting for the invention of a musical version of *Les Misérables* that has given a fresh impetus to Hugo's novel over the last thirty years.

Oliver Twist is the first major work of literature that puts a child at its centre, and among the first to introduce the colourful language of the underclass, including many words borrowed from cant, or thieves' slang. What brings it closer still to *Les Misérables* is its generosity of spirit. It is no mere coincidence that an adaptation of Dickens's novel should have led to the most widely seen reworking of Hugo's masterpiece to date.

g

Hugo probably never read *Oliver Twist*, but he did get to meet its author, who visited Paris with his comrade John Forster in 1847. He granted an audience to the Englishmen in his splendid apartment in Place Royale. There's not a trace of the visit in any of Hugo's records, which suggests that Charles Dickens didn't make a strong impression on the literary star of the day, but it was a memorable occasion the other way round. In Dickens's eyes, Victor Hugo looked 'like the Genius he was'; his wife Adèle had such a glowering air that he thought her capable of putting poison in the poet's breakfast any day; and the daughter who brought in the tray looked so sinister that Dickens suspected her of carrying a sharp poignard in her stays 'but for her not appearing to wear any'. In this lugubrious atmosphere that must owe something to Dickens's wish to entertain his correspondent, Hugo addressed 'very charming flattery, in the best taste' to his English guests.[13] That's not surprising. Hugo may have had the status of a rock star, but he didn't behave like one at all. He was always neatly and soberly dressed, and his manners were exquisite. It's part of what made him the perfect ladies' man.

At the time of Dickens's visit Hugo had already drafted the basic narrative of most of what are now Parts I and II of *Les Misérables*, and the manuscript was most likely lying on the writing shelf just a few feet away from the deep sofa where the English writer sat. But the two great novelists did not talk about it. Despite all the feelings and ideas they shared, despite the parallel tracks they were following in their work, the conversation between them could only be an exchange of pleasantries. Hugo had never learned English (and never would), and Dickens knew no Latin, which was Hugo's second tongue. They were stuck with the conversational French that Dickens learned quite late in life, for he had not been to the right kind of school. If only he had had a proper education . . . but then he would not have written the novels of Charles Dickens.

The real conversation between Dickens and Hugo didn't happen in 1847, but fifteen years later. In 1861, the English writer completed his story of an ex-convict, Magwitch, transformed by an act of kindness into a power of good. Just a few weeks later, Victor Hugo brought the story of Jean Valjean to its conclusion. *Great Expectations* and *Les Misérables* say more to each other than their authors ever could.

Oliver Twist brought the lives of workhouse orphans and criminal gangs to attention in England, but in France, the lower depths were brought to the surface most spectacularly by Eugène Sue. His *Mystères de Paris*, published in daily instalments in a mass-circulation newspaper in 1842–3, were read by maids and mistresses, bootblacks and bosses, teenagers and adults, students and workers . . . It was such a huge success that it transformed the economics of newspaper publishing; and because it was often read aloud in cafés and bars, it reached beyond the literate to create the first mass audience for fiction in France.

In each episode of the *Mystères*, the recurrent hero, Prince Rudolph of Gerolstein, delves into a corner of *Paris misérable*, the hidden city of the poor. There he encounters prostitutes and pimps, exploited workers and oppressed artisans, crooks and dealers, single mothers, orphans, beggars and cripples. To each of the social ills that he finds, he brings some noble, practical or charitable relief. Rudolph is more like a figure from popular theatre or pantomime than what we expect to find in a literary novel: he's an aristocrat and a master of disguise who can pass himself off as a bourgeois, a worker or a crook, as required, because he's also as fluent in street slang as he is in the dialects of artisans or the language of the court. Hundreds, perhaps thousands of readers recognized their own situations in the serial and wrote letters to the author begging him to tell them how their own lives would work out, or else asking him to insert episodes they had written themselves.[14] Such was the popular impact of Sue's novel that nobody could pretend any more not to know about the poor. It wasn't the only thing that drew Hugo's eyes towards the problem of poverty, but it surely confirmed that it was the burning issue of the day. Not just in France, moreover. In Russia, Gogol's *Petersburg Tales* focused on the lives of the lowest ranks in the civil service; Dostoevsky's first full-length novel, *Poor Folk*, was written in 1845, just as Hugo was beginning the first draft of *Les Misérables*; and in London, Bulwer Lytton's *Paul Clifford* (1830) and Disraeli's *Sybil* (1845) created a new awareness of the 'condition of England' and its two nations of rich and poor. The only one of these that Hugo is likely to have known about is *Les Mystères de Paris*. Sue was just a little ahead of Hugo in responding to a sea change in literary and social sensibilities across Europe as a whole.

I find *Les Mystères de Paris* turgid and boring to a degree, but as it was read with enthusiasm by such a wide public the fault must surely lie with me. The French novelist Honoré de Balzac objected to it for other reasons besides. He was jealous of Sue's earnings, for a start, but he also deplored the appeals to 'social justice' that its episodes contain. Unlike Hugo, Balzac saw French society in decline and thought that only a return to the legitimate monarchy and the rule of the church could provide 'a complete system of repression of the depraved tendencies of the human race'.[15] His response to *Les Mystères de Paris* came in two sombre masterpieces gathered together under the topical title *Poor Relations* 'to overthrow the false gods of that bastard literature,'[16] by which he meant serial fiction in the manner of Eugène Sue. Hugo's response, which he never acknowledged as such, took much longer to work out. But it is buried just under the surface of the prose work he began in 1845 and which eventually turned into *Les Misérables*.

There are some obvious parallels between the two works. Like Prince Rudolph, Jean Valjean dies and is reborn many times: sent down for the theft of a loaf in 1796, he loses his name and becomes 24601; on his release in 1815 he goes to Montreuil-sur-Mer, where he changes into M. Madeleine; after owning up in 1823 to being a wanted man, he is reincarcerated as convict 9430; then he jumps off a mast into deep water and is given up for dead, but is spotted by Javert in Paris a few months after that; he flees, then disappears over a wall into a convent. But to have the right to stay there he first has to leave it in a coffin, and is nearly buried alive. He becomes 'Ultime Fauchelevent', and when he leaves the convent five years later others know him by the names of 'Monsieur Leblanc' and 'Urbain Fabre'. Valjean vanishes and reappears under new names more times than the Count of Monte Cristo, more often than Princess Bari, like the hero of some ancient saga – or of a modern one, like Sue's.

2.

Fantine

It is Christmas Day 1855, and the Hugos are living in a large rented house in Hauteville Street, overlooking Havelet Bay. As the house does not yet belong to them, the remodelling and interior decoration that eventually made it into a showcase for Hugo's strange imagination have not yet begun. What has begun, however, is the routine of family dinners prepared by Marie, a commandingly competent cook teasingly called 'Mary Sixty', as if she was one of the island's *seizeniers*, or local bigwigs. Hugo always sits at the head of the table, as befits a paterfamilias, and he usually holds forth on some topic or other. On this day, he talks not of politics or science, but of his own work. 'What I'm going to read to you came to me at the House of Lords in 1845, and I even began writing it in the chamber, on this piece of paper . . .'

In those years, Hugo's still unmarried twenty-five-year-old daughter Adèle (called Adèle II to distinguish her from her mother) kept a meticulous diary in which she noted down almost everything her father said. Her summary of her father's recitation on that 25 December describes a poem about a young woman who loses her family and has to fend for herself sewing clothes. When winter comes and days are short, the high cost of lamp oil plunges her into debt. She pawns her watch, her coat, her ring, even her father's war medal, but these do not meet her needs. She has no option but to go on the streets, where she's laughed at by urchins and told to move on by police. The second topic in the poem that Hugo's dutiful daughter recalled expressed horror at the cruel treatment of working animals, and the third section protested the use of child labour in factories.[17]

The summary leaves no doubt that Hugo was reading his family a version of the poem called 'Melancholia', which is now included in *Les Contemplations*, a collection first published in 1856. In the published edition, the poem is dated 1838; however, because Hugo frequently changed the dates of his compositions (for all kinds of reasons), the date of 1845 given by Adèle is much more likely to be the right one. That is when Hugo joined the Chambre des pairs, and the year when he started writing *Les Misérables*, which also tells the story of a poor woman who turns to prostitution for want of any other way to earn a crust. The tale of Fantine has the same outline and many of the same details as the subject of the first part of 'Melancholia'. The 'abuse of child labour' is also a shared theme – Cosette's suffering at the hands of the Thénardiers may seem more like a retelling of the Cinderella story now, but it highlights the general issue of how poor children were treated. Cruelty to working animals is also described in *Les Misérables* in a short but touching scene in front of Bombarda's restaurant in 1817.[18] It is therefore quite reasonable to see 'Melancholia' as springing from the same set of feelings and ideas as the prose work begun around the same time that eventually turned into *Les Misérables*, which, on Christmas Day 1855, was still only a draft and a plan. In any case, Hugo made no secret of the relationship between the two. When he finished reciting what was at that stage probably only about 110 lines of the 300-line poem, he told his family that it contained 'the germ of his unpublished novel'.[19]

Hugo expressed himself with equal ease in prose and in verse, though he tended to concentrate on one type of writing at any one time of his life. What we can guess from the hints provided by Adèle's account of the Christmas recitation at Hauteville House is that the 'germ' of *Les Misérables*, planted in Hugo's mind and heart around or shortly after April 1845, as the new 'lord of the realm' took his seat in the Chambre des pairs, came to him more or less indistinctly in verse and in prose. His eventual decision to use that material for a prose work rather than a narrative poem is the real 'source' of the greatest novel he ever wrote. And if *Les Misérables* has aspects and dimensions that take prose into the realm of poetry, that is partly because some of its subjects were indeed expressed in verse.

Hugo does not describe the life of a sex-worker in 'Melancholia', and he says no more about it in *Les Misérables*. Fantine's 'fall' is dealt with in just seven words:

> 'Well,' she said, 'let's get on with it and sell the rest.'
> The poor girl went on the streets. (I.5.x, adapted)

These clipped sentences contrast with the opulence of Hugo's habitual style and, partly because of that, they make a stronger impression in context than they do when quoted on their own. They ask readers to imagine what it meant to 'go on the streets' in a garrison town in 1823. What Hugo leaves out has been put back in by film-makers, graphic artists, adapters and the writers of fan fiction ever since, and some representation of Fantine's life as a prostitute has become an almost obligatory sequence in modern adaptations of *Les Misérables*. These more or less explicit portrayals of nineteenth-century sex work are inventions that owe nothing to what Hugo wrote. They are best taken as mirrors of the attitudes prevailing in the time and place where they were made.

Les Misérables also offers no criticism of capitalism or of the conditions of industrial labour. Quite the contrary: far from being one of the causes of poverty, 'wage-slavery' is presented in the novel as a providential cure. The only material and moral respite Fantine ever gets comes from packing beads at Madeleine's factory in Montreuil-sur-Mer: 'When Fantine saw she was making a living, she enjoyed a moment of happiness. To live honestly by the work she did – what a blessing! She truly regained a liking for work' (I.5.viii, 163).

These lines answer those who followed Malthus in thinking the poor were naturally lazy. Hugo demonstrates that even a 'lost woman' regains a liking for work once she is given a job to do. The implication is that the alleged moral depravity of the poor comes simply from the fact that there are not enough jobs to be had. The natural corollary is that men like Madeleine are to be admired for providing the work that allows poor people to become honest folk.

This apologia for industrialism is a sentimental fantasy, even a sinister one, for some modern readers. The growth of manufacturing in the decades that followed *Les Misérables* gave rise to political ideologies focused on the needs and rights of the labouring masses, and they in their turn changed perceptions of the meaning of Hugo's novel. Madeleine's model factory at Montreuil-sur-Mer and the philanthropic munificence that its profits allow suggest there is nothing wrong with exploitation. The manufacturer may behave in a superficially kindly manner to the workers and citizens of Montreuil, but what he's really doing is grabbing the fruits of their labour for himself – he amasses 630,000 francs (equivalent to 200kg of gold) in only six years. From this point of view the 'objective meaning' of *Les Misérables* is no more than propaganda on behalf of the robber barons of the industrial class.

Overall levels of prosperity have multiplied a hundredfold since the days of Fantine, but poverty hasn't disappeared, under any political regime. The big questions asked by Malthus, by Tocqueville and by Victor Hugo – why do poor people exist, and how can we be rid of them? – have been answered again and again, but never so well as to make them disappear. Is welfare itself the cause of poverty? Should income support and unemployment benefit be merged? Is there an irredeemable underclass that will always be poor, whatever laws are passed? How much of a benefit seeker's personal circumstances are relevant to assessing his or her needs? How much responsibility should be taken by the state for the relief of poverty, and how much left on the shoulders of the poor themselves?

Indeed, the social mechanisms that condemn some people to poverty today are not very different from what Hugo lays out in the plot of *Les Misérables*. The factors identified by modern social scientists as the main contributors to the cycle of poverty are these: loss of close family members; loss of financial support; unwanted pregnancy; low educational achievement; unemployment; falling rates of pay; ill health; being a victim of violence; and involvement with the law. Hugo put his finger on all those self-reinforcing disasters in his imagination of the life of Fantine. She is illiterate (the only illiterate character in the whole novel, I believe), has an unexpected pregnancy, is abandoned by the father of her child, loses his financial support, becomes unemployed, sees the rate of pay for piecework as a seamstress collapse, is physically attacked, gets arrested and falls ill. Her life is a classic example of the poverty trap.

We may want to take comfort in the tools that have been developed since the time of *Les Misérables* to prevent such an outcome. Universal primary education means that no modern Fantine has to rely on a tipsy letter-writer to correspond with the foster-parents of Cosette, so the existence of her illegitimate daughter would not be blabbed about around town. Birth-control methods make unwanted pregnancies less likely in any case, but when they occur, scoundrels like Tholomyès can be traced and obliged to provide child support. Anti-discrimination laws do not allow factory managers to sack employees just because they are single parents. If rates of pay fall below subsistence levels, some kind of income support is now provided by most states in the developed world. Caught in a squabble with a rough customer on the streets, prostitutes are no longer assumed to have lesser rights than members of the bourgeoisie, and the chest complaint that killed Fantine can be dealt with by antibiotics. We can congratulate ourselves on living in a less brutal age. We can relegate Fantine's horror story to a past that's been mended and made all right.

We really should not. In housing schemes, in the *banlieues*, in the de-industrialized wastelands of Europe and the slums of Mumbai, the disasters that fall on Fantine continue to make many lives utterly miserable ones. The destitute are not as numerous as they were in 1845 and not as visible in the centres of cities like Paris or New York. But even if Fantine's story points indirectly to all the progress that's been made to limit the impact of life events to which women remain more vulnerable than men, it also underscores the need to carry on.

g

In Hugo's youth, jails and dungeons were considered picturesque, and tourists in Paris visited all kinds of places that modern visitors shun. A prim Swiss student who came to Paris in 1830, for example, whiled away a Sunday afternoon at the women's ward in a lunatic asylum and then dropped in at the morgue, just to see.[20] Fashionable interest in ruins and medieval remains and a widely shared taste for the quaint and the bizarre – the main components of Romanticism when reduced to a statement of style – provided respectable cover for interests now served by the noirest genre of film.

In 1828, as a young man of his times and a maker of them, Victor Hugo went with his friend the sculptor David d'Angers to visit the prison of Bicêtre, where men condemned to death and hard labour were held. A serious interest in the preservation of the gothic past made Hugo keen to see the ancient prison buildings, but to do so he had to join a crowd of well-heeled gawkers who were permitted to watch what went on in the jail. The visitors were placed just behind the prison guards to get a close-up view of a detachment of men recently sentenced to hard labour being led out into the yard. The prison blacksmith set up his brazier and anvil and used a mallet to drive a red-hot rivet into the iron collar placed around each convict's neck.

It is a dreadful moment that makes even the boldest go pale with fear. Each hammer blow struck on the anvil set up behind the man's neck makes his chin bounce: the slightest movement forward or backward would have his skull cracked open like a nut.[21]

Once linked together in this humiliating and terrifying way, the convicts or *forçats* were made to mount open carts and sit face outwards on a bench in the middle to begin their long journey south to the *bagne* (prison) at Toulon. That is what Jean Valjean endured on 22 April 1796:

As the bolt was riveted into his iron collar with heavy hammer blows behind his head, he wept; his tears choked him, they prevented him from speaking, all he managed to say every now and then was 'I was a tree-pruner at Faverolles'. (I.2.vi, 80)

Valjean's ensuing twenty-seven-day journey to Toulon is not described in the narrative sequence of the novel, but it is brought back to life in an elegant and moving way some thirty-five years later on. When living in Rue Plumet, Valjean and Cosette go for an early-morning walk and encounter a grotesque and frightening scene: a procession of oxcarts bearing a ragged and filthy crew belting out a popular song. It is the chain-gang, on the first leg of a journey that Valjean had made twice over. People come out to watch, and urchins hurl abuse at the poor men.[22] Cosette sees without knowing what sort of a man her 'father' had been, and the reader is reminded that the gentle philanthropist had once been no more than a human beast providing entertainment to a heartless crowd. From the iron-smithing scene in *Le Dernier Jour d'un condamné The Last Day of a Condemned Man,* written in 1828, to the last part of *Les Misérables,* composed in 1861, Hugo did not cease to be saddened and angered by man's humiliation by man.

On his visit to Bicêtre, Hugo was also taken to inspect death row, and what he saw there shook him to the core. He imagined what it would be like to be a 'privileged' prisoner with a neck free of chain because it would soon be severed by the guillotine. Instead of writing a report, he composed a fictional, day-by-day diary of the thoughts of a man about to die. *The Last Day of a Condemned Man* doesn't reveal the identity of the writer or the nature of the crime that earned him his sentence of death. The direct, almost deadpan tone and the absence of explanation made this short first-person novel more shocking to readers than the facts it conveyed. It came out in 1829 without Hugo's name on it and was attacked in the press as a deplorable example of nerve-jangling Romantic excess. After the July Revolution of 1830, however, Hugo republished it in his own name, with a new preface making clear that he viewed capital punishment itself as a crime. From then on, he never wavered in his call to abolish the death penalty. It was finally done away with in France in 1981, after a century and a half of campaigning that had its source in the visit made by Victor Hugo to the prison of Bicêtre.

Brigands, outlaws, adventurers and tricksters figure in popular entertainment probably in every age, but the early nineteenth century seems to have invented contemporary crime as a social and literary topic. However, most of the 'literature of crime' of the Romantic era deals with spectacular and sinister forces of evil lurking just beneath the surface of polite society – Balzac's Vautrin, for example, is the banker of the underworld, pulling a thousand unseen strings to manipulate otherwise respectable young men. Hugo's contribution to the genre is entirely different: a sober, only lightly fictionalized report of a real case, that of a prisoner provoked to commit even greater crimes by the unmerciful application of unjust rules. *Claude Gueux*, which appeared in 1834, allowed or prompted Hugo to become quite knowledgeable about the system of justice and the organization of prisons, and it is in this short quasi-novel that he first formulated the view that he elaborates on a grander scale in *Les Misérables* on the link between poverty and crime: 'Why did this man steal? Why did he kill?' are the questions asked at his trial, and Hugo replies, 'The people are hungry, the people are cold. It is poverty that leads men to crime and women to vice.' [23]

In *Les Misérables*, however, Hugo refrains from explicit comment on the injustice of the law that sent Valjean to prison. He deals with the trial in just a few words: 'Jean Valjean was found guilty. The terms of the Penal Code were mandatory . . . What a fateful moment it is when society . . . irredeemably casts adrift a thinking being! Jean Valjean was condemned to five years' hard labour' (I.2.vi, 80).

Hugo lets the imbalance between the crime and its punishment speak for itself, but adapters of the novel for stage and screen often feel the need to spell it out. Richard Boleslawski, for example, the director of the classic Hollywood film of *Les Misérables* made in 1935, imagines a trial by jury in which the defendant takes the witness stand and delivers an impassioned, almost Shakespearean speech against not only the unfairness of the law, but the injustice of poverty that drives men to steal bread. It is a fine early example of that quintessentially American film genre, the courtroom drama, and the actor Fredric March surely speaks more for the victims of the Great Depression than he does for any eighteenth-century French *misérable* (especially because there were no jury trials at that time, and under the civil law system defendants cannot take the witness stand or make speeches on their own behalf). Many subsequent film versions have followed Boleslawski's lead, contributing to a general impression that Hugo's story begins with a denunciation of the injustice of the law. In the literal sense, it does not; but the attitudes and emotions expressed in these anachronistic and invented courtroom scenes are not contradictions of what Hugo expected his readers to understand.

Les Misérables treats Valjean's nineteen years of life in jail with equivalent brevity. We learn only that the poor convict acquires the nickname of 'The Jack' because of his strength, illustrated by his ability to hold up a falling stone column on the town hall in Toulon; that he learns to read and write; that he tries to escape four times; and that he is cheated of some of the money due to him on his release in 1815.[24] What we certainly do not see in the novel is Valjean pulling on oars as a galley-slave – but it is with just such a scene that the Broadway version of the musical by Boublil and Schönberg begins.

The adapters of the musical did not invent the idea: they got it from Boleslawski's film, which shows a dozen bearded giants heaving-ho to a rhythm beaten out by a glistening black man on a huge gong, seen through the low, slant angles that Welles used to such effect in *Citizen Kane*. As a substitute for the episode illustrating Valjean's strength at the town hall in Toulon, Boleslawski's Valjean lifts a broken beam that has trapped a man below decks, and the overseer – Javert, in his first manifestation as a prison guard – comments aloud to himself that he's never seen a prisoner so strong. That is where the opening chorus of the musical comes from. But why did Boleslawski invent a scene of seaborne labour in the first place?

It comes from a single word in the text. It is said by Valjean to Bishop Myriel, to make sure his unexpected host knows what kind of man he has allowed into his home: 'Avez-vous entendu? Je suis un galérien. Un forçat. Je viens des galères' ('Did you hear? I'm an ex-convict. Sentenced to hard labour, I come from the prison hulks') (I.2.iii, 71). This translation is taken from the currently available English edition, but earlier versions such as those available in the 1930s reproduced the French with English words that look more like them: 'Did you hear? I am a *galley slave*; a convict. I come from the *galleys*.' The older translation can't be called wrong: the French word for 'galley' is indeed *galère* and 'galley-slave' is *galérien*. From the founding of the naval port of Toulon in 1679 to the middle of the eighteenth century, moreover, men sentenced to hard labour were sent there to serve as oarsmen on military vessels powered principally by sail. That's why hard labour was called 'the galley punishment', *la peine des galères*, and convicts were called *galériens*. Around 1740, however, new kinds of cannon were fitted to warships. These much heavier pieces had to be housed below decks, otherwise the ships would have become unstable in bad weather. That left no room for the galley-slaves, and from then on the French navy relied on sail alone until the introduction of steam around 1830. The literal *peine des galères* was formally abolished in 1748, and by 1796, when Valjean was sent down, galley-slaving was not even a memory in Toulon any more – except in the words used to refer to the prison and its inmates, *les galères* and *galériens*. You could say that the words changed their meaning, but that's not really true, since the original meaning of the words survives to this day if you need to speak of galleys and slaves (in Ancient Rome, for example). What changed was the world in which they were used.

It's possible that Boleslawski knew this – he had been trained in theatre and film at the Moscow Academy of the Arts and most likely understood French very well – and chose to misinterpret the words to justify a much more dramatic prison sequence than any that Hugo provides; but as 'galley-slave' has never been an English code-word for 'convict' it's also possible that he simply didn't know what the words referred to at the time Valjean was sent down.

The 'maritime mistake' incorporated into Boublil and Schönberg's musical set Tom Hooper an interesting problem when he came to make a film version of it in 2012. His crafty solution was to replace the opening scene below decks with a grand view of convicts haul-ing a ship into dry-dock beneath the cruel eye of their overseer, Javert. A back-breaking task of that kind is historically plausible – Valjean and his comrades were put to mending roads, breaking stones and shifting ammunition around the naval dockyard (Hugo saw them at it himself when he visited the *bagne* at Toulon in 1839); and it is also true that in the absence of powered tools the only way of getting a ship into dry-dock was to use a large crew of strong men. A reasonably full circle is therefore now complete, taking Valjean from his actual prison to an imaginary seafaring one and back to dry land again.

Hugo barely mentions it, but there was a maritime aspect to the hard-labour prison all the same. Convicts were for the most part housed on decommissioned naval vessels and brought ashore each morning by rowboat to do work on land. It solved the problem of housing so many men, and the idea was copied in England, where men sentenced to transportation were parked on rotting hulks in the Thames until there was a vessel ready to take them to the end of the world. One more thing that Dickens's Magwitch has in com-mon with Jean Valjean.

3.
The First Draft

On 17 November 1845, Hugo took a fresh sheet of writing paper and wrote: 'In the first days of October 1815, about an hour before sunset, a traveller walked in to the little town of D.' Since this very sentence opens the second book of *Les Misérables* there is no doubt that the manuscript page marks the start of the work completed on Guernsey sixteen years later.

Why did Hugo begin *Les Misérables* at that time? Why did he choose to write *Les Misérables* at all? His daughter's diary entry from December 1855 tells us that the social issues raised in the story of Fantine had been present in his mind ten years before. Pairing the story of a fall into prostitution with a story of a man forced into a crime makes Valjean the male complement of Fantine, if we go by Hugo's claim in *Claude Gueux* that poverty was the underlying cause of both catastrophes. He must have been as aware as Balzac was of the immense appeal of Sue's saga of the underside of the city in *Les Mystères de Paris*, which deserved a response from his own very different artistic and moral perspective. He also had a contract with his publishers for a 'second novel' to follow on from *Notre-Dame de Paris*, but as he had been steadfastly ignoring it for thirteen years that commitment may be the least important of the reasons why he set himself to writing *Les Misérables*. But among these various factors there must also have been the sense that, having now accepted responsibility for the nation as a member of its legislature, he had a duty to exercise it in a way that he was uniquely equipped to do: by writing a book.

All this is speculation, for Hugo left no direct trace of what led him to invent *Les Misérables*, nor did he leave any record of how he began. There's no sketch, plan or preliminary synopsis of a novel about a convict, a priest, a prostitute or an orphaned child – at any rate, no such document has been found, and because Hugo hung on to every last scrap he ever wrote, it's not at all likely he threw any such thing away. Hugo was such an obsessive keeper of his own writing that he even archived notes written on the backs of envelopes. One, addressed to him at the Chambre des pairs (therefore written after April 1845), has the nearest approximation to an 'idea' for *Les Misérables* scrawled on it. It is very short:

> The story of a saint
> The story of a man
> The story of a woman
> The story of a doll[25]

The 'saint' is presumably Bishop Myriel, the 'man' must be Jean Valjean, the 'woman' Fantine, and the doll must be the one that Cosette admires and that Valjean buys for her from a stall at the Christmas bazaar at Montfermeil.[26] But this jotting isn't necessarily the 'first origin' of *Les Misérables*. It could equally well be a retrospective checklist of topics noted down when the writing of the novel was already underway.

The year 1845 was marked by Hugo's rise to a position of great honour and also by an embarrassing fall. Since 1833, he had pursued a stable and not at all secret extramarital liaison with a former actress, Juliette Drouet, who loved him dearly and stayed by his side for the rest of her life. But he was also a serial philanderer. On 4 July, he was found 'in crumpled attire' by two officers of the law in an apartment rented under the name of 'Mr Apollo'. His consort, Léonie Biard, was a married woman. Because adultery was a criminal offence in France at that time, both lovers faced a trial.

Adultery abounds in novels of all periods and is especially prominent in French fiction of the nineteenth century. On the other hand, trials for adultery are almost unheard of in fiction and they were quite rare in real life too, principally because disappointed spouses were reluctant to make their marital misfortunes public knowledge. But this case was different. Léonie was already seeking a divorce on grounds of cruelty, so her husband – a painter of no great importance – seized his wife's affair with a celebrity as an opportunity to strike back. He pressed the charges that the law allowed him to make. Léonie was tried, found guilty and sent to the women's prison at Saint-Lazare, then confined to a convent for several months. She wasn't free until the end of the year.

The name of the co-respondent in the trial of Léonie Biard was supposed to be secret because he was such a prominent man, but it was leaked very soon, and then everyone knew who it was. Within months, Balzac started on a novel about sexual obsession and resentment centred on the life of an obsessive skirt-chaser called Hector Hulot. One episode in *Cousine Bette* is borrowed directly from life when the hero is found in bed with a woman by police tipped off by her wretch of a spouse; the sergeants in the novel follow exactly the same procedures as the real ones did on encountering 'Mr Apollo' in bed with Léonie Biard. The name Balzac chose for his philanderer is so close to that of Victor Hugo as to make the source of the story quite obvious. Libel laws didn't apply in the same way as they do now, but Balzac was lucky not to have had to face a duel.

Hector Hulot arranges to have the husband of his mistress paid to drop the legal charges against him. Victor Hugo did not face a trial either, but for a different reason. As a *pair de France* he could only be tried by his peers, that is to say, in the Chambre des pairs. The king was furious. He did not want parliamentary time wasted on a trivial scandal, and he did not want his judgement called into question by the trial of a man he had only just elevated to high rank. He took immediate action by giving Léonie's husband a commission for wall-paintings at Versailles. It was the order of a lifetime, and Biard accepted the sole condition – to drop charges against Hugo. The miscreant lover, for his part, was told to make himself scarce and leave town.

Hugo told his wife Adèle what had happened. Perhaps surprisingly, she took it in her stride. She invited Léonie to dinner at Place

Royale once she was out of jail. Adèle even seems to have liked her – at any rate, she treated her as an improvement on Juliette Drouet, who was kept in the dark about the whole affair. But Hugo was incorrigible in that domain. Throughout 1846 and 1847 he weaved his way between three wives. Balzac's imagination of the sex life of Hector Hulot was not far from the truth about Victor Hugo.

In the course of the summer, there were rumours that the poet had started a book about a saint, and people joked that he must be doing penance for his unsaintly behaviour. I don't believe Hugo really suffered pangs of guilt about his sex life at that time or any other. He was certainly embarrassed and confused by seeing his lover go to jail while he was let off because he was of high rank. He didn't think he should be above the law, even if the law was so stupid as to make amorous passion a criminal act. Some commentators have presented the 'Biard Affair' as a shipwreck in Hugo's personal and social life that led him to take refuge in an uplifting tale, but I'm sceptical of that moralizing approach. Hugo's colleague and fellow poet Alphonse de Lamartine put it more rationally with his famous quip 'On se relève de tout, même d'un canapé' ('You can disentangle yourself from anything, even bed sheets'). Hugo overcame that awkward affair very fast.

But *Les Misérables* is unusual among nineteenth-century French novels for not talking at any point about adultery or even sex. Its main characters are celibate: Valjean never marries, falls in love or has relations with a woman; Javert likewise; and the only mistress the idealistic Enjolras entertains is *Patria*, the feminine Latin noun meaning fatherland.[27] Marius and Cosette are virgins before their marriage, and although Gillenormand likes to boast of amorous exploits in times gone by, he doesn't indulge himself in that way in the course of the novel's action. That, surely is the main impact of the Biard Affair on Hugo's intention as he started the first draft of *Les Misérables*: to write about everything *except that*.

Hugo wrote the first draft in fits and starts over twenty-seven months, between November 1845 and February 1848. At times his engagement with the project was so intense that he didn't get to bed until 1 a.m., which was very late for him (he always rose at dawn). Although the chronology of its composition can be tracked fairly precisely from Hugo's routine of dating his manuscript sheets, the first draft itself no longer exists as a physical entity. Its pages were overwritten, moved around and woven into the far longer manuscript of the final version, completed twelve years later in a hotel room in Belgium overlooking the site of the Battle of Waterloo. However, a century of scholarly endeavour has allowed the 'original' version of *Les Misérables* to be reconstituted to a high degree of certainty. Thanks to Guy Rosa and his team at the University of Paris-VII, a typeset image of Hugo's first draft is now accessible to all on the web.

The reconstructed first draft shows that the *story* that Hugo invented when he was one of France's most eminent men is not significantly different from the plot of *Les Misérables*. The released convict, the charitable bishop, the model factory, the single mother, the evil innkeepers, the exploited waif, life under cover, the escape to a convent, a hesitant courtship, the cheeky urchin, the ambush, the band of students with high ideals, the rumblings of discontent, the riot and the construction of the barricade are all there. Of course, a lot is missing, since the story in first draft is incomplete, stopping before the barricade is assaulted, and therefore prior to the escape through the sewers, the reconciliation of Marius with his grandfather and all that follows. In addition, many of the sub-plots and all the essay chapters of the corresponding parts of *Les Misérables* are absent, and few of the characters have the name by which we know them now (the principal exception being Thénardier). Even so, it is a substantial work of around 200,000 words, which would make a 600-page paperback doorstopper nowadays. As it is incomplete, it seems clear that Hugo intended it to be a very long book from the start.

Once Victor Hugo had got his teeth into a plot that he must have worked out in broad outline in his head near the start, life came up trumps and threw in his path material of just the right kind. But he was also a co-conspirator with happenstance, taking more or less conscious steps to get hold of the right details in time.

'I can't say why the idea occurred to me', he wrote, but on 10 September 1846, on his way home from a meeting at the Chambre des pairs, he dropped in at the Conciergerie, the prison next to the law courts on Ile de la Cité. He showed the medal he carried to prove he was a *pair de France*, and the prison director, Lebel, promptly gave him a guided tour of the gothic pile, with a running commentary on the obscene graffiti, the old torture chamber, death row, the women's quarter and the section where under-age children were kept, often for trivial offences like stealing peaches from a tree. Lebel also told him about a spectacular escape. A prisoner had jammed his back into the corner made by two walls meeting at an angle of ninety degrees. Using only his elbows and heels as levers, he had hoisted himself to the roof by muscular strength alone. The anecdote went straight into the work in progress, but not for a prison escape. It explains how Valjean got himself *into* the convent of Petit-Picpus 'as surely and steadily as if he had ladder rungs under his feet'.[28]

Not long before or after his visit to the central prison, as he was crossing the courtyard of the building where the Académie française met, Victor Hugo was accosted by a white-haired fellow in rags who claimed to know him well. He had to look twice to remember: it was an old schoolmate of his, called Joly. What a change! At school, Joly had been a pretty, pampered boy who always gave freely to his friends. He was the only child of rich parents who had died young, leaving him a fortune of 800,000 francs. After his school years, however, Joly spent and gambled it all away and then got into debt. Too accustomed to idleness to get a job, he turned to forging the money he liked to throw about. Short of murder, forgery was the most heavily punished crime in nineteenth-century France. Joly was caught, convicted and given the obligatory sentence of hard labour. He wrote to his old school friend Hugo and asked him to intercede. Ever generous, Hugo approached the minister of justice, who reduced Joly's sentence by four years. On his release, the ex-convict was given a residence order confining him to the small town of Pontoise (north-east of Paris), just as in *Les Misérables* Valjean has a residence order for Pontarlier, an industrial town on the Swiss border. However, Joly took no notice of it and went to live among vagrants in Paris. (Valjean also disregards his residence order and settles in Montreuil-sur-Mer, hundreds of miles to the north.) To keep out of sight of police patrols at night, he slept under the bridges on the muddy and often dangerous banks of the Seine (as Paris's famous *quais* hadn't yet been built, the river had rapid rises and falls, depending on rain). When Joly had finished his tale, Hugo put his hand in his pocket to give the man a coin, but the ex-convict stopped him. A hand-out could be construed as begging, and begging was a crime that could have him sent down for life because it would be a second offence. (The same consideration applies in *Les Misérables* to the man mistaken for Jean Valjean, put on trial for stealing the branch of an apple tree.) Hugo asked Joly to call on him at Place Royale, where he could give alms more discreetly. The reprobate came more than once and soon proved to be an insistent and insolent scrounger. Hugo urged him to mend his ways and was quite baffled by Joly's resistance. He went on giving money to the old crook for months, but by the end of 1846, Hugo had had enough.[29]

The story of Jean Valjean looks like Joly's turned upside down. Starting from the bottom not the top, guilty of a lesser crime but paying a higher price, Valjean is a model of upward, not downward social mobility, and an example of moral improvement, not of persistence in low life and crime. It is likely that Hugo learned or checked up on details of prison administration and the constraints placed on ex-convicts in conversation with Joly, but it is not possible that he invented the entire story of Valjean as a response to this striking example of a fall, since he had already written quite large parts of what is now Part I of *Les Misérables*. However, when he was revising his presentation of the student activists and of the barricade scenes in Parts IV and V at Hauteville House in 1861, the story of Joly came back to his mind, because he told it all again over dinners at Hauteville House to his wife Adèle, who put it down in her precious account of 'Victor Hugo as told by a witness of his life'. Perhaps in memory of the peculiar fellow, Hugo borrowed his name for one of the 'Friends of the ABC'.

Hugo gathered other material more actively, by asking for stories and details from people he knew. In June 1847, at Hugo's request, a naval officer he'd come across wrote down a gripping account of the heroic action of a convict working on a naval vessel undergoing repairs at Toulon. A sailor aloft in the rigging loses his footing and nearly falls to his death but manages to cling on to a spar. None of the crew – press-ganged fishermen all – dares go to his aid, but a convict on the chain-gang that was also in the dockyard at the time asks permission to rescue the sailor. He's detached from his chain, clambers up the mast, ties a rope around the man's waist, winches him up to the yardarm and then carries him in his arms back to the forecastle. After performing this extraordinary and generous feat, he goes back down and is reattached to his chain.[30] Hugo copied this note by Roncière le Noury almost verbatim in II.2.iii, the chapter explaining how Valjean escaped from his second incarceration at Toulon, but he gives it a different ending. Instead of going down to rejoin the gang, Valjean jumps into the sea and disappears.

Hugo knew he could not write the convent episode without help, because no man could know what life was like behind those high walls. He turned to his beloved Juliette Drouet and also to Léonie (who had resumed her maiden name d'Aunet after her divorce from Biard), with whom he was still having a parallel affair. Juliette wrote out four pages of notes on her life at school in the convent of the Dames de Sainte-Madeleine; Léonie, who had been educated by nuns as well, supplied Hugo with a longer description of the convent of the Perpetual Adoration of the Holy Sacrament, situated at 12, Rue Neuve-St-Geneviève, also in the Latin Quarter.[31] Her description of the convent garden is repeated almost verbatim in *Les Misérables*, but her other memories are blended with Juliette's to produce an account of convent life that would not strike convent-educated readers as far-fetched or false.

Two women, a school friend, a naval officer, a prison governor . . . there were surely many others who, knowingly or not, gave Hugo a detail, an episode, a memory or a piece of technical information that found its place in *Les Misérables*. Within a decade Émile Zola would build a whole 'theory of the novel' on data trawling of just this kind. Hugo never claimed to have a system, but his magpie approach brings *Les Misérables* closer to the documentary novel than might at first appear.

In the early stages Hugo referred to his work in progress simply as the novel he was writing. In 1846, he started calling it *Jean Tréjean*, by the name of the ex-convict who had not yet become Jean Valjean. By 1847, punning on the title of Sue's *Les Mystères de Paris*, he was calling it *Les Misères*. That is the name the first draft had from then on, and still does now. It is no easier to translate than *Les Misérables*.

ℊ

Victor Hugo was obliged to put his novel to one side in February 1848, when street protests in Paris turned into a violent revolution followed by months of chaos and change.

The later parts of *Les Misérables* also hinge on a moment of revolution in Paris, but it is not this one. Yet the two – the historical event, and a fiction that partly resembles it – are intertwined in compelling and complicated ways. Whether you want to understand how Hugo's novel was written or what it has to say, revolution is an unavoidable theme.

'Revolution' means a turn of 360 degrees – in car engines, for example, where a revolution is a full cycle, or in astronomy, where a revolution of a planet around its sun brings it back to where it was a year before. In politics, too, 'revolution' used to mean an event that put things back where they had been before: the 'Glorious Revolution' of 1688, for example, ensured that the English throne would not pass to a Catholic line of descent. In the eighteenth century, however, the word started to be used for something rather less (or more) than the restoration of an original state by a full turn of a wheel. In its new meaning, a 'revolution' became a turn of 180 degrees, putting things not where they had been but in an opposite state. However, not all processes of change in the political sphere are considered revolutionary. The word acquired its modern senses largely because of the particular history of France.

Hugo was born too late to experience the great upheaval of 1789 that swept away the French monarchy, introduced the Rights of Man, descended into the Great Terror and ended up empowering Napoleon Bonaparte to liberate most of continental Europe from the feudal monarchies that ruled it. As that founding event was dubbed 'the Revolution', the word 'revolution' acquired senses that derive directly from specific aspects of the popular uprising of 1789 and its dramatic sequels. The French Revolution of 1789 is not the subject of *Les Misérables*, but one of the novel's larger purposes is to make it the well-spring of nineteenth-century civilization and so to heal the bleeding wounds that it bequeathed to subsequent generations of French men and women.

Hugo was an adolescent when Napoleon fell and the monarchy was restored in 1815. When the new (but fairly old) king, Louis XVIII, died in 1824, the throne passed to his younger brother, Charles X, a stern and religious man, whose rule became ever more backward-looking. Hugo, who had adopted his mother's royalist views in his teens, composed verses for Charles's faux-medieval coronation at Rheims in 1825. Meanwhile, pressure from the middle classes for a more liberal regime led the king to take increasingly repressive measures. When he reimposed censorship of the press and restricted the electorate by decree in July 1830, protesters came out on the streets, led by print-workers, who saw a threat to their livelihoods in the new censorship rules. Attempts by troops to restore order were bungled. Some detachments got lost in the labyrinth of streets around Les Halles, and the king fled to his palace in Saint-Cloud, outside Paris. The long-serving Marquis de Lafayette – the French hero of the American War of Independence – appeared on the balcony of the Hôtel de Ville, the Paris town hall, and for a moment it seemed as if a new Republic were about to be declared. However, a group of notables, among them the banker Jacques Laffitte, moved quickly behind the scenes to bring back to France the exiled head of the junior branch of the French royal family. Louis-Philippe d'Orléans accepted their invitation to become the constitutional monarch of a more liberal France.

This revolution, known as the July Revolution or the 'Three Glorious Days' of 27, 28 and 29 July 1830, celebrated in Delacroix's huge painting of *Liberty Guiding the People*, is the first that Hugo experienced for himself. But it is also not the subject of *Les Misérables*.

By 1830, Hugo's political views had shifted towards the liberal cause, and he wrote stirring verses in retrospective support of the coming of a new and freer regime. All the same, he had many good reasons for not centring *Les Misérables* on the events that brought Louis-Philippe to power. First, he had taken no part in the uprising and hardly saw any of it with his own eyes. That was because his wife Adèle was about to give birth to their fourth child, and Hugo's main concern when the first shots could be heard was to get his family out of town as fast as he could. His daughter, also called Adèle, was born at Montfort l'Amaury on 29 July 1830. Hugo had another important reason beside parenthood to be absent from the turmoil of the world: he was behind schedule on a book that he owed to a publisher who had paid him an advance. A week before the July Revolution erupted he had locked away his going-out clothes and donned a woollen body-stocking so as to settle down to an intense period of literary work at home. He was determined to stay at his writing shelf until *Notre-Dame de Paris* was done.

Beyond these personal and practical reasons for avoiding 1830 in real life, there were also commonsensical reasons why Hugo did not place the barricade scene of *Les Misérables* in 1830. The three-day overturning of the Bourbon monarchy was a remarkably brief and relatively bloodless civic rampage that quite surprisingly allowed the country to switch to a regime under which Hugo prospered and rose to high rank. He wasn't the only one of his generation to do well out of the 'Three Glorious Days'. Among those who benefited were the historian Jules Michelet, made head of the National Archives by the new king; the short-story-writer Prosper Mérimée (the author of the original *Carmen* that Bizet later turned into an opera), who was parachuted into a new and equally important position as inspector of national antiquities; the liberal bookseller Louis Hachette, who won the contract to supply all the new primary schools that were founded in 1833 with slates and chalk; even the unclubbable Stendhal landed a job that he wanted, as French consul in Civitavecchia, in Italy. A whole generation of talented and ambitious young men found their places under the rule of King Louis-Philippe, who led a far less pompous and cloistered life than his predecessors on the throne of France. Had Hugo decided to focus his novel on the barricades of 1830, he would have been stepping into a moral minefield, for the regime they brought about was still in power in 1845. A retrospective apologia for how the status quo had come to be was not what he had in mind.

The July Monarchy, as Louis-Philippe's eighteen-year reign is called, was more favourable to commerce and to the professional middle classes than its predecessors had been, but the slowly rising wealth of the nation was not equally distributed. In addition, many rival factions contested the policies and even the legitimacy of the regime. Civil disorder was frequent, some of it fomented by those who remained faithful to the Bourbon line of descent represented by Charles X (living in exile in Edinburgh, which is how Royal Terrace got its name), some from Bonapartists plotting to restore an authoritarian and modernizing regime, and some from a scattering of groups with still-vague socialist and utopian ideals; but most of all from the often desperate, disgruntled and volatile poor. The painter and cartoonist Honoré Daumier made some memorable images of the ugly slaughter that followed one such riot, the 'Massacre in Rue Transnonain', in 1834. For *Les Misérables*, Hugo chose an equally doomed moment of civil strife in the early part of the reign of Louis-Philippe: the riots of 5 and 6 June 1832. It's an episode that would now only be recalled by specialist historians of nineteenth-century France if

Hugo had not made it the centrepiece of *Les Misérables*. It had no identifiable consequences and no measurable effect on the real world, but Hugo wanted to believe that it was not a meaningless event. Unburdened by any impact on the course of events, the micro-revolution of June 1832 was a better vehicle for explanations *in principle* than any more historically significant moment of change.

Hugo drew on authentic historical documentation and on the accounts of contemporaries for his reconstruction of the events of 5–6 June 1832, but he also made many changes to the facts. Not out of sloppiness or disrespect, but because fiction is the vehicle of truth. Derealizing the actually rather sad and sordid events of that night allowed him to bring out the higher and more important meanings of 'revolution' for the past and future history of France.

In February 1848, Hugo's story was near to its dramatic climax. Marius, despairing of ever marrying his beloved Cosette, has joined his student friends at the barricade in Rue de la Chanvrerie, a small street in a working-class area of central Paris (a street that had long ceased to exist). Shots have been fired, there are dead and injured already, but as night falls on 5 June most of the militants behind the barricade are still alive. Should they fight on? What will dawn bring? That's where Hugo's first draft stops because, at that precise time in the writing of *Les Misérables*, an entirely non-fictional riot erupted in the streets outside. In the space of forty-eight hours the government collapsed, barricades went up, and the king threw in the towel. Victor Hugo, a peer of the realm, could not simply stand aside. He put away his pen and turned to finding out what his duty was. He had no plan of his own to change the world and no clue what the chaos would lead to, but he had to be part of the fight. It was a new moment and called for new kinds of action on his part. Nothing affected Hugo's life and mind – or the composition, structure and sense of *Les Misérables* – more profoundly than what happened next. The narrative of the novel may be focused on 1832, but what it has to say cannot be properly understood outside Hugo's experience of the revolution of 1848.

It was a year of revolutions throughout Europe. 'The Spring of Nations', as 1848 is called, brought major political changes in Denmark, Holland, Austria, Hungary, Germany, Poland and Italy. These uncoordinated uprisings had local and particular causes, but all were inspired and encouraged by what happened first in Paris. In that year, the city of light truly filled its legendary role as the political and intellectual centre of the world.

The events in Paris had two converging causes: the general desperation of the poor, and a particular political mess. In the 1840s, Louis-Philippe felt obliged to take repressive measures against republican and other opponents of his reign. Unorthodox opinions about the way France should be governed were expressed by a small handful of elected representatives and through newspapers aligned with them, but their freedom was increasingly curtailed. Prominent republican figures were jailed and all political parties were banned. Some of them survived as clandestine clubs, but they were not all of like mind. Some were still calling for the restoration of the Bourbon monarchy; some were socialists; and the long-established Bonapartist underground had its secret network too. What was obvious to them all was that no change could be achieved by parliamentary means without giving the vote to a wider circle of electors. By the mid-1840s, extension of suffrage had become the focus of otherwise incompatible forces seeking the end of the reign of Louis-Philippe d'Orléans.

A way round the ban on political associations was found in 'banquets', where prohibited political views could be expressed in coded terms in pseudo-ceremonial toasts. A large one was planned for 14 January 1848 to promote the cause of electoral reform. The prime minister, Guizot, banned it. The organizers put it off until 22 February. The plan was to have 'diners' accompanied to the hall by 'companions', a subterfuge that would create a public demonstration flouting the spirit but not the letter of the law. On 21 February, Guizot repeated the order banning the banquet, but it was too late. A crowd of people who had been planning to accompany the diners came out on the streets and assembled in Place de la Concorde. Guizot called out the National Guard, a civilian reserve force drawn mostly from the middle classes. Unhappily for him, most of its members were sympathetic to electoral reform, and they took no action against the crowd. Guizot saw that he had failed, and so he resigned. The crowd held a noisy celebration outside his home, scaring Guizot's personal guards. Desperate to disperse them, the guards opened fire and killed several men. The bodies were paraded on carts through the streets of Paris, arousing the anger of the masses. Barricades went up, and by dawn on 24 February an uprising was in full swing. Louis-Philippe tried to form a new government, but each of the men he asked to lead the country in its time of need backed out within hours. France had no government, and the people knew it. Rioters moved ever nearer the Tuileries Palace, where the king lived. Louis-Philippe did not want to end up on the guillotine like Louis XVI, or at war with his own people like Charles X. He stepped down and passed the crown to his grandson, who was only nine years old.

Victor Hugo did not try to escape involvement in the crisis. On 22 and 23 February he strode back and forth between his home in the Marais quarter and the Luxembourg Palace, where the peers were meeting in almost permanent session. In the afternoon of 24 February, Odilon Barrot – prime minister for just a few hours – told him to announce to the people in his area that power had been transferred to the queen, as regent of the new child-king. Hugo spoke to the crowd from the balcony of the local town hall in Place Royale and then went on to Place de la Bastille, where there was a larger, angrier and now armed mob. To be seen he had to stand on the plinth of the monument to the July Revolution (the Column of Liberty, which is still there today), to be heard he had to shout at the top of his voice, and everything he said was cheered, booed, contested or drowned out.

A man in a worker's shirt shouted out, 'Shut up the *pair de France*! Down with the *pair de France*!' And he trained his rifle on me. I stared at him hard and raised my voice to such a pitch that everyone else fell silent. 'Yes, I am a *pair de France* and I speak to you as a *pair de*

France. I took an oath to serve not a royal person but a constitutional monarchy. Until such time as another government is established it is my duty to serve it. And I always believed that the people don't approve of breaking promises, whatever they are.'[32]

The crowd didn't want a regent, or any kind of king. 'No regency? But what then? Nothing's ready, absolutely nothing! It would be a complete collapse, ruination, poverty, maybe civil war; at any rate, it would be a leap into the unknown.'[33]

Hugo did not know at that moment that Alphonse de Lamartine, whose politics had turned towards the left more sharply and much earlier than his own, had already set up a provisional government at the town hall, the traditional seat of people's power since the days of the first revolution in 1789. The next day, after tramping through dangerously chaotic streets from the Marais to the Luxembourg Palace in the Latin Quarter and back again, he dropped in at the town hall.

Lamartine stood up as I entered . . .

'Ah! You are joining us, Victor Hugo! A fine recruit to the Republic!'

'Hang on, my friend!' I said with a laugh. 'I'm just coming to see my old friend Lamartine. Perhaps you don't know that yesterday, when you were bringing down the Regency at the Chambre des pairs, I was defending it at the Bastille.'

'Yesterday, sure. But today? Today there's no regency or royalty left. It is not possible that in his heart of hearts Victor Hugo is not a republican man.'

'In principle, yes, I am for the republic. In my opinion a republic is the only rational form of government, the only one worthy of nations. A universal republic will be the last stage of progress. But has its time come in France? It's because I want there to be a Republic that I want it to be a viable one, I want it to be definitive. You're going to consult the country, aren't you? The whole country?'[34]

The royal family went into exile and settled in Twickenham, while the exiled relatives of Napoleon Bonaparte were allowed to return. A provisional government was declared, and it declared itself to be a republican one. It quickly brought in reforms implementing several of Hugo's more or less recently acquired principles: universal male suffrage, abolition of the death penalty (but only for political crimes) and of slavery in the French colonies. Hugo wasn't so naive as to think that the last would bring racial discrimination to an end by itself:[35]

> When the governor [of Guadeloupe, a French colony in the Caribbean] proclaimed the equality of the whites, mulattoes and blacks, there were three men on the podium, representing as it were the three races: a white man, the governor; a mulatto, holding his parasol; and a black man carrying his hat.[36]

The problem of mass poverty was addressed by a jobs-for-all scheme paid for from national coffers. However, the economic slump that had brought discontent to boiling point and was now exacerbated by political instability meant that the *ateliers nationaux* or 'national workshops' didn't have any work to hand out. The idea of setting the men to building railways ran into objections about interference in private enterprise, so the newly employed unemployables hung about on the streets playing quoits. Political restraints on clubs and associations were lifted, and at times it seemed as if the city was engaged in a permanent political talk-in. Even so, order had to be kept. The provisional government established a new National Guard, which ceased to be organized on a local basis and manned by middle-class volunteers. It was now a professional paramilitary force that could move to any part of the city as needed. Elections by universal male suffrage for a constituent assembly of 900 delegates, whose job would be to write a new constitution, were set for April. The result was not a landslide for socialists and republicans, despite their apparent victory on the streets. The newly enfranchised countryside, where the mass of the French population still lived, chose local notables to represent them, often the same ones who had served in the national assembly under the previous restricted electoral regime.

The upper chamber was abolished along with the old parliament, so Hugo ceased to hold the rank of *pair de France*. In the April elections he won 60,000 votes, but not a seat. He stood again in a by-election on 4 June, garnered 89,695 votes and was elected to the constituent assembly as a representative of the people of Paris.[37] He attended the first session on 10 June 1848 and took a seat on the right-hand side, signalling that he was not 'on the left'. In his first speech on 20 June, he attacked the scandal of the jobs-for-all scheme that was ruining the nation and not doing anything to help the poor. Although he probably didn't quite realize it at the time, his speech was the last drop that brought to overflowing the cup of fury among elected conservatives at the continuing chaos of republican and revolutionary France. Two days later, the provisional government, which was now more 'right' than 'left', abolished the *ateliers nationaux*, introduced compulsory conscription for able-bodied unemployed men under the age of twenty-five and banished all other jobless men to the provinces so as to get them off the city's streets. That was more than a labour market reform. It was a purge, and it was taken by the poor as a declaration of war. Working-class areas of Paris erupted in protest, and rioters built barricades larger and more solid than any that had been seen before.

> The first barricade went up as early as Friday 23 [June] in the morning and it was attacked the same day . . . When the assault force . . . came within range, a huge volley blasted out from the barricade, and the ground was strewn with National Guards. More irritated than intimidated, the soldiers stormed the barricade at a trot.
>
> At this point a woman appeared on the crest of the barricade. She was young and beautiful with unkempt hair and a fearsome sight. The woman, who was a prostitute, raised her skirt to her waist and bawled at the guard, in that frightful bawdy-house slang that can

only be given in translation, 'Cowards, shoot if you dare at a woman's belly!'

Here things turned horrific. The National Guard didn't hesitate. Squad fire brought the woman down. She fell with a loud scream. Silence passed over the barricade and the attackers.

Suddenly a second woman emerged. She was even younger and even more beautiful – almost a child, seventeen at most. What profound *misère*! Another prostitute. She raised her skirt, showed her belly, and yelled, 'Shoot, you villains!' They shot her. Riddled with bullets, she fell on top of the first woman.

That is how this war began.[38]

In the draft novel he'd left at home on his work shelf, Hugo had only sketched out the start of a barricade scene. But even in the version he completed twelve years later there is nothing as sad and shocking as this.

On 26 June, a state of siege was declared. The constituent assembly ordered sixty of its members to go to different places around the city to inform rioters of that fact and to persuade them to leave their barricades. Nine representatives were shot dead before reaching their destinations. Hugo made his way to the entrance to the Faubourg du Temple, where he declared the state of siege to an armed and angry mob entrenched behind a huge barricade. He was a dutiful man.

He wasn't wearing any uniform, as he had never been a soldier of any kind. Nonetheless, the bewildered troops facing the barricade took his order to open fire. Hugo seems to have suddenly become a different man. For the next thirty-six hours he stayed in command, shouting advice, giving orders and risking death many times under a hail of fire. (Some of the bullets might have come from the poet Charles Baudelaire, who was having the time of his life taking pot shots at anyone who might have been his hated father-in-law.) Such behaviour was completely unexpected from an exquisitely courteous literary celebrity and ladies' man. At all events, it was an experience like no other Hugo had ever had, and not easy to square with his views, his feelings and his position. By dawn on the third day, the barricade fell. Hugo, exhausted but unharmed, had a lot of thinking to do.

It would be hard to guess from film and stage adaptations of *Les Misérables* that it was written not by a man who fought on a barricade but by the impromptu commander of a military unit that took one down. But it isn't very hard to grasp the reality from the text of the novel itself. The 'wrong-headed violence' of a mob 'against the principles that are its life', he says in his essay on the meaning of 1848,

> must be quelled. The man of probity dedicates himself to this, and out of his very love for the mob he fights against it . . . June 1848 . . . had to be combatted, as a matter of duty, for it attacked the Republic. (V.1.i, 1,052)

What 'the man of probity' considered his duty in June 1848 was at odds with his convictions, for Hugo certainly did not believe he had the right to kill. Yet the rioters were a threat to the republic and to civilization. As a citizen and representative, he had no choice but to put them down. The sight of the rioters' huge and ugly barricade in Rue Saint-Denis was an affront in itself: 'Nothing can be more chilling or more sombre than the hideous heroism of abjection, displaying all the strength of the weak; nothing more chilling than civilisation attacked by cynicism and defending itself like a barbarian.'[39]

Not many of us have to face brutality, or learn how brutal we could be. That was the real catastrophe for Victor Hugo. It's hardly surprising he could not return to the draft of a novel suspended on a different barricade straight after those terrible days, or for a long while after that.

⁋

After the June days, Hugo put his energy into the work of the constituent assembly, labouring to produce a new constitution while the still provisional government moved steadily towards the right, in the name of law and order. There were many fundamental questions to be answered. Should there be two legislative chambers or one? Was universal suffrage such a good idea after all? Should members of former French dynasties be eligible for office? In fact, the nephew of Napoleon I, an unremarkable, rather hesitant man with a German accent, had returned to Paris already and had even started attending the Assembly. Many conservatives openly admitted to having royalist sympathies. Hugo sat through all-night sessions and stuck to the principles of universal male suffrage and eligibility for all. But as there was a continuing risk of civil disorder in his still volatile land, he was not averse to strong leadership. He actually met Louis-Napoléon Bonaparte at a dinner party in November 1848. The man seemed:

> distinguished, cold, gentle, intelligent with a degree of politeness and dignity, a German look, black moustaches, looking nothing like the emperor. He ate little, said little, laughed little, though the dinner party was very jolly . . . [While others were talking politics] Louis Bonaparte fed fish fritters to Mme Barrot's greyhound pup.[40]

His name alone made him a figure of authority, and Hugo thought he might be able to keep a new Assembly in check . . . When the constitution was passed and presidential elections were called for November 1848, the newspaper that Hugo's sons ran under his guidance didn't back the former left-wing president, Lamartine, who was wiped out, as was his successor, the repressive General Cavaignac. *L'Évènement* called on its readers to vote for Louis-Napoléon Bonaparte, who won with a massive majority and took the title of *prince-président*. The Second Republic was entering a new phase.

In May 1849, there were elections for the new legislature. Among a tidal wave of support for the 'party of order', a significant minority returned candidates from the socialist left. French politics was becoming ever more polarized. Hugo became the deputy for the

Department of Seine (effectively, the city of Paris). But where did he stand?

The new Legislative Assembly proposed to install a commission to look into means of alleviating the mass poverty that many felt was the root cause of the turmoil of the previous year. The bill came up for debate on 9 July, and Hugo was the first to speak.[41] He began badly, accusing unnamed deputies of thinking that the only way to deal with unruly mobs was to come down on them hard, that outside main force there was no solution to the problem of order and that everything else was just socialism in disguise. Hugo was heckled and challenged to name names. It took him some time to extricate himself from the tangle of accusations and counter-claims, but he eventually got down to his prepared oration in which he declared that the duty of the nation was nothing less than to 'destroy poverty'. The actions and the talk of the last eighteen months, he said, had produced nothing. It was now time to move towards reconciliation. Socialism (by which he meant the jobs-for-all scheme) had failed but it expressed a hidden truth – man's aspiration to better his lot. If the plight of the poor could be made less dire, then all that was frightening and bad in the socialist project would vanish. Just as leprosy was a disease of the body, poverty, he went on, was a social disease, and like leprosy it could be made to disappear. Hugo gave shocking examples of abjection – people living in rags, scraping morsels of food from rubbish dumps, dying of hunger on the streets. The government had succeeded in re-establishing order, but in truth it had done nothing.

> You have done nothing as long as able-bodied workers are without bread! As long as seniors who have worked all their lives are without homes! . . . As long as you have no fraternal, evangelical laws that give assistance of all kinds to poor and honest families, good peasants, good workers, those of good heart! [He got applauded for that.] You have done nothing, nothing at all, as long as in the persisting subterranean project of darkness and destruction the wretched stand shoulder to shoulder with the evil!

In his rousing conclusion he declared that a body that could pass laws against anarchy must now pass laws against poverty.

Hugo's heart was with the poor and he insisted that *something* had to be done for them, though he was unable to say what. At the same time his head was with order. He had seen civil war close up, and it was not good. He would not budge on the sovereignty of the people and accepted that the results of elections by universal (male) suffrage had to be respected, whatever they were. But he also defended civil liberties, particularly freedom of expression, and became wary of the creeping authoritarianism of the state under its new and still sphinx-like *prince-président*.

Disturbances in June 1849 prompted the expulsion of some left-wing deputies from the assembly. Yet another state of siege gave the government powers to ban public and private meetings of political clubs. In July, a press law made offending the president a punishable offence. In the autumn, the church was given back some of its former role in schools and higher education. Hugo was opposed to most of these changes. When the president summarily dismissed a government approved by the assembly and appointed ministers more amenable to his own views, democracy seemed to be slipping away. In by-elections in March 1850, the country swung firmly behind the 'party of order', but Paris returned a trio of left-wing candidates. That alone persuaded the conservatives in charge that the rabble hadn't yet been 'compressed' enough. In June, a law was passed to restrict the right to vote to men who paid tax, cutting the electorate by about 30 per cent. However, although he had won by a landslide in November 1848, Louis-Napoléon, who was from one point of view no more than the tight-lipped beneficiary of an illustrious uncle, would be obliged to step down at the end of his four-year presidential term. Starting in 1850, the *prince-président* launched a campaign for a constitutional revision to allow him to extend his rule. Victor Hugo, now thoroughly disenchanted with the presidential regime, thundered against the idea of imperial restoration in debates in the Assembly on the proposed constitutional change. 'Just because we had Augustus,' he asked, in a typical repurposing of Roman history, 'do we have to have Augustulus? Because we had *Napoléon le Grand*, do we have to have *Napoléon le Petit?*'[42] The quip provoked 'an inexpressible tumult' of cheers and catcalls. 'Little Napoleon' turned out to be Hugo's best-known political barb, and a nail in his coffin. Louis-Napoléon Bonaparte never forgave Hugo for an insult that hit home. From then on, it was war between the two men.

The first sally targeted Hugo's son Charles in his role as editor of *L'Événement*, a newspaper written exclusively by Hugo's relatives and close friends. For criticizing the way the death penalty had been carried out in a recent case, Charles Hugo was found guilty of 'contempt' and sentenced to six months in the Conciergerie. Then his brother François-Victor and Paul Meurice, a close friend of the family, were given nine months in jail for having invited the government to give political asylum to foreigners (implicitly, to the leaders of national uprisings that had now been suppressed in the Austrian Empire and in Italy). These warning shots were loud and clear. Hugo was in the president's black book.

Louis-Napoléon lost the vote in the Assembly over the constitutional amendment that would have allowed him to stand for president a second time. His riposte was a proposal to restore universal suffrage, since he knew he could rely on a personal majority among the rural masses. He lost that vote in the Assembly too – but this second defeat at the hands of 'mere politicians' was what he needed to justify the action he'd been planning all along.

At dawn on 2 December 1851 – the anniversary of Napoleon I's coronation at Notre-Dame in 1804 and of his victory at the Battle of Austerlitz the following year – placards were posted throughout Paris, under armed guard, announcing the dissolution of the Legislative Assembly and the drafting of a new constitution that would be submitted to a plebiscite with all (men) entitled to vote. During the night a police dragnet had already put eighty democratic militants behind bars along with twenty elected deputies, including all military officers in the Assembly. Troops moved into the parliament building to prevent the remaining deputies from assembling, but some of them – republicans and democrats in the main – managed to get together in the town hall of the tenth *arrondissement*. They voted to unseat the president for having infringed the constitution and ordered prison governors to release all those arrested in the night. They were arrested in their turn and led to prison by soldiers obeying the orders of Louis-Napoléon Bonaparte.

Hugo was tipped off when he was still in bed. He dressed, rushed out and started haranguing workers to take up arms against the *coup d'état*. He had proclamations printed and bills posted. On 4 December, protesters were massacred in the streets, with troops shooting civilians almost randomly. Hugo was a prime target, and he went into hiding. Friends and associates started to slip away over the border. Hugo did not want to leave. Both his sons were in jail, and he still hoped that France would rid itself of the monster who had violated its trust. He was given shelter by friends, but his best 'minder' by far was his lover Juliette. She kept her eyes and her ears open, warned him of risks, led him away from potential traps. He almost certainly owed his life to her. Hugo went unshaven, he didn't change his clothes, he hardly slept. But by the end of the first week, it was clear there was no point in further resistance. Paris was in the firm hands of the army and of Louis-Napoléon Bonaparte. On 10 December, Juliette borrowed a passport from a print-worker she knew. Next day, a man in a top hat and false beard with identity papers in the name of Jacques Lanvin sat at Gare du Nord, waiting for the night train to Brussels. Checks by police at stops in Amiens and Arras went by without incident. By dawn Victor Hugo was in Belgium. He hadn't waited to be thrown out, but only a few days later the *prince-président* declared him a *proscrit*, along with thousands of other republicans, democrats and citizens simply outraged by the coup. They were all banished men now. They would never be allowed back into France.

Interlude: Invisible History

Les Misérables was already a 'historical' novel when it first appeared because its story is set in the past. It begins in 1815, thirty years before the first line of it was written, and ends after Valjean's death in 1835, twenty-five years before the last page was composed. The gap of a human lifespan between the story and its publication allowed it to be read as an exercise in nostalgia for a vanished world. Much more of it has vanished now, of course, in ways that Hugo could not have foreseen. As a result, *Les Misérables* has become 'historical' in another sense besides, as an unintended guide to the way things used to be.

Reading novels as historical resources is not a way of paying attention to what the author meant to say, but a matter of identifying what was once so obvious that it didn't need to be said. For example, Jules Maigret, the recurrent hero of Georges Simenon's series of detective novelettes from the 1930s, often has to buy a token at the bar of a café so as to use the telephone at the back, telling us now that there was a time not so long ago when there were no public telephones in the street, let alone mobile ones. As there is no way of knowing which details of everyday life will be overtaken by change, the truly historical dimension of a novel like *Les Misérables* is to be found in details so ordinary that Victor Hugo didn't even think they needed explaining. Without an explanation, however, later readers can easily miss the point of what Hugo's characters do, think and say. About colours, for example, or about coins, or carriages on the streets.

Hugo had no reason to know that the publication of *Les Misérables* coincided with an advance in chemistry that would rapidly change the very meaning of colour. A young English student, William Henry Perkin, accidentally discovered in his home laboratory in Cable Street that aniline (extracted from coal) could be used to produce a substance with an intense purple colour. Further tests showed that the new compound, called mauveine, could be used to dye fabrics, including silk. Other colours followed in quick succession, and the modern world of cheap and varied colours was born. As we have become entirely accustomed to it, the far drabber colour-world of *Les Misérables* has become hard to understand.

Before synthetic dyes, colours in fabrics and paints were limited to hues that could be extracted from vegetable, animal or mineral sources, some plentiful and others rare. Colour choice in 1862 was not a statement of taste, because the (rather few) hues available for clothes and flags had symbolic meanings related to their cost. Naturally enough, Hugo takes it for granted that you know what the colour codes were – except that few people do any more. Here's a basic guide I've put together to help with the reading of all fiction written in France before around 1865.

White was the field colour of the flag of the French monarchy before 1789. Because of that, the use of white was always associated with the royalist cause. Until 1830, white was also the colour of military uniforms in France, in contrast to the red worn by Wellington's troops at Waterloo.

Blue was also a royal colour, used in the insignia of the Bourbon monarchy when it was restored to the throne in 1815. Because there is no source for it in the flora of northern Europe, it was extracted from an oriental shrub, *indigofera tinctoria*, which had to be imported at great cost. In *Les Misérables*, the botanist-cum-bookseller Mabeuf pins his hopes on experiments to naturalize the plant. If he had succeeded, he would have solved his money problems at a stroke, because 'blue' signalled wealth and high standing all on its own. Alongside white and gold, blue meant 'regal', 'rich' and 'rare'.

At the other end of the code-spectrum was *yellow*, associated with poverty and shame. That's why it was used for the internal passport issued to Jean Valjean on his release from jail. Later on, he persists in wearing a yellow greatcoat even when he is able to afford a more expensive hue. To keep under cover, he needs to be seen as a common man.

Green was a colour of social distinction, just below aristocratic or regal rank. Members of the Académie française wore it, as did politicians and bankers in formal attire. Victor Hugo had a green going-out suit for grand occasions, but he usually wore grey.

In the twentieth century *red* became the symbolic colour of the political left, which is why it was used on the flag of the Soviet Union and the People's Republic of China and by trades unions and socialist parties all over the world. That wasn't yet true in 1862. The story of how red came to mean what it does hangs in no small part on how Hugo used it in *Les Misérables*.

Red is cheap. Extracted from the madder flower, which grows easily in southern Europe, it has been used for millennia for colouring clothes. In Ancient Greece, slaves wore a red cap (known as the 'Phrygian bonnet') to distinguish them from citizens, and red continued to be used to mean 'submission' down to the days of *Les Misérables*. In jail in Toulon Valjean has to wear a 'red blouse', a slight that he never forgets. 'Humiliation' was the primary meaning of the most widespread of all dyestuffs.[43]

In military signalling, however, red had a more specific function. Waving a red flag in battle on land or at sea told the other side that 'no prisoners will be taken', that the engagement would be a fight to the death. After the Bastille was stormed in July 1789, for example, royal troops waved the red flag at rioters to warn them to disperse or be shot on sight. The raucous mob seized the signal and turned it around, using it to provoke troops into confronting them. In a flash, red ceased to be a sign of order and became the symbol of the revolutionary crowd. In a similarly ironical reversal of meaning, the mob also adopted the red cap of Greek slaves to proclaim that the oppressed were now in charge. Red switched its meaning to become the banner of the revolution itself.

That is why the red flag never became the flag of France. The First Republic proclaimed national unity in the blue, white and red tricolour, which was retained by Napoleon down to 1815. On his fall, it was replaced by the blue and white colours of the Bourbon monarchy, and the tricolour became the icon of the republican movement, which was of course banned. The Goddess in Delacroix's *Liberty Guiding the People*, for example, holds the tricolour aloft to show not that she is a French patriot, but the herald of a republic that did not come about. To placate disappointed republicans, the new king, Louis-Philippe, restored the tricolour as the flag of France in August 1830. It was dropped by Louis-Napoléon when he made himself emperor in 1852, of course, but was reinstated as the flag of France when it became a republic once again in the 1870s.

From around 1794, the red flag disappeared outside of military signalling, but it re-emerged as a violent provocation in the events of June 1832 as they are portrayed in *Les Misérables*. Hugo reports in the novel on the funeral of the republican general Lamarque on 5 June:

> This was a touching and solemn moment . . . Suddenly, in the middle of the group a man on horseback dressed in black appeared with a red flag – others say, with a pike and red liberty cap on top of it. Lafayette turned away . . . This red flag raised a storm, and was swallowed up by it. (IV.10.iii, 953)

The German poet Heinrich Heine kept a detailed record of what he saw and heard during his stay in Paris that year. He wasn't at the funeral himself, but informants assured him that it wasn't a red flag that was waved a moment before the riot erupted, but the red-gold-black emblem of a visiting German student group.[44] Right or wrong as his information may be, it's clear from his account and from Hugo's mention of it that raising a red flag was tantamount to a declaration of civil war. Hugo has a couple more red flags waved in Rue du Temple and in Cour Batave, because he does see the uprising as a 'war within four walls' (IV.10.v, 956, 958).

Shortly after the Revolution of February 1848, some members of the provisional government proposed adopting the red flag in memory of the rioters of 1789, but they were overruled by the president,

Alphonse de Lamartine. The nation had to stick with the tricolour, he said, or else fall apart. For him, the red flag was a declaration of unending revolt, not an emblem of popular rule.

However, in *Les Misérables* if not in historical fact, the student group led by Enjolras hoists the red flag over the barricade in Rue de la Chanvrerie.[45] Even for them, of course, it is not yet the 'workers' flag'. It signals, first of all, that they will fight to the death (as they do), and in the second place, that they are fighting for a republic, since the tricolour, formerly the republicans' flag, had been adopted as the national flag by the monarchy of Louis-Philippe. However, the aspirations expressed by the student leaders on the eve of their deaths make this the first real appearance in French history of the red flag as the emblem of broader hopes for a better world.

The pole of the red flag flying over the barricade is shattered by a shell fired by the National Guard. Enjolras asks if there is anyone brave enough to raise the flag again. The destitute bookseller Mabeuf volunteers for this suicidal task and he is shot and killed as he puts it up. When his body is recovered and brought to lie in the front room of the café, Enjolras says that Mabeuf's blood-stained jacket will be hoisted as the revolutionaries' flag from then on.[46] Dried blood doesn't stay red for very long, and no doubt ceased to be visible from a distance very soon. What could be seen at dawn on 6 June was a flag that looked entirely black – and black meant something far worse than red. From Hugo's notes on a day in March 1848: 'Last night four men went through the Saint-Antoine [working-class] area carrying a black flag with these words on it: *War on the Rich!* . . . The flag was made from a woman's skirt.'[47]

A similar incident occurs in *Les Misérables* in a passage written twelve years later with its reference backdated to 1832: 'In Rue St-Pierre-Montmartre, some bare-armed men were carrying a black flag on which these words could be read in white letters: *Republic or Death*' (IV.10.iv, 955).

In the context of revolution and war in nineteenth-century France, 'black' was not the opposite of white, but a darker shade of red. That's why the black coat flying over the barricade provokes the impatient commander of the National Guard to commence the assault before he has received orders to go ahead. He is 'infuriated by the successive appearance of the red flag and the old coat that he mistook for a black one' (V.i.xii, 1,085). He's putting down not just republican militants, but terrorists flaunting the colour of death.

ᵍ

The coinage of *Les Misérables* also allows us to enter a mental world that is as different from our own as the colour codes of a world without modern dyestuffs – despite the fact that France pioneered a currency system that almost all countries have copied since then. In 1803, Napoleon replaced the confusing multiplicity of coins used under the old monarchy with a decimal system based on a single unit, the franc, divided into one hundred centimes. The new French franc was a silver coin weighing 5g, and other silver coins (25 centimes, 50 centimes, 2 francs and 5 francs) were of proportionate weights. The standard of value was gold, fixed at 15.5 times its weight in silver. The new twenty-franc coin, the only gold piece in common circulation, therefore weighed 6.7g, which made it the size of an American dime. Nothing could be simpler in theory, but the practice was something else.

There are around 300 sums of money mentioned in *Les Misérables*, all of which have a specifiable value in francs and centimes. However, Hugo's characters rarely use the official names of the coins that they handle. The language of money in nineteenth-century France was vastly more complicated than what it designated in monetary terms.

There were four different ways of naming money.[48] The sets of words that people used for the coins they exchanged or kept in their purses reflected the class to which they belonged and the kind of transaction they were engaged in. As a result, the way money is counted out in *Les Misérables* reflects and reinforces the structure of the society it depicts.

59

Poor people counted in *sous*, not in francs. The *sou* was not a coin, but a mental unit inherited from the past. The word *sou* is used in proverbial expressions in modern French ('to be penniless' is to be *sans le sou*, for example) but only in French-speaking Switzerland does it still mean what it did 200 years ago, which is five centimes.

After leaving Digne with Myriel's gift, Jean Valjean steals a coin from a mountain lad on his way to earn a living as a chimney-sweep and street entertainer (he has a hurdy-gurdy and a trained marmot with him). Petit-Gervais begs Valjean to give him back his *pièce de quarante sous*, 'forty-sou coin'. 'Forty sous' wasn't embossed on the coin, since all currency was denominated in francs, but even though he'd never been to school, Petit-Gervais could multiply two by twenty and divide 200 by five.[49] Like all other poor people in France, he never used the proper name of the money he had in his hand, but that did not stop him knowing how much a two-franc coin was worth.

The middle classes used different words. For income received from dividends, interest, rents and stipends and for the capital values of property and land, they spoke in *livres*. These were exactly equivalent to francs, so they don't imply the mental agility required to count out small change in *sous*. All the same, the word *livre* is a class-distinctive term of the same general kind. Taken together, *sou* and *livre* make it clear that the money of the rich and the poor were different kinds of thing.

The largest silver coin in circulation was worth five francs and had '5 francs' embossed on it. For people who reckoned in *sous*, its name was the *pièce de cent sous*, the 'one-hundred-*sou* coin'. In transactions reckoned in *livres* – when larger sums of money, or richer people, were involved – the five-franc coin was called an *écu*. When Thénardier tries to sell Valjean the signboard from his old inn at Montfermeil for an outrageous price, he inflates the tone by asking not for 5,000 francs, but for 1,000 *écus*.[50]

Between the 'low' language of *sous* and the 'high' speech of *livres* and *écus* there was a third set of names based on the image on the head side of the coin. Throughout the seventeenth and eighteenth centuries coins had been minted with the head of one Louis or another, so *louis* became the other name of the five-franc piece, which was a *pièce de cent sous* and an *écu* as well. Five francs, 100 *sous*, five *livres*, one *écu*, one *louis* are all the same thing. Hugo makes no effort to explain this confusing multiplicity of names because their meanings were part of the mental equipment all his readers had. What is not said, although it may leave modern readers perplexed, speaks volumes nonetheless. The fact that it went without saying that rich and poor used different words for money is both sign and substance of the social injustices that *Les Misérables* sought to dramatize and to protest.

The highest-value coin in general circulation was the twenty-franc gold piece, first minted when Napoleon was emperor and showing Napoleon's head, and therefore called a *napoléon*. In 1815, Louis XVIII minted new twenty-franc coins showing not the head of 'The Usurper', but his own, and they obviously had to be called *louis* as well. But these new *louis* were worth four times what an *écu*, a *pièce de cent sous*, in other words, a *louis* was worth. A gold coin of 6.7g can hardly be confused with a silver one weighing 25g when you have it in your hand, but in a novel that gives you words in place of things, you can easily lose the thread. Only context and mental arithmetic can tell you whether what is at stake is a *louis d'or*, a golden one, or a silver *louis* worth a quarter of that.

Napoleon Bonaparte also minted a small number of double *napoléons* with a value of forty francs. They seem to have been treated as collectibles from the start, and were not often used for everyday transactions. All the same, you have to keep your eye on the arithmetic when a character in a novel loses his 'last *napoléon*' in a gambling den.

The official term of 'franc' was used to refer to fines, taxes and public expenditure – for anything involving the state, except for sums less than five francs, which were always counted out in *sous*. For example, Valjean says that the purse he received on his release from Toulon consisted of 'one hundred and nine francs and fifteen *sous*' (I.2.iii, 72), not seventy-five centimes, which is what it was.

However, to make a strange system perfectly obscure, the term *franc* was also used, inconsistently, for everything else.

The social and political weight of the way money is named is taken to a comical extreme by Marius's aged grandfather, Luc-Esprit Gillenormand. When he asks his daughter to give the young man an allowance to save him from starvation, he tells her to take him 'sixty *pistoles*' (III.3.viii, 582).[51] The *pistole* was an obsolete Spanish coin no more current in 1829 than the ducats and doubloons of Alexandre Dumas's musketeers. What Gillenormand means to say by using the term is that he has no truck with revolutions or empires and new-fangled decimal nonsense. However, he is using the term not to name a coin (any real *pistole* found in a cupboard or tip was worth either nothing as legal tender or quite a lot to collectors) but as an antiquated equivalent for ten francs. Marius finds the sum in a casket on his desk but as he is too proud to accept a hand-out he returns it to sender. He can't send back 'sixty *pistoles*' in any literal sense, of course, but puts thirty *louis* in a roll to have delivered to his grandfather. But which kind of *louis* were they? The answer makes a difference to the plot. Was Marius playing fair or short-changing the old man? As the computation was already arcane in 1862, Hugo steps down to explain the sum.[52] This comical juggling of alternative names for 600 francs makes a general point that readers of *Les Misérables* need to grasp: that the meaning of money in nineteenth-century France lay in the way it was named, and that the names that individuals used for the coins that they handled always revealed something about their social positions, their attitudes, assets and needs.

The way money was named also tells us that people of all classes could multiply and divide by five and twenty in their heads. That doesn't put them on the level of their British contemporaries, who handled twelve pennies to the shilling and twenty shillings to the pound, counted out in coins as ten florins or eight half-crowns, and it leaves them far behind Guernsey folk who counted in *doubles* worth one-eighth of a penny whilst using coins minted in Jersey worth one-thirteenth and one-twenty-sixth of a shilling. Our forebears must have been rather good at doing sums in their heads.

⁋

France's first railway, from Paris to Versailles, opened in 1837, so *Les Misérables*, set in 1815–35, portrays a world without steam (except for the memory of an experimental river craft that made a noise like a dog paddling and was dismissed as 'a plaything, the fantasy of an impractical inventor' (I.3.i, 111) in 1817). The various means that people used to get from place to place were even greater markers of difference in wealth and rank than cars and buses are today.

Rich people owned their own horse-drawn transport. 'Having a carriage' meant having a coach house, a stable, a coachman and a groom – in other words, you had to be not just a millionaire, but a rich one too. The grandest such vehicle was the four-wheeled *carrosse* with an enclosed cabin and rudimentary suspension. Louis XVIII is glimpsed in the royal carriage on his way back from his daily hunting expedition, but no others are seen in *Les Misérables* until Gillenormand hires two to take Marius and Cosette to get married in church. It was the equivalent of renting a Rolls-Royce for a wedding party nowadays.[53]

The *calèche* was a lighter version, and the niftiest of all carriages was the two-wheeled *tilbury*. Like the *carrosse*, these vehicles required housing, staff and maintenance, and were therefore restricted to people of substantial means (or to outrageous borrowers like Honoré de Balzac, who ran a *tilbury* for a few months until his creditors closed in). Hugo never owned any kind of carriage, even when he was a *pair de France*. He walked, or else he took a cab.

Cabs, called *fiacres*, waited for hire on street corners in Paris round the clock. They were four-wheeled, half-covered, one-horse conveyances driven by a coachman sitting in front of the passengers. There were also two-wheeled *cabriolets*, driven by a coachman standing on an open platform at the back. These were more manoeuvrable and therefore more expensive, but like *fiacres*, they all had identification numbers and charged fixed rates.

Taking a cab did not imply the great wealth required to have a *carrosse*, *calèche* or *tilbury*, but it was not something common folk could afford. When Éponine tells her father that a charitable old man she'd approached in church had taken the bait and was about to come to their hovel in a cab, Thénardier is so delighted that he exaggerates what it means far beyond its real significance: 'In a cab! He must be Rothschild!' (III.8.vii, 676)

Cabs did not venture beyond the gates of Paris. What took people to the suburbs were slow-moving one-horse jalopies painted yellow, with up to six inside seats and space for several more on the roof and the rear. There were as many as 500 of these *coucous* in service before the railways came. Like collective taxis in Israel nowadays, they left their ranks only when full. As a result it was hard to guess when you would get to places like Saint-Cloud or Montfermeil.

Public transport between towns came in several forms. The speediest was the four-horse *malle-poste*, or mail coach, with passenger seats only half-protected from wind and rain. A seat inside a fully enclosed *diligence* was more comfortable, but you could also travel for a lesser fare on the roof. That's how Marius travels to Vernon to find his father, whereas his swanky cousin Théodule snoozes inside.[54]

Along with the several different bone-shakers that Madeleine hires to get him from Montreuil to Arras in time for his trial, these are all the forms of vehicular transport that arise in *Les Misérables*. The only other ways of getting around were on foot or on the back of a horse.

Many people in London and Paris rode horses around town, and riding was even more common in the countryside. Poor folk, however, did not have the opportunity to learn how to ride. It is presumably to express solidarity with his flock that Bishop Myriel uses a donkey or an ass but never a horse to reach remote parishes in his mountainous diocese.[55] Hugo's readers must have taken it as obvious that all Madeleine's tribulations on the road to Arras (the *tilbury* rented from Maître Scaufflaire loses two spokes, the swingle-bar of the wicker cariole hired from an old lady in Hesdin breaks) would have been avoided had he ridden a horse all the way. It's true that he asks the innkeeper at Hesdin if there's a horse to be bought or hired (I.7.v, 224), but despite being the mayor of Montreuil-sur-Mer, M. Madeleine is still Jean Valjean, and people of that class just don't have horses to ride. The unnatural absence of horse-riding from the whole of *Les Misérables* except in the Waterloo scenes is a transparent, perhaps provocative but now almost invisible way of demonstrating what it meant to be among the *misérables*.

For all other purposes everyone walks, and walks to a degree it is hard to credit nowadays. In *Great Expectations*, Pip walks from London to Putney just for dinner; David Copperfield, for his part, walks from London to the coast of Kent; in *The Old Curiosity Shop*, a stunted teenage girl and her half-demented grandfather walk from London to the dark satanic mills of the North. Jean Valjean beats even those sturdy English striders. He walks all the 200 kilometres from Toulon to Digne, covering fifty-eight of them (twelve leagues) in a single day, across hilly terrain.[56] From Digne to Montreuil-sur-Mer is another 900 kilometres, and he walked all the way.

'There is no trivial fact in the affairs of man, no trivial leaf in the vegetable world,' Hugo writes as if to excuse himself from the strange hodgepodge of facts he recalls from his youth (I.3.i, 112). But if history perhaps legitimately neglects some of the details provided in 'The Year 1817', it should not leave aside the colours, coins and carriages of *Les Misérables*, which tell us even more than Hugo could have guessed about the world that his novel depicts.

PART TWO
Treasure Islands

4.
The Money Plot

Fantine's daughter Cosette has an unpromising start in life. The orphaned child of a destitute mother, she is exploited by harsh foster-parents who aren't likely to provide her with education, employment or any prospect of economic advancement later on. She would surely grow up to be a nameless member of the mass of *misérables* but for Jean Valjean, who rescues her from the Thénardiers and gives her a life of a different kind. By the age of eighteen, she is the wife of a prosperous lawyer and has a substantial fortune in her own name. The 'happy ending' of *Les Misérables* may be a miracle from Cosette's point of view, but Hugo doesn't simply pull it out of a hat. The combination of assets and income in the hands of M. and Mme Marius Pontmercy after their marriage in 1833 results from a mostly plausible sequence of economic steps that show how money can be made and lost, kept safe and poured down the drain. The plot of *Les Misérables* is constructed on the basis of a wide grasp of the economic realities of nineteenth-century France – which are significantly different from our own.

One big difference is inflation. It isn't mentioned in *Les Misérables* because it didn't happen in the real world either. The fortune Jean Valjean made at Montreuil-sur-Mer lost none of its value when it was hidden in a hole in the ground for ten years. Had Cosette kept her dowry intact and left it to grandchildren at the end of the nineteenth century, it would still have been worth the same as the wad of banknotes Valjean drew from the Bank of Laffitte in December 1823. Thanks to the bimetallic system introduced by Napoleon, France enjoyed a century of monetary calm.

Valjean's fortune comes from a factory making cheap black beads. It's a strange business to choose as the foundation stone of a novel seeking to present the social history of the nineteenth century. Madeleine's enterprise isn't typical of the new industries from which great fortunes were made at that time – it is not based on coal, iron or steam, it is not related to transport or textiles, and it is not an application of new technology. It is an obscure industrial niche that could have been carved out at almost any time, since the raw materials, the process and the product were all available before 1816 and are just as available now.

However, when *Les Misérables* appeared in 1862, Valjean looked like a business genius. A few weeks before publication date, the Royal Consort, Prince Albert, died. Queen Victoria vowed to wear mourning apparel for the rest of her life – not just black dresses and robes, but black jewels too. Regal diamonds and pearls were shut away and replaced with black gems. Jet, the only true gemstone that is entirely black, became very precious, and black glass, which looks very similar but costs a fraction of the price, was manufactured in great quantities to allow others to follow style. Black glass could in turn be simulated by even cheaper materials, and decorative items that looked more or less like jet could be sold by the shipload in 1862. For the first readers of *Les Misérables*, it stood to reason that Hugo's ex-convict would make a fortune in no time at all, because what he made in his factory at Montreuil-sur-Mer was imitation fake jet. Among all the harsh criticisms made of the novel by newspaper critics at that time, not one took aim at the story of how Madeleine's fortune was made. But fake black gemstones weren't hot products in 1845, when Victor Hugo first invented his story of Valjean's transformation from a pauper into an industrial entrepreneur; nor were they in 1816, when the story of the black bead factory is set. The basis of the main money plot of *Les Misérables* goes deeper than that.

Jean Valjean travels to Montreuil-sur-Mer after a transformative encounter with the bishop of Digne. Thanks to the priest's generosity he has a set of silver plates in his sack, and they provide him with initial capital. It cannot have been very much: as a gram of silver was worth four *sous* (see p. 59 above), 1,000 francs was equivalent to

5kg of silver at the official price, and a set of six even quite substantial plates can't have weighed much more than that. The silver could not have supplied all the working capital needed to build premises, hire workers, lay in machinery and raw materials for a business large enough to generate millions within a short space of time. Actual entrepreneurs of the day would have been financed by their families or by a loan from a bank. But there is not a word about Valjean borrowing money in *Les Misérables*. There is a reason for that. Implausible as it is, the story of a fortune made without recourse to credit corresponds to a belief laid out at great length in the rest of the novel, namely, that borrowing leads not to the creation of wealth but to a downward spiral of debt.

The fall of Fantine, for example, which mirrors and parallels Valjean's rise between 1815 and 1823, is mapped out by the progression of her debts. She leaves Paris in 1817 with eighty francs to her name. At Montfermeil, she pays the Thénardiers fifty-seven francs in advance for the care of Cosette and arrives in Montreuil-sur-Mer with just a pittance in hand.[1] She gets a job straight away at M. Madeleine's bead factory, which allows her to borrow money for rent in advance and to furnish her room. Her outgoings rise as the Thénardiers demand ever higher charges for the upkeep of Cosette, so she falls behind in repayments for the furniture and then with her rent. Her descent into debtor's hell starts even before she is sacked, but it accelerates thereafter as piecework rates fall. Physically, Fantine dies of a chest complaint, but the sale of her furniture, her hair, her teeth and 'the rest' are the fatal consequences of her spending money she did not have.

Marius, on the other hand, avoids the trap. He leaves his grandfather's home with no immediate prospects and just fifteen francs in his pocket, but when his new friend Courfeyrac asks him if he would like a loan, he gives a simple reply: *Never!* Marius manages to get by from selling his smart clothes and gold watch, then from fees for translating from German and English (languages he learns on the job, so to speak). He is a bit of a prig, and a lucky young man as well, but it's important to realize that he is the carrier of the novel's economic morality. Despite having a tiny budget for a couple of years, he never gets into debt. Why does he avoid forward financing so strictly? Because in his mind, and Hugo's too, debt is 'the beginning of slavery' (III.4.vi, 611 and III.5.ii, 616).

It is also the beginning of crime. Thénardier haggles fifty-seven francs out of Fantine in 1817 as down payment for the care of Cosette, but they go straight out the window to pay a bill falling due the next day for 110 francs. But the respite doesn't really help. When Valjean comes to the inn to rescue Cosette six years later, Thénardier's immediate debts have increased to 1,500 francs. In the end, he loses the business entirely to 'a squalid puddle of petty debts' and moves on to outright crime. When he crosses the path of Valjean once again in the Gorbeau tenement, he doesn't have a penny to his name, he is behind with the rent and scrapes by on scams and who knows what other paltry resources the underworld provides. His ingenious rapacity as master of the house at Montfermeil had got him nowhere, and his bid to extort a fortune from Valjean results only in his arrest. Thénardier's legal and illegal business careers are serial disasters. What drives him to crime is the fact that he can't pay his debts. What made him borrow in the first place is the fact that he was a crook from the start. Debt and crime in Hugo's book are two sides of the same coin.[2]

Madeleine's factory is therefore established without recourse to credit so as to avoid a contradiction in the novel's economic morality. But what of the morality of the business itself?

By comparison with most industrial products and processes of the early nineteenth century, making small trinkets out of fake black glass must have seemed utterly benign. Beads do no harm, and their manufacture doesn't send men underground or produce palls of smoke or piles of slag. Madeleine's factory is a model that stands as a reproach to dark satanic mills such as those denounced in Dickens's *Hard Times*. But it is not a fairy-tale.

Madeleine did not invent the idea of simulating black glass, he only found (or borrowed) a new way of doing it. Previously, imitation black glass masquerading as jet had been made from tree resin diluted with alcohol. Madeleine substituted shellac for tree resin and turpentine for distilled spirit. The switch of raw materials lowered production costs, cut the wholesale price, increased the market and allowed handsome profits to be made.

Shellac is excreted by *kerria lacca*, a bug native to the forests of South-east Asia.[3] It is scraped off the trees where the bugs feed, then processed into flaky sheets that may be amber, red or pure black in colour, depending on the host. When diluted with a solvent and warmed, shellac forms a putty suitable for moulding and pressing, and as it cools it turns rock-hard. It has had many uses since the days of M. Madeleine: early gramophone records, oil pipelines, paste jewellery and so on. In liquid form, shellac is the main ingredient of many varnishes and lacquers.

The reason why Madeleine's beads are cheaper than others is that in place of a home-sourced raw material, namely tree resin, he uses a colonial product; and in place of a manufactured solvent, he uses a natural one, turpentine, which is distilled from the sap of the terebinth tree. Both of his raw materials were easy to obtain since wholesalers stocked shellac as an ingredient of sealing wax and turpentine as one of the constituents of household paint. But there is a problem about handling them together. When mixed with shellac and warmed, turpentine gives off noxious vapours that damage the respiratory tract; and until it is cool, turpentine-shellac putty is a major fire hazard. 'When these materials ignite,' a standard work on glassmaking states, 'it is hardly possible to extinguish them. If water is poured on them, they explode like gunpowder, and can easily set fire to everything within range.'[4] The only fire that occurs at Montreuil-sur-Mer is burning hard when Valjean first arrives there.[5] He must have devised a very stringent safety routine, because none occur over the following six years when tons of highly flammable material are processed under his eyes.

In the draft novel written between 1845 and 1848 no explanation is given for the financial success of the bead business, but in passages written on Guernsey in 1861, Hugo has Valjean give Cosette and Marius a fuller account of how he had earned the money that is now theirs. He tells them that his unit cost for manufacturing one gross (that's to say, a dozen dozen, or 144) fake jet earrings was ten francs, for a wholesale price of sixty.[6] That is a huge margin of profit, and it helps to explain why Valjean grew rich. (Because there were no taxes on income, profits or sales, gross margins were net.) What remains to be explained is why such a large mark-up could be had.

Beads of real jet, glass beads painted black to look like jet, and various non-precious stones that have a black or near-black sheen have been prestige objects for millennia. Egyptian mummies are decorated with black beads, and Viking warriors were buried with black glass beads beside them. In more modern times, black beads were used as trim on the mantillas of Spanish *dueñas*, and it is to Spanish buyers that Madeleine sells 'immense quantities' each year. But could Spain have consumed a million or more beads from Montreuil every year just to trim its ladies' apparel? That seems unlikely: the country was bankrupt after 1815 and sank into such turmoil that France decided to invade it in 1823, at the time when Madeleine's business was at its peak. Hugo reminds us of this indirectly in his criticism of the Spanish invasion, and again when Valjean pretends to be a *rentier* reduced to poverty in the Gorbeau tenement by the collapse of Spanish government bonds.[7] The 'immense quantities' of black beads shipped to Spanish ports were probably not intended for resale in the country, but destined to travel further on.

Bilbao, San Sebastian and Cadiz were regular ports of call for ships en route to West Africa to pick up wood, ivory and human cargo from Arab and African middlemen. With what currency? Mostly, black beads. Also called trade beads, or slave beads. Like cowrie shells, they were used as tokens of exchange across the continent. Germany and England manufactured trade beads in great quantities, and it's reasonable to suppose that Madeleine's cheaper knock-offs were picked up in Cadiz to fill the *pacotillas* or 'small packets' that were taken on to Africa and used in exchange. There too the mark-up was outrageous. One slave purchased on the

African coast for a sixty-franc bag of beads would fetch $1,000 when landed in Virginia on the second leg of the infamous Triangular Trade. Perhaps Victor Hugo knew without knowing that the rapid accumulation of wealth in Europe was connected with the horrors of colonial trade, and that Madeleine's laudable relief of poverty in Montreuil-sur-Mer was part of a global network responsible for the most wretched form of human life at that time.

Had Madeleine been an ordinary member of the French middle class, even a philanthropic one, he would have put most or all of his personal savings into French government bonds, which gave a return of around 4 per cent. That was the standard way to acquire an income safe from commercial and political risks and to join the class of *rentiers*. Hugo himself put his savings into government stock and tried to live on the income they produced. But Madeleine could not do that.

Nominally, the French state did not pay interest on treasury bonds because its debts were held to be unredeemable loans. This fiction had few practical consequences, except that instead of buying bonds from brokers, investors had their names 'written down in the Great Book' and were 'granted a pension' in return. Such pensions, called *rentes*, could be awarded only to named individuals with documented identities. Despite being the mayor of Montreuil-sur-Mer, Madeleine had no identity document under that borrowed name, so the path to *rentier* status was closed to him. He had lots of cash, but he was an outcast nonetheless.

His solution was to put his savings into an open account with the bank of Laffitte. It's not a fictional institution, but an important part of the economic and political history of France. Jacques Laffitte was a carpenter's son who started out as a bank clerk and ended up being the main financier of Napoleon Bonaparte and governor of the national bank. After the Restoration he continued to run one of the main French competitors to the Rothschild Bank (which had made a fortune out of Waterloo) and made many major investments in new industries. That's why Madeleine goes to Laffitte rather than another bank for assistance in keeping his profits safe.

But Laffitte got into politics too. In 1830 he headed the coterie that brought King Louis-Philippe to power, who made him his first prime minister in return. Politics proved ruinous to his business, however, and by 1831, Banque Perregaux, Laffitte et Cie was on the brink of liquidation. It's lucky that Valjean withdrew his savings in 1823. He might have had nothing to pass on to Cosette ten years later had he left it in the bank of Jacques Laffitte.

Madeleine withdraws the cash immediately after owning up at the courthouse in Arras to being the wanted runaway ex-convict Valjean. After making his statement, he says he has 'several things to do' (I.7.xi, 256) and walks out. In an exploit worthy of Sue's Prince Rudolph of Gerolstein, he stays free for three days before handing himself over to serve his second sentence in jail. He knows his bank account would soon be seized by the authorities because it was held under a false name. So Valjean's main task at that point is to get to Paris, draw his money from the bank and put it in an even safer place.

He could have drawn it in coin, which would have saved some of the trouble he runs into later on. He can't do that, of course, because 630,000 francs in silver weighed more than three tons, and he would have needed a wagon train to take it away. Even in gold coin, Valjean's nest egg came to 211 kilograms, more than even a strong man could deal with discreetly. Valjean has no choice but to take out his life savings in paper money. Six hundred and thirty 1,000-franc banknotes of that era make a package the size of a large dictionary that could plausibly be hidden in a chest and quickly buried under a few spades of earth.

But what was easy to handle was not easy to use.

Nineteenth-century France was allergic to paper money. The first French republic that arose from the Revolution of 1789 inherited empty coffers, and it tried to keep going by issuing paper money secured not against gold but against the assets it had seized from the church. However, the authorities did not limit the issue of these promissory notes, called *assignats*, to the presumed value of the assets. Between 1789 and 1796, revolutionary governments printed all the money they needed to fund the state, and the result was inflation of almost Zimbabwean proportions. In the west of France, the Catholic resistance to the revolutionary regime also issued paper money, which similarly became worthless in no time at all. This history is commemorated in *Les Misérables* by the counter-revolutionary *assignat* pasted on the wall of Fauchelevent's hut in the garden of the convent where he works and by Enjolras's alcoholic side-kick Grantaire asserting his political credentials by keeping a revolutionary *assignat* in his desk drawer.[8] These souvenirs remind the reader why post-Napoleonic France was reluctant to use banknotes. But as Valjean has no choice but to use them, they are also tiny threads in the finely-wrought web of *Les Misérables*.

After his Batman-like escape from the *Orion*, Valjean makes his way back to Montfermeil, takes some of his money out of the buried chest where he has hidden it, rescues Cosette from the Thénardiers and settles in a squalid apartment in a poor part of central Paris. Now and then he goes back to Montfermeil to draw another 1,000-franc note. He sews it into the lining of his coat before returning to town. When he needs to use the money, he unstitches his coat lining in an unoccupied room in the tenement, out of sight of Cosette, but he does not realize that the landlady is spying on him. She sees him extract from the opening he's made in his coat 'a yellowish piece of paper that he unfolded'. 'She realized with alarm that it was a one thousand franc banknote. It was the second or third such thing she'd seen in her life. She fled in great fright' (II.4.iv, 400).

She's scared because it means her tenant is not what he seems – he must be a crook, or else a millionaire. Valjean compounds the drama by asking her to take it to the Banque de France to get it changed into coin, with the feeble excuse that the banknote is his quarterly *rente* (if that is what it was, then he could have changed it on the spot when he'd drawn it at the same bank). The landlady naturally gossips about this extraordinary event, and soon the whole street knows there's a mysterious millionaire living as a pauper in the Gorbeau tenement. The rumour comes to the ears of the police, and that is why Javert sets the trap that obliges Valjean and Cosette to flee to the convent of Petit-Picpus. At bottom, the banknote – with the fear that it inspires – is the narrative prompt for a major turn in the plot of *Les Misérables*.

§

Valjean's cash is nonetheless kept safe for ten years and provides a substantial dowry for Cosette, but her marriage is not quite the end of the money plot. Thénardier catches sight of Cosette and Marius on their way home from the wedding when their carriage is stuck in the Mardi Gras parade, then inveigles his way into the new household to put a proposal to the young lawyer. He believes that the mysterious father of Cosette who had made Marius rich was an ex-convict (he is right about that) who had stolen the fortune from a man called Madeleine (wrong). He's willing to destroy what he believes is proof of the crime in return for a slice of the dowry. Like Balzac's arch-criminal Vautrin, Thénardier believes that 'the secret of great fortunes with no apparent source is a forgotten crime'[9] – but he's wrong again, and Marius knows it. Valjean has told his adoptive son-in-law who he really is and has explained the origin of the wealth he handed on. But the irremediably crooked Thénardier with his half-baked scams remains a blot on the landscape, and Paris would surely be better off without him. Marius gives him part of what he wants – not in coin, but in the form of a promissory note drawn on a bank in New York. That's where Thénardier wants to go – to become a trader in slaves.

Hugo's villain is wrong yet again, because the State of New York had freed its last remaining slaves in 1827. Six years later, after the wedding of Marius and Cosette, the now comical villain of *Les Misérables* leaves the scene planning a new career in a business that no longer exists. For him, at least, crime will never pay.

In its first composition of 1845–8, *Les Misères* tells the story of an ex-convict's transformation into a prosperous manufacturer of black beads who despite great obstacles preserves 630,000 francs in banknotes hidden in the ground. However, all the more intricate details of the money plot were added during the second period of composition of Les Misérables between January and June 1861.

On 15 April 1861, the first shots rang out in the American Civil War. The plot of Les Misérables may not venture outside of France, but the story of a fortune begun in 1845 and completed seventeen years later takes us from the unspoken end-use of trade beads in Africa to the nightmare it unleashed in the New World.

In between those dates Hugo's own fortune had taken a battering. How it was restored is part of the story of the making of Les Misérables.

ʃ

In the 1840s Victor Hugo lived in a large rented apartment in a grandiose square in a run-down part of central Paris that was predominantly working class. He lived on the product of his writing, the most profitable part of which was his work for the theatre, and he was doing very well. He spent lavishly on antiques but held back substantial sums that he put into government bonds. In the first days of the revolution in February 1848, when Hugo was dashing back and forth to the Chambre des pairs, his opulent apartment was a sitting target for the rioting mob, which broke in when he was out of the house. Angry men were on the brink of ransacking it when one of them noticed a petition lying on top of a paper pile. It was a call for clemency for mutineers in the fleet at Le Havre. Hugo's bold signature at the foot of the page persuaded the invaders that the great poet was a true friend of the people, so they turned around and left the place intact. That was a close shave for Victor Hugo and for us. The paper pile beneath the petition was the whole of Les Misères.

Four years later, Hugo was a banished man living in exile in Brussels. He had lost access to his investments in France and had no way of retrieving the treasures at Place des Vosges. As he had stopped paying rent for the apartment, its contents were seized and sold off. This sentimental, aesthetic and financial blow was softened a little by friends who bid for some of Hugo's objects at the auction with the aim of returning them to the poet one day. However, no manuscripts came up for sale. Every scrap of Hugo's writings had been piled into a trunk in December 1851 and taken over the border to Brussels.

In Paris, Louis-Napoléon had the army, police, the middle class, prisons, money and guns. In Brussels, all Hugo had was his pen. But he would make it spit fire! The first salvo was an incendiary pamphlet titled by the same quip that caused such an uproar in Paris in 1850: *Napoléon le Petit*, 'Napoleon the Small'. It is vindictive, insulting and over the top, and that was the point: to use rhetoric as a weapon of war, to rally the masses and bring down the illegitimate dictator of France. It could not be published or printed in France, of course, but that was not a problem. Belgium had a thriving book industry based on the production of unlicensed material for smuggling into France. Many tens of thousands of copies of *Napoléon le Petit* were circulated in this way, and it was quite foreseeable that Paris would soon ask Brussels to clamp down on the trade and on the man who had produced such a severe irritant to the new regime. Hugo did not wait for the order to leave, which was sure to come. He moved on as soon as he could, like a man on the run. Money was one problem, of course, but the main one was finding a place to go.

England was the obvious choice. It had no immigration laws and was notoriously tolerant of firebrands and refugees from abroad. (That's why Karl Marx found safe haven in the British Library at that time.) But London was expensive, especially for a man who had a wife, two sons, a daughter and his beloved Juliette to care for and no certain source of future income. In addition, the whole city was an affront to a French patriot: the very names of Trafalgar Square and Waterloo Station were reminders of national humiliation. Worse still, almost everyone spoke English.

America would have welcomed him, but it was largely English-speaking too. Portugal was tempting because it was cheap and warm; Spain too, and it had the advantage of speaking a language that Hugo knew from the year he had spent in Madrid as a child. But they were too far away. Hugo still hoped that Louis-Napoléon's detestable regime would not be tolerated by French citizens for very long. He wanted to be close by when it fell, perhaps even to be the tool of its richly deserved collapse. Some political refugees (such as Eugène Sue) crossed into the Kingdom of Savoy (the area around Annecy and Chambéry, which was not yet part of France); others went to Baden-Baden in Germany, and yet others followed the path of Voltaire and Madame de Staël by moving to the Republic of Geneva. Hugo stumbled on an even better idea.

The Bailiwicks of Jersey and Guernsey belong to the British Crown, but they are not part of England or of the United Kingdom and have never been part of the European Union. They have been inhabited since prehistoric times, but their modern population descends from the Normans who also conquered England in 1066. When King John gave up his claim to the continental part of Normandy in 1204, he retained ownership of the islands in the Channel (with the exception of Chaussey), which have been 'particulars' of the British Crown ever since. These charming islands are all that's left of the once-great Duchy of Normandy. They are self-governing and make their own laws, which are written in French. In the nineteenth century educated Channel Islanders spoke standard French (with some local variations), and that meant that Hugo would not have to learn another tongue. The farmers and fishermen who made up most of the islands' population still used a dialect directly descended from the Franco-Norman language spoken by William the Conqueror ten centuries before.

Hugo heard of the Channel Islands because small groups of political exiles from Italy, Hungary and Germany had already found refuge there. So with his wife, his children, his lover and his manuscript trunk, he travelled by coach, train and boat via Ostend, Dover, London and Southampton and landed at St Helier on 5 August 1852. He soon found a large house to rent on Marine Terrace, next door to where an eccentric utopian, Pierre Leroux, lived. Other *proscrits* followed Hugo's lead and formed a community that saw itself as a vanguard of moral and verbal resistance to Louis-Napoléon. Some among them even saw St Helier as a base for real action, since Jersey lies only a few miles from the coast of France. However, the only invasion Victor Hugo imagined would be led not by guns but by words.

The first thing Hugo did on Jersey was to turn the angry prose of *Napoléon le Petit* into the biting verse of *Les Châtiments* (*Chastisements*). The poetry collection has a broader sweep, and its vicious rhymes swat not just the 'little man' at the top but all the scoundrels, turn-coats and money-grubbing careerists who had helped put him there and were keeping his cardboard castle standing up. Hundreds of thousands of copies were printed outside France and got over the border inside crates of fruit and ladies' boots, stuffed into linings and stitched into cloaks, landed on beaches by fishermen and hauled over passes on carts. *Les Châtiments* were read by thousands, and Hugo was right to think a large part of the nation was with him. But Louis-Napoléon's regime, now renamed the Second Empire, kept on failing to fall apart.

Les Misères had been on the shelf for five years but had not been forgotten. Hugo had read excerpts to relatives and friends in 1847 in the drawing room of his apartment, raising expectations that the work would soon be finished. On 31 July 1848, Hugo's sons used the first issue of their newspaper to declare that 'in 1848, we shall have *Les Misères*'.[10] The year passed, then another, and another, without any sign that work on the novel had resumed, let alone been completed. In the summer of 1851, 'three years and seven months after being interrupted by a revolution', Hugo did at last appear to be ready to return to work on his novel. In October, he consulted the Muse about what he should do next, and she shouted back at him: 'Finish Your Book!'[11] However, the confiscation of the Second Republic by Louis-Napoléon Bonaparte on December 2 got in the way of even her plans.

These largely involuntary deferrals allowed a change to take place in the back of Hugo's mind. It came to light in 1853 on the back panel of the first printing of *Les Châtiments*, in the customary list of the author's 'forthcoming works'. Among them would be a new novel 'entirely unconnected to contemporary political issues' that would constitute 'in dramatic and novelistic mode a kind of social epic of poverty'.[12] The title to which that description was attached was no longer *Les Misères*, but *Les Misérables*. However, the new and definitive title was not quite a key to the gate to the book. Hugo had many more troubles and trials to overcome before he could open it up.

At Marine Terrace a stream of visitors from France brought news, gifts, friendship, even a few curios saved from the liquidation sale. One among them brought to the island a new American craze that was sweeping through Paris and that allowed you to communicate with the deceased. All it took to talk to the other world was a wooden-top table with three metal legs. Intense concentration was needed, but once you got the hang of the thing you could talk to the past.

Hugo was fascinated and learned how to speak through the 'turning table' with a host of old friends, among them Moses, Virgil, Dante and Shakespeare, who had most conveniently learned French in the ample leisure they had had in the beyond. Participants in these spiritist séances sat around the 'turning table' and asked it if anyone was there. The table responded with taps on the ground apparently made by one of its legs. One tap for yes, two for no; for longer messages, one for A, two for B, three for C, in a kind of celestial Morse. Delphine de Girardin, who had brought the idea to Jersey, soon went back to the mainland, but the Hugos carried on calling up absent spirits almost every night for more than a year. Adèle II wrote down what they said, and her transcriptions allow us to follow the strangest of all the adventures of Hugo's mind.

Even in the shadow-world, Hugo did not forget what he still had to do. When he asked the Spirit of Civilization what his task was in the years that remained, the answer came straight from the shoulder, in a rather long sequence of taps: 'Great Man, finish *Les Misérables!*'[13]

The 'table-turning' phase of Hugo's Jersey years has persuaded some people that the writer was out of his mind. If so, then millions of other members of the European middle class were just as insane. From 1853 until the end of the century, communication with the other side was a common pursuit in parlours far and wide. Competent scientists tried to explain away talkative ghosts, but they made barely a dent in the Victorian preference for mystical gurus who claimed that souls live on and also come back. Hugo had plenty of company in his wish to believe that he could have conversations with the deceased.

He was nonetheless wary of being thought foolish by readers of a rational bent. There are plenty of 'spectres' and 'ghouls' mentioned in *Les Misérables*, but almost all of them arise as metaphors and are not intended to be taken literally. Nonetheless, the return from their graves of all the leading characters to sing the finale in the musical that has been made from the book isn't entirely false to the beliefs and wishes of Victor Hugo. Many of the things that Boublil and Schönberg did to the story of *Les Misérables* might have had the author storming out of the theatre in rage, but if he managed to wait until the finale his view of the show might have softened. For he does bring a revenant into the room in the last act of his hero's life.

Jean Valjean is on his death-bed in his bare apartment in Rue de l'Homme-Armé. The doctor can see there is nothing he can do and asks the patient if he wants him to call a priest to say last rites. Valjean says no. This would have been a mildly shocking refusal in nineteenth-century France, except for the follow-up. Waving his hand towards the mantelpiece, where two silver candlesticks stand, Valjean says he has a priest already. The narrator comments: 'It is likely that the bishop was indeed present at this hour of death' (V.9.v, 1,301). As the charitable bishop who had made a gift of the candlesticks had been dead for many years, the priest in the room at the close of the novel can only be the ghost of Monseigneur Bienvenu.

When he was not entertaining guests, holding séances or walking on the beach, Hugo was a busy man. He was the most prominent member of the exile community, its principal spokesman in relations with island officials, and the only person of authority who could maintain some degree of cohesion and order among a fractious and often desperate bunch of men. Friction between the islanders and the refugees had several causes. The least tractable was the ancient hostility these strict Protestants felt for the predominantly Catholic French. Their rigid observance of the Sabbath irritated continentals used to a more relaxed regime, but it was so important to the islanders that it overruled even loyalty to the British Crown. When Queen Victoria made a state visit and came ashore on a Sunday, all the islanders turned out to watch her carriage process – but not one in ten men took off his cap, in silent protest at Her Majesty's failure to respect the Lord's Day. The queen smiled graciously at the few who did acknowledge her as she passed, but it's not likely she ever learned that one of them was Victor Hugo.

But it wasn't just a matter of having to tolerate papists in St Helier. The refugees were mostly penniless and they brought nothing to the island's trade. Some of them wore beards, others had long hair, and some were probably atheists as well. A few of them had been seen eyeing up boats they probably planned to steal for an amateur invasion of France. As in many situations of this kind today, ordinary residents viewed the migrants as an alien and untrustworthy lot. There were spies among them, that was for sure. But were their paymasters in London, in Paris, or further afield?

The breach between the host and migrant communities was exacerbated by the outbreak of a distant war. In a disastrous attempt to defend Turkey's hold on Crimea against a Russian advance, Britain became an ally of the new emperor of France. Napoleon III was given a lavish welcome when he made a state visit to London, and it seems that he took the opportunity to ask the British government to deal with the nuisance on Jersey. Westminster could only meet the French request in a roundabout way because it had no direct power over the internal affairs of the island. Parallel orders also came from Paris to the French Consul in St Helier to find a way of getting Hugo and his consorts thrown out. French agents pressured exiles to spy on their comrades and rivals, British agents kept close watch on the French while pulling their own strings among the island's elite to increase tension between the community and the refugees. By 1855 the imbroglio in this otherwise quiet and orderly place reached a level of complication worthy of a novel by Le Carré.

The trigger for the showdown was an open letter to Queen Victoria asking her not to flatter Napoleon III by making a return visit to Paris. Written by a French exile in London, it was published in *L'Homme*, the journal of the French exile community. It was taken to be offensive to the queen, to whom the islanders were intensely loyal. It took the lid off the resentments that foreign agents had been stoking as best they could, and all of a sudden the townsfolk of St Helier wanted the French exiles to leave. Victor Hugo had had almost nothing to do with the letter itself, but he made a show of standing shoulder to shoulder with his comrades, provoking a flicker of a riot that nearly turned into a lynching party. To preserve public order, the authorities ordered the great man and his sons to leave. The name of the document that was handed to him only made sense to Victor Hugo when he'd repeated the main word in it to himself with the diction appropriate to the 'great language of the human race': *Expieulcheune*.

Where could he go now? With his family, and his manuscript trunk?

5.
Hauteville House

Jersey and Guernsey had much in common but had always led separate lives, with different legislatures, customs and coinage. There was even a degree of animosity between them, and it was this quirk in the history of the Anglo-Norman Islands that gave Hugo his new place of abode. It stood to reason that a victim of Jersey's *expieulcheune* would be welcome on Guernsey's shore. It was a stroke of luck that heralded many more. The steamer that took the thrice-exiled group from St Helier to St Peter Port on 31 October 1855 was certainly buffeted by high seas, but the winds of Hugo's fortune had begun to turn.

In 1855, Guernsey was not the holiday resort and tax haven of today. Its population of about 40,000 worked in three small industries (a quarry, a shipbuilding yard, and the knitting of 'garnseys' with imported wool) or in farming and fishing, with a bit of smuggling on the side. Smaller than Jersey and even more blessed by the Gulf Stream, it has an exceptionally mild climate that allows geraniums and tomatoes to grow year round out of doors. For a nature-lover like Victor Hugo, it was close to paradise. Wild flowers bloom on gentle slopes and dramatic cliffs, seabirds of every kind wheel in the sky, and from almost every high point there are views of the sparkling, raging, magnificent sea.

Hugo arrived there with a work almost completed on Jersey. Not *Les Misérables*, but a substantial body of lyrical verse that he organized into a kind of poetic biography of himself. He completed it in early 1856 and had it published in Brussels by his old friend and fellow exile Pierre-Jules Hetzel. *Les Contemplations* came out in 1856 and was immediately recognized as a milestone achievement. It contains many of the best-known and most-loved lyrics written in French. By the time Flaubert's *Madame Bovary* and Baudelaire's *Les Fleurs du mal* (*Flowers of Evil*) appeared the following year, the delicate, enchanting, eerie and memorable poetry of *Les Contemplations* was in everybody's ears.

Unlike *Napoléon le Petit* and *Les Châtiments*, *Les Contemplations* was not a clandestine publication. Its sale was permitted in France, and Hugo was able to receive payment for it. The book made Hetzel a rich man and replenished Hugo's coffers too. After three years drawing down and nearly exhausting his reserves, he could now return to living within his means, and living quite well.

Soon after coming ashore at St Peter Port, Hugo found a vacant large house to rent. It hadn't been lived in for some time because of fears it had been visited by one of the island's undead. Hugo learned of this after he moved in when the cook told his wife that the only tenant in the last four years had had to move out because of the knocking that could be heard at night. The servants were sure they could hear the ghost moving about, and Hugo himself was woken up by 'something like the noise that dwarves running up and down a wooden staircase would make'.[14]

Hugo didn't think of moving out when he learned that Hauteville was a haunted house. Perhaps he'd grown sceptical of his own pursuit of the undead, or perhaps he liked the idea of having a visitor. As he already had an advance for *Les Contemplations* and was confident that more was on its way, he approached the owner and bought the place outright. Like most French people in that period Hugo was not accustomed to owning his own home, and Hauteville remained the only property that ever would be his. However, he had a special reason for using his cash in that way. Owning a house made him a taxpayer, and on Guernsey, taxpayers had an inalienable right of abode. After four years of moving ever on, Hugo now had a permanent home.

Hauteville was large enough to house the whole clan: the writer, his wife Adèle, his elder son Charles and his younger son François-Victor (both bachelors still) and his equally unmarried daughter,

Adèle II. Her suitor, Auguste Vacquerie, who was a fervent disciple of Victor Hugo, also needed a room. A household of that kind required live-in servants – a cook, Marie Sixty, and two maids, who rotated quite often. Hugo organized the house and its inhabitants from bottom to top. The ground floor supplied the public rooms (dining room, billiard room and the guest suite, initially reserved for Vacquerie). The first floor was for the two Adèles, each with her own bedroom, and two large reception rooms facing on to the garden and the sea. The second floor was allocated to the young men, Charles and François-Victor, with a bedroom each and a shared bathroom, and a similarly imposing salon with views to the sea. Only the top floor, by far the least grand, was Hugo's own retreat. His bedroom was small and gave on to a junk room and to an antechamber where the maids slept (Hugo insisted they sleep nearby). The space he set aside for writing was hardly luxurious and must have been difficult to heat, as it gave directly on to a roof terrace through glazed doors. He called it his 'Look-Out', variously spelled by Juliette and others as *loocout*, *loukot* and so on. Juliette herself was part of the ménage, but had to be housed elsewhere. The agreement with Adèle rested on strict territorial respect, and the 'other woman' was never allowed into the house. For his lifelong lover Hugo rented La Fallue, just a few steps away, across a garden and over a wall. Juliette could see Hugo when he stepped out on the roof terrace every morning to take an open-air bath in a tin tub. He insisted that 'hydrotherapy' did him good, and she fussed about him catching cold in the morning air. They loved each other a lot.

Hugo set about making his home unique. He had gas lighting put in and then redecorated the place from bottom to top. The dining room was done in blue-and-white tiles with Latin mottoes and logos incorporating the letters 'V. H'. The first-floor lounges were lavishly decorated with red and blue fabrics and all kinds of exotic objects found in sales. The second-floor salon was the most bizarre: panelled from floor to ceiling in dark oak with carvings of medieval inspiration, its main exhibit was a huge wooden bed on which Hugo said he would spend his last hours. Throughout this exercise in gothic interior design

Hugo installed *objets d'art* and pieces of furniture he thought up himself and had made by a local craftsman, Tom Mauger. This Victorian wonderland has been left more or less as it was and can be visited in the summer months. The conception and installation of this richly detailed and self-obsessed interior decor was Hugo's consuming passion from 1856 to 1859. He even got to the point of wondering whether he had chosen the wrong career. Maybe he should have devoted his energies not to literature and politics, he mused, but to decorating homes. Thank goodness it was only a thought.

The remodelling of Hauteville was not the principal reason why *Les Misères* stayed in the manuscript trunk for so long. Jersey and the sight of the sea had sparked off an intense burst of creation in poetry that had not yet run its course, and when he got to Guernsey Hugo continued to produce large amounts of narrative and increasingly philosophical verse. He had always been an occasional painter, and on Guernsey he also put more time into watercolours, pen-and-ink sketches and unclassifiable visual works in other media. It's as if he was giving himself a protracted holiday from prose before settling down to what he had known for many years would be an immensely challenging task.

On 25 April 1860, Hugo finally went to his manuscript trunk in the Oak Room of Hauteville House and took out the work he'd broken off in February 1848. He looked at a few pages of *Les Misères* and took them with him to read aloud that evening when he went over the road to have dinner with Juliette at La Fallue. Next morning, as every morning, Juliette's first thought was to write a letter to her lover in the big house over the way.

> Did you sleep well, my dear great man? Did your little Cosette not make too much of a noise in your head last night? . . . My mind is still quivering with affection and joy as if I were expecting the return of a real daughter of our own we'd been parted from for twelve years.[15]

The campaign to turn a draft into the greatest novel of the nineteenth century was about to get underway.

6.

The Beliefs of Victor Hugo

Les Misérables expresses the beliefs that Hugo held, which were quite particular to him. He was never reluctant to say that he believed in God, but he did not subscribe to any established tradition or cult. Contrary to the impression that *Les Misérables* may make on some readers, Hugo was not a Catholic. Unlike most French people of his age he had never been baptized or confirmed and had never taken communion; he never attended religious services and never went into church to pray.[16] But pray he did. And he was adamant that *Les Misérables* was 'a religious book'.

At the start of the story, in October 1815, a fierce-looking ex-convict that no innkeeper will house is offered a meal and a bed by a priest. Valjean wakes up in the small hours, puts the silverware he's seen at dinner in his kitbag, climbs over the garden wall and runs off. Local gendarmes arrest him and bring him back to the bishop's palace. Myriel stuns the policemen and the ex-convict by saying (untruthfully) that he had made a gift of the silverware to the outcast, who had overlooked the two silver candlesticks that he'd meant to give him as well. This exceptionally charitable act strikes to the heart of the rough customer just out of jail. He resolves to turn himself into a different man and to be as good to others as Monseigneur Myriel has been to him.

Hugo's elder son Charles, a rationalist and a republican through and through, did not approve of this portrait of a saintly priest. One evening at Marine Terrace, fulfilling his half-official role as the winder-up of his father's after-dinner talk,[17] he declared that the uplifting 'candlestick story' at the start of *Les Misères* was a dreadful way to begin. Adèle II's record of the ensuing flare-up is almost fit for the stage:

> CHARLES: Priests, especially Catholic ones, are the enemies of democracy. To make a Catholic priest a model of perfection or understanding is to do a favour to the Catholic church, it's like saying that Catholicism and the ideal of the good can be one and the same thing.
>
> *He finished up by saying his father should use, in place of a priest, another kind of man, a modest professional like a doctor, for instance.*
>
> VICTOR HUGO: First, in general, there will always be religions and priests. There are different ways of being a priest. Whoever teaches about the invisible world is a priest. All thinkers are priests.
>
> CHARLES: Well, take a thinker then, a priest of times to come, not a priest of times past, the enemy of the future.
>
> VICTOR HUGO: You can't put the future in the past. My novel is set in 1815.
>
> *Charles Hugo used as a secondary argument in the conversation the bad impression that the glorification of a priest would make on republicans, who would not understand the book's aim.*
>
> VICTOR HUGO (*loud*): You call Myriel a Catholic priest? I would say that the portrait of a pure, great and real priest in my book is the most savage satire imaginable of real living priests today.
>
> *Charles Hugo then raised the objection that it would nonetheless irritate a number of blinkered and obstinate republicans.*
>
> VICTOR HUGO (*louder*): I don't care about the opinions of crazy or blinkered republicans! What I care about is doing my duty. At my time of life, having scaled every peak, having been a member of the Académie and the Chambre des pairs, having served in two parliaments [. . . and] having even turned down a ministerial post, here I am, in exile. Here I am no longer a man, I am an apostle and a priest. I am a priest. Mankind needs religion. People need God. I'm not afraid to proclaim that every night I pray.[18]

Hugo's after-dinner outburst about religion and prayer wasn't directed just at the audience round the table. Behind Charles's bid to steer *Les Misérables* away from favourable representation of a member of the Catholic church lay the wider community of unbelieving socialists and republicans in exile on Jersey and elsewhere, who hoped that the most famous *proscrit* among them would pin his flag to their mast. Many of them went so far as to think that Hugo's attachment to religion was unhinged. Kessler, a loyal hanger-on who followed Hugo from Jersey to Guernsey, called the great man a cretin to his face for believing in God. Pierre Leroux, the utopian philosopher who lived next to the Hugos at Marine Terrace, made a sport of poking fun at Hugo's beliefs during their long walks together on the beach. (Hugo privately dubbed that notorious scrounger a *philousophe*,[19] blending the words for 'crook' and 'philosopher'; in *Les Misérables*, he goes so far as to transfer the insult to Thénardier).[20] An adulating scribe, Martin-Dupont, felt it proper to say that Hugo's beliefs were childish and could be summed up as diluted Catholicism. 'Either you believe or you don't, and that's that,' was Hugo's conventional conversational riposte.[21] But the fact is that in 1845, at the start of the work, in 1854, in argument with his son, in 1862, in the final version of the novel, and at all other times in his life, Hugo was respectful of all those who had faith but had no interest in what faith that was.

Bishop Myriel (whose character is based on the historical Bishop Miollis of Digne) is certainly not an average ecclesiastical dignitary of the era. He lies without a qualm, and to the police; he sells stolen property recovered from a bandit; his beliefs do not appear to include the divinity of Christ or the Virgin Birth. His refusal of pomp and his charity towards the poor and the oppressed are silent reproaches to the regular behaviour of the Catholic hierarchy. That's why Catholic readers of the first edition of *Les Misérables* in 1862 were outraged more by the character of Myriel than by almost anything else in the book. The nephew of the real Miollis protested in a letter to the press: Hugo had no right to refer so transparently to his uncle, he said, and especially not to add 'details entirely contrary to the truth and of a libellous nature', namely the 'odious, absurd, fantastical and abominable' scene where Bishop Myriel kneels at the feet of the political outcast G.[22]

Charles was the first in a long line of readers who have tried to bend *Les Misérables* to fit political agendas and ideas alien to Victor Hugo. Because he put in his oar before the book was finished – while it was still the incomplete draft suspended on 21 February 1848, with only its new title in place – he was more effective than anyone else in making the novel even more firmly what it is. In the work Hugo did later on to complete and expand his draft, he paid special attention to broadening and deepening his image of the godly man of the church. Partly to show Charles who was in charge, and partly to make sure he would be completely understood.

Myriel gives away 90 per cent of his stipend, leaving himself only 1,500 francs a year to live on. That certainly justifies calling him *un saint homme*, which means a little less than 'a holy man' and rather more than 'a good guy'. However, it is not the saintliness but the *fairness* of Myriel that Hugo foregrounds in the title he chose for the first book of *Les Misérables*, 'Un Juste'. Meaning something more than 'good', the word *juste* points more specifically to righteousness. (The 'Righteous Among Nations' honoured by the State of Israel at Yad Vashem are called *Les Justes Parmi les Nations* in French.) Myriel is an example not of what a priest might be, but of how a just man – a fair and righteous man – can mitigate the injustices visited on others by the social practices of nineteenth-century France.

The world depicted in *Les Misérables* is far less marked by religious customs and objects than real France was at that time. No wayside crucifixes or shrines decorate the streets of Hugo's Paris or the countryside around Digne; no character in Hugo's novel turns to 'the eternal book for all the weary and the heavy-laden, for all the wretched, fallen and neglected of this earth', as Dickens calls the Bible in *Dombey and Son*;[23] Bishop Myriel is seen officiating at no formal ceremony; Valjean refuses last rites; he never takes communion, although he goes into churches to pray after dark – but Marius, Enjolras, Gavroche, Thénardier and so forth don't even do that. On Christmas Eve at Montfermeil, the millers and hauliers drinking at the inn don't think of attending Midnight Mass. The wedding of Cosette and Marius – which has the potential to make a grand theatrical denouement to the whole plot – is dismissed in a couple of sentences.[24] Hugo really does not want to take *Les Misérables* inside a church, so as not to let the church think it has a role in the 'indefinite but unshakeable' religious slant of *Les Misérables*.

Film directors often put back in what Hugo so pointedly omits. In a 1952 remake of Boleslawski's film version, for example, Lewis Milestone has Valjean repent for his theft of forty *sous* from Petit-Gervais under a shrine to the Virgin Mary. Tom Hooper chose to shoot some scenes in his 2012 adaptation of the musical in Winchester Cathedral, and he places church-like candles in many other frames. These ecclesiastical decorations can be justified if the aim is to provide a plausible vision of nineteenth-century France, but they introduce ideas that Hugo took care to avoid. Films of *Les Misérables* that display the conventional symbols of the Catholic faith suggest that the work has a religious meaning to match. Hugo's strongly held beliefs were much less specific than that.

A few months after reading a few pages from *Les Misères* to Juliette in April 1860, Hugo wrote two new chapters to insert near the start of the book. They contain the episode in which Myriel dines with an atheist senator (I.1.viii) and the story of his encounter with a dying radical holding views that were abhorrent to the church (I.1.x). Their aim is to establish in crystal-clear terms the religious position of the bishop and, by implication, the ideal faith of the whole book.

The main role of the atheist senator is to be knocked for six. This loquacious gourmand regurgitates a well-known eighteenth-century argument that human beings are no more than machines. On this view, which has no place for a god, the purpose of life is to have as much pleasure as possible.

What is there to do on this earth? To suffer, or to enjoy. I have the choice. Where will suffering take me? Nowhere. But I will have suffered. Where will enjoyment take me? Nowhere. But I will have had some pleasure. (I.1.viii, 31)

In this pre-Darwinian view, life is being created all the time, so questions about its origin are irrelevant. The senator also rejects renunciation and sacrifice: wolves don't do it, and nor should we. He does not believe in a god or in the message of Jesus Christ, and, more generally, he denies that any moral law exists. There is no punishment after death, he says, because nothing can be done to a pile of old bones. However, something is needed to keep the poor in their place, and that's where religion comes in. The soul, immortality, paradise and so on are human inventions that aim only to placate *les misérables*. They lap it up since it's all they have to spread on dry bread. God is for the people, he tells Myriel, but not for us.

To modern ears, Hugo's cynical senator seems to have been reading Karl Marx. That is obviously not possible, because Marx's dismissal of religious faith as 'the sigh of the oppressed creature, the heart of a heartless world . . . the opium of the people' was written in 1844, decades after the senator's dinner with Myriel, and it hadn't been translated into French when Hugo wrote this chapter. However, the senator's atheistic creed alludes directly to the probable source of what Marx said about faith. In 1793, the revolutionary leader Maximilien Robespierre (the man blamed for the Terror of 1793–4, and anathema to the church) rejected a proposal to set up a godless Cult of Reason as the official creed of the new French state. Why so? Because 'atheism is an aristocratic creed, whereas the idea of a supreme being who offers succour to the oppressed and the innocent while punishing the triumphs of crime comes from the people'.[25] At the dinner with the atheist, Myriel turns the tables by enlisting Robespierre: yes, he says, my congratulations, you have views entirely in keeping with your exalted position in society. Hugo scores a double hit in this witty banter. By putting Robespierre's words in the mouth of a bishop to say that the rejection of faith is a typical invention of the idle rich he slams the door on the fingers of his unbelieving left-wing friends.

Hugo is accusing them of being objective allies of the gut-stuffing upper bourgeoisie.

In the second inserted chapter, Myriel calls on a dying radical, G., who had been a member of the Convention, the body that fashioned the constitution of the first French Republic after 1789 and voted to execute Louis XVI. This political past makes G. a bogeyman in post-revolutionary France, which is why he lives in a shack far away from town. Myriel challenges G.'s past actions and tries to make him repent, but the old radical won't apologize for anything he did. Abolishing the monarchy was the only way to abolish its crimes, he says; he hadn't voted for regicide, but he didn't think the death of a monarch more deplorable than the death of any other man. Myriel plays his last card: 'Progress must believe in God. The good cannot be well served by the ungodly. He who is an atheist is not a fit leader of men' (I.i.x, 43, adapted).

The dying man raises a finger to the sky, a tear comes to his eye, and with a shiver of ecstasy he addresses 'the ideal' directly, as if he could see someone there: 'You alone exist,' he confesses. This epiphany in extremis is what Myriel and Hugo both seek: a recognition that some kind of higher being exists beyond the material world. The bishop can now ask for the man's blessing, because faith is what matters, not the form that it takes.

These two chapters provide the philosophical underpinning of Les Misérables: materialism and atheism exacerbate the opposition between rich and poor, but natural religion can reconcile even a man of the church with an anti-clerical radical. The broadest purpose of the novel is to encourage precisely this movement from conflict to harmony by representing it in the life-story of one man.

Les Misérables does not engage with any more specific religious topics, but one question raised by many faiths was never far from Hugo's mind: where do people go when they die? He had always found it hard to accept that loved ones could cease to exist (which partly explains his willingness to experiment with turning tables). He and Juliette Drouet had both lost children to premature deaths. Claire Pradier, a daughter of Juliette's by her lover James Pradier, died of tuberculosis at the age of twenty, in June 1846; Hugo's first daughter, Léopoldine, had died even younger, at nineteen, in a freak boating accident on the Seine. At the time, he was on a jaunt with Juliette under a false name, so he only learned of Léopoldine's drowning from a newspaper handed to him at an inn. Guilt combined with grief to make the loss of his daughter the gravest emotional wound in Hugo's life. He wanted Léopoldine to come back and was sometimes on the brink of believing she would. In a poem that he wrote to honour Juliette's lost child, he made it all but explicit that lost children never really go away:

> Car ils sont revenus, et c'est là le mystère;
> Nous entendons quelqu'un flotter, un souffle errer
> Des robes effleurer notre seuil solitaire
> Et cela fait alors que nous pouvons pleurer . . .[26]
> (For they have come back and that's where the mystery lies
> We can hear someone hovering, a breath moving about,
> Dresses brushing over our lonely front step
> Which is what makes us able to weep . . .)

Les Misérables mostly conforms to our expectations of realist fiction, and, with the exception of Monseigneur Myriel, none of its characters actually rises from the grave. Yet the art of the novel did provide Hugo with a hidden tool for resuscitating the most loved of all the loved ones he missed. Léopoldine and her husband, who tried to save her, drowned in the Seine on 4 September 1843, when their sailing boat flipped over in front of her in-laws' family home, not far from where the motorway bridge at Tancarville now stands. In *Les Misérables*, Valjean escapes from the sailing ship *Orion* in a feat of daring borrowed from Roncière le Noury. He disappears, and a local newspaper reports the death by drowning in the naval dockyard of prisoner No. 9430.

The digits of Valjean's second prison number are there to signal to those who care to know it the date of the disappearance of

Léopoldine. It may not be much, but it is one way of having her live on.

❡

In 1858, a purulent sore broke out on Hugo's back: it was wool-sorters' disease, a painful malady without an antidote at that time.[27] The poet was lucky to survive, and when he recovered, he was keen to get all his work done while he still could. This reminder of his own mortal frailty wasn't the only spur that led him to resume the writing of *Les Misérables*. On 16 August 1859 – the feast of Saint-Napoléon – the man who now called himself Napoleon III granted amnesty to political exiles who had been expelled for opposing his seizure of power in 1851. For eight years the *proscrits* in the Channel Islands had been living on grants and gifts and the few odd jobs the islands could provide; many of them were glad to be able to go home to pick up their careers and provide for their families again. Hugo did not stand in the way of their return but he would not accept the amnesty for himself. If France was not free, then it was nothing at all. He would go back only when freedom did. Hugo came close to sounding like Charles de Gaulle in 1940: real France was where *he* was and nowhere else.

Victor Hugo was getting on for sixty and beginning to feel his age. He now had to wear spectacles to read after dark, and his mind turned towards making a will. His brush with an unpleasant disease reminded him that the hated dictator was six years younger and might not die before he did. The rejection of amnesty therefore meant that the Guernsey idyll could last the rest of his life. Neither the grandeur of Hauteville House nor the inspiration that Hugo drew from the sea would ever make St Peter Port a real home. He now needed a means of making himself present in France, whilst accepting he might never set foot in the country again. Completing his unfinished novel was the most powerful tool that he had to show who was the tallest tree in the land.

It was no simple matter to come back to a story written so long ago. Another writer might have put a line through the draft and started all over again. Hugo took a different approach, which was not obviously a less demanding one. He read through the manuscript slowly once more and made detailed notes on what he needed to do to adjust it to changed circumstances and times, and then set about turning the text that he had into the crowning glory and vindication of his life and work.

The title had already changed from *Les Misères* to *Les Misérables*. The new wording shifts the focus from the abstract issues of poverty and woe to characters afflicted by them, signalling unambiguously that what it names is a novel, not an essay or tract. (A secondary effect of the change is to silence the phonetic echo of Sue's *Les Mystères de Paris*, which was irrelevant to readers of the 1860s and to the project in hand.) Even so, it is not immediately obvious what either of the two titles meant to Victor Hugo, or what he meant his readers to understand by them. That is probably the main reason why *Les Misérables* keeps its title in French in the English-speaking world, joining a small handful of translated religious works, national epics and novels and films labelled in English by the names they have in their original tongues.

La misère is the French word for 'poverty', and *misérable* often serves as the adjective associated with it, meaning 'poor'. Some translations of Hugo's title restrict the meaning in exactly that way: *Nyomorultak*, which means 'poor people', is the standard Hungarian name of the novel *Les Misérables*. Hugo uses the word more than a hundred times in the text of the novel as well, and in many cases it means no more than 'short of cash'. When Marius tells Cosette that he can't follow her to England because he is '*un misérable*', for example, he means that he is an 'impoverished wretch' and cannot pay the fare (IV.8.vi, 922).

However, *misérable* isn't actually an adjective based on the noun *misère*, just as English 'miserable' isn't derived from 'misery'. The ending *–able* (or *–ible*) is always used in English, French and Latin to make adjectives not from nouns, but from verbs: 'doable', 'thinkable', 'regrettable', 'edible' and so on are things that can be done, thought, regretted, eaten, etc. 'Miserable' and *misérable* are not exceptions to the rule. What has happened is that the verb that lies behind them has disappeared.

These words all have their ultimate origin in the Latin adjective *miser*, 'unhappy', and the noun *miseria*, 'misfortune' or 'woe'. *Miser* has found its way into English with its meaning restricted to avarice, just as *miseria* narrowed its meaning to 'poverty' as it turned into French *misère*. Latin was Victor Hugo's second tongue – he read Latin every night in bed before going to sleep, he knew thousands of lines of Latin verse by heart to the end of his life, and he frequently used Latin phrases and quotations when writing and speaking in French. He gave a Latin title to a pen-and-ink sketch of a haggard woman that he thought might be used as a frontispiece of *Les Misérables*. It could be a portrait of Fantine, but its title *Miseria* does not mean that it is a picture of poverty. It is an image of woe.

Latin *miseria* can be put in the plural, *miseriae*, just as in English we can talk of 'the miseries of life'. In French, however, plural *des misères* most often means 'a trifling sum', 'peanuts', and it is not at all common in other senses. Hugo's original title, *Les Misères*, obviously doesn't mean 'peanuts', but it is hard to say what it signifies unless we hear behind the French formulation the Latin word in Hugo's mind. *Les Misères* is Latin *miseriae* in French dress, and it means something like 'all the woes of the world'.

French *misérable*, like English 'miserable', is a direct import of Latin *miserabilis*, an adjective formed from the verb *miserere*, 'to feel sorrow for', 'to take pity on' or, in the usage of the King James Bible, 'to have mercy'. In English the meaning of 'miserable' has been narrowed to refer to the psychological state of someone on whom we might (perhaps) take pity, and now refers to roughly the same inner state as 'glum', 'sorrowful', 'downcast' or 'depressed'. That process of specialization has not affected the meaning of its French twin *misérable*, which never means 'miserable'. Even now the French word retains some of the senses it had in classical and church Latin: 'deserving of pity and sorrow'. These meanings were even nearer the surface in the mind of a man who was as good as bilingual in the two tongues.

The Latin meaning of *misérable* was all the more present in nineteenth-century France because *miserere* and *miserabilis* were constantly heard in a country where Latin remained the language of the church. *Vermis sum, miserabilis sum* ('I am a worm, I am a wretch . . .') were commonly recited homilies, and the opening of Psalm 51, read or most often sung at funerals, weddings and masses, begins: 'Miserere mei, Deus, secundum magnam misericordiam tuam'.

Hugo reminds readers of the root meaning of his title when the retired bookseller Mabeuf has his peaceful evenings disturbed by his housekeeper's tomcat. The animal's vocal range is so wide and the volume so high, the narrator jokes, that his yowling could have filled the Sistine Chapel with the sound of Allegri's setting of the Psalm. In other words, if you don't know the *miserere*, you're in a class lower than Mme Plutarque's pet.[28]

When Jean Valjean laments the sin he has committed by purloining Petit-Gervais's two-franc coin outside Digne, he calls out 'Je suis un misérable!' (I.2.xiii, 103). Here, most obviously, but also elsewhere, he does not mean 'I am poor,' but 'I am a moral wretch.' Latin frequently lies behind the French words of Hugo's text.

But it is more complicated even than that. *Misérable* is one of those many words that can switch their value from positive to negative without notice. There are many similar cases in English too: a wretched person is worthy of pity but may just as well be beneath contempt. *Un misérable* is similarly two-faced. Context and common sense usually tell you, but taken on its own *misérable* may refer either to a scoundrel to be scorned or to a soul in distress.

A novel called *Les Misérables* could therefore be about many different things: poor people, of course, but also people deserving of our pity, people who have sinned, and contemptible wretches. The broad arguments of Hugo's time about how to deal with the poor and with crime discussed on pp. 8–14 above were focused on making *distinctions* between those different groups and, implicitly, on separating out the different strands in the meaning of *misérable*. Hugo's huge, subtle, overpowering response is to lump them all together. That is the true significance of the new title of his book. It came to him on Jersey when, despite his eminence and his bluster, despite his good health and his multiple partners, despite his beliefs, his gifts and his hopes, he was an outcast too. It took time to work out what he had done by reinventing his novel of the poor as a novel of *Les Misérables*, but in the end he was able to make it completely explicit. When revising his description of the wretched lives of the wretched Thénardier clan, the novel's *mauvais pauvres* or 'villainous paupers', he inserted a broad reflection on what poverty and crime have to do with each other on a page that turned out to fit in at the exact mid-point of the whole book:

> They seemed very depraved, very corrupt, very debased – heinous, even – but rare are those who fall without sinking into vice. In any case, there is a point where the poor and the wicked become mixed up and lumped together in the one fateful word: *les misérables*. And whose fault is that? (III.8.v, 671, adapted)

It's a truism that you can't change the meaning of a word on your own. Except that sometimes you can, and in this central redefinition of the meaning of the title word of *Les Misérables* you can see it being done. Henceforth it will mean not 'poor' or 'pitiable' or 'despicable' and not even all three in turn. It becomes a way of naming what these groups have in common: a moral and social identity that had no name before. 'The Outcast'? Maybe. 'The Wretched'? Quite plausible. 'The Oppressed', 'The Humiliated', 'The Downtrodden' . . . there are many strands that can be picked out and named, but no way of reinventing Hugo's inclusiveness in any other tongue. That's why *Les Misérables* remains *Les Misérables*.

Hugo does not say that the cause of the Thénardiers' depravity and corruption is poverty, though many readers project that meaning on to this passage. He does not say directly that uncommon moral strength is needed to stay honest when you are debased and cast down by financial woes, but it's a meaning that can be extracted from the passage equally well. What he certainly does say is that the awful are as worthy of pity and sorrow as anyone else. That generous and utterly unorthodox claim is offered as the foundation of a new social morality.

Hugo does not answer the question he puts at the end. Catholic readers of his day might have wanted to exclaim: the fault lies with the decline of religion. Socialists and progressives might have wanted to say: the fault lies with capitalism, or with the economy, or with society as a whole. But there is one answer that all readers most likely want to resist, though it can hardly fail to arise from the direct form of address that Hugo uses: that somehow or other, the fault lies with us.

7.

Hugo Gets Back to Work

Victor Hugo took the month of May 1860 to read through *Les Misères* and to list the points that needed attention. There were nineteen in all:

1. Modify the philosophical side of the bishop. Bring in the member of the Convention.
2. Check if there's a need to use the map of Digne.
3. Maybe Thénardier's inn: 'The Federal Soldier of 1815'.
4. Move the convent. (Should I mention that Cosette becomes a happy girl while she's there?)
5. After the convent, prayer. Describe the absurd monastic regime and say: as long as women are legal minors, as long as the problem of women remains unsolved, the convent is only a secondary crime. Marriage with God is not a bad deal (an acceptable plan B). Claustration on earth is an escape into heaven.
6. Try to replace *gamin de Paris* with another word: hooligan? Or else the people of Paris when still a child is called *le gamin*.
7. Touch up the portrait of M. Gillenormand.
8. Perhaps make a very sentimental scene out of the colonel who can't see his child any more and is obliged to leave him to M. Gillenormand (but without encroaching on Jean Vlajean's last pain).[29]
9. Explain how the grandfather splits with his grandson, thus: tradition of antique paternal severity; he'll have to come back and then we'll see!
10. Get to the bottom of Mabeuf.

11. For the barricade, note that I have to look at a map of Paris.
12. Don't give Cosette a silk dress.[30]
13. Point out it's nearly dark when J. V. goes into Jondrette's hovel, which explains why J. V. doesn't recognize anyone there.
14. Explain why the brazier doesn't suffocate; because of the broken window pane. Size of the hovel. A vague smell that is unpleasant but bearable.
15. Explain that because of the thickening snow the coming and going of the cab which brings M. Leblanc to the Jondrette hovel can't be heard (would be better if he came on foot).
16. That's contradicted by Thénardier's cab that is heard later on. Sort this out.
17. Explain why Marius only goes to Gillenormand's in the evening. He remembers it's the only time the old man was in the habit of having guests, in accordance with old fashions: making day of night and night out of day – or find some other reason.
18. Say that at dawn Chavroche got his kids out of the elephant.
19. Be wary of the word *piller* ('to pillage'), overused in the riot.[31]

Hugo's 'to-do' list of May 1860 hardly seems commensurate with the scale of *Les Misérables,* and it doesn't mention most of the changes and additions that were eventually made and which more than doubled the length of *Les Misères.* At best, it gives us access to Hugo's idea of how novels should be made. He reminds himself to check on the accuracy of references to the real world (points 2 and 11, use of maps) but also to alter reality so as to mask material borrowed from other hands (point 4, shifting the convent). He is attentive to finding the 'right word' (point 6) and avoiding verbal repetition (point 19), which is even more of a style fault in French than in other languages. He tells himself most of all that he needs to enhance the psychological plausibility of his characters (points 7, 8, 9, 10 and 17) and prop up the least credible turns of the plot (points 13, 14, 15, 16). And, remembering the opinions of Charles and others, he plans to strengthen and make more explicit the philosophical side of the book (points

1 and 5). These notes are points for tidying up an existing draft. There is no hint of a plan for bringing its story to completion.

Before Hugo took his first steps in that direction, however, he had other business to attend to. He had been invited to address a fundraising event on Jersey in support of the champion of Italian unity, Giuseppe Garibaldi. He was reluctant to go back to an island that had thrown him out, but his political friends raised hundreds of signatures on a petition begging him to return, and he felt obliged to accept. The crossing was unpleasant, but the welcome loud and warm. Placards were posted all over St Helier saying VICTOR HUGO HAS ARRIVED!, the banquet was packed out, and the writer was fêted like a conquering hero for three days. This rewarding interruption was followed by another, a charity bazaar launched by his wife Adèle to raise money for the children of Guernsey's poor. Hugo had always been a willing giver of alms. It went with his status, of course, and was also part of what it meant to be a middle-class man. On Guernsey he never walked down to Fermain Bay for a swim without small change in his pocket, which he gave freely to poor folk he met on the way (though he also used it to pay girls for sex, a pursuit no less important to him at that age than decorating his home). The bazaar was the first of the family's ventures into organizing charity on a larger scale. Adèle, who was not a banished person, spent weeks in France collecting items for sale from friends. Hugo donated autographs, books and photographs of himself; he even served at a stand for a few moments and bought another heap of curios to decorate Hauteville House.

At the end of June 1860, Hugo started on the next stage of work on *Les Misérables*. For forty days and forty nights (or so he said) he pondered the reasons he had for writing a book about the wretched, the outcast and the poor. However, the product of his immersion in the underlying meaning of the work he had not yet started redrafting for real was a fifty-page ramble dealing with almost everything *except* the meaning of *Les Misérables*. Hugo realized that his draft was not a real preface but an exercise of the mind: 'The author could not have not written [these pages], but it is easy for the reader to skip [them],' he confessed.[32] There's no disrespect involved in taking the hint, but two things need to be rescued from this false start. The first is that it contains a lengthy attempt to justify belief in the existence of God, boiled down in *Les Misérables* to a bafflingly dense paragraph put in the mouth of the outcast revolutionary G.:

> The infinite exists. It is there. If the infinite had no selfhood, selfhood would set a limit upon it; it would not be infinite. In other words there would be no such thing. Yet exist it does. So it has a self. That selfhood of the infinite is God. (I.1.x, 43)

The second is that when, just before abandoning the preface at the end of August, 1860, Hugo finally asked himself how 'a dreamer of this kind' could have written *Les Misérables*, he explains (to himself) that such a work has to be based on two beliefs: 'belief in the future of man on earth, that is to say, his improvement in human terms; and faith in the future of man beyond earth, that is to say his improvement on the spiritual plane'. He ends his essay with the much-quoted and often misapplied assertion that 'the book you are about to read is a religious one'.[33] The problem in applying this definition of the novel of Valjean and Cosette is that Hugo's idea of 'religious' is not like anyone else's understanding of the term.

§

Hugo was physically robust, and he kept himself fit through regular exercise and a healthy diet. On Guernsey he went walking and swimming most days of the year; he ate a light diet and took hardly any drink. He was good for another twenty-five years, but he didn't know that when in December 1860 he came down with a sore throat and bad cough. He had such a high temperature that he thought he might die and wondered how long he still had. In a note written on 23 December, he fixed his remaining span at no more than five years. You can tell what his mood was like from the first pages he wrote when at last he got down to completing *Les Misérables*:

Alas, if despair is a dreadful thing when the hair is black . . . what is
it like in old age, when the years rush on, ever more wan, to that
twilight hour when you begin to see the stars from the grave?
(IV.15.1, 1,037)

As part of his recovery from his throat-and-chest complaint, he
made two changes to the way that he lived. He moved his narrow
bed from the 'Look-out' to the Oak Room, one storey down, clear-
ing the top floor of the house for two writing shelves and tables for
the manuscripts and materials he would need to have at hand.

His second innovation was to stop shaving. Unlike other members of the Romantic movement, Hugo had not grown a beard in
his younger years. He remained smooth-cheeked even when beards
became the uniform style of democrats and republicans in the 1840s.
The Second Empire became so suspicious of facial hair that it
banned bearded teachers from schools. Hugo was not averse to signalling his solidarity with other victims of Louis-Napoléon
Bonaparte, but that was not the reason he stopped shaving before
restarting the main engine of *Les Misérables*.

Public speakers have to take care of their throats, and in the 1850s
the sermon-giving clergymen of England came up with a new way
of staving off coughs, colds and the loss of voice. A 'Beards
Movement' swept through this traditionally smooth-chinned group
and reached the shores of Guernsey too. Hugo must have heard
about it from a local curate, or else from the press.[34] Hugo's beard
quickly turned into a snow-white extension of his face, with a wisp
of black persisting on the upper lip. Charles took many photographs
of his father on Jersey in the 1850s, and we can still see what Hugo's
face looked like without a beard: well-proportioned, with a famously
high forehead and small, penetrating eyes. However, because of the
immense popularity he enjoyed after the publication of *Les
Misérables*, most of the photographs used on book jackets, hung on
the walls of French town halls and propped on mantelpieces all
over the world were taken after Hugo had transformed himself into
a whiskery patriarch who would fit into a Father Christmas parade.

It wasn't a fashion statement, even less a desire to look like God Almighty. Hugo grew a beard to protect himself from diseases that might prevent him finishing *Les Misérables*.

By the last days of December, he was feeling better and ready to get down to work in his newly cleared Look-out on the top floor of Hauteville House. We know exactly when Hugo took up his quill and started on the mammoth job of revising and completing the story of *Les Misérables*, because he marked it quite explicitly in the manuscript. On the page that has Gavroche setting off from the barricade to take a letter from Marius to Cosette – and which must therefore be the last page of the original *Les Misères*, the one written on or just before 23 February 1848 – Hugo erected a milestone in his own life, in the history of this novel and in the history of world literature:

> This is where the *pair de France* broke off and the exile carried on.
>
> 30 December 1860, Guernsey.

g

Hugo wrote standing at one of his two writing shelves in the top-floor room overlooking the harbour and, beyond it, the often choppy sea breaking on the shore of the island of Sark. He wrote with a goose quill on loose blue-tinted sheets that were roughly the size of A4. The stationery bought in St Peter Port did not quite match the sheets he had used in the 1840s for *Les Misères*, so the growing manuscript of the novel had a ragged edge. As the writing involved insertions as well as additions, it was especially important to keep track of the sequence in case the pile was disturbed by a gust of wind from an opened window or door. Hugo numbered his sheets from A to Z, with W omitted (as it only occurs in non-French words, W can be considered as not a letter of the French alphabet). The twenty-sixth sheet was number A^1, the twenty-seventh B^1, the fiftieth Z^1, the seventy-fifth Z^2, and so on. At some periods Hugo used both sides of a sheet, but his routine for the continuation of

Les Misérables was to leave the verso blank. He always left a broad margin for corrections and additions, but much of the new material that turned *Les Misères* into *Les Misérables* was far too voluminous to fit in that way and called for a refinement of the numbering scheme. An extra sheet inserted into the sequence after sheet B^2, to take an imaginary example, would be numbered B^2A, and if this insertion ended up being twelve pages long, it would end on B^2L before the pre-existing sequence of pages resumed with C^2. In principle, it is no more difficult to learn to count Hugo's pages than it is to count nineteenth-century coins, but practice is needed before either becomes handy to use. The most practised person of all was Juliette Drouet, who had long before abandoned her career as an actress to be her great man's copyist. Her job was to transcribe finished sections on to a fair copy that incorporated corrections and additions indicated in the left-hand margins and brought the longer insertions with their branch-numbered pages into the 'main line' from A to Z^n.

❡

When Hugo took up his pen on 30 December 1860 the narrative of *Les Misérables* was exactly where he had left it in *Les Misères* in 1848. The immediate context out of which new adventures were waiting to be spun was as follows. In her dying moments Éponine (still called Palmyre) has handed Marius (originally, Thomas) a letter from Cosette saying that her 'father' has moved from Rue Plumet (not the present-day Rue Plumet, but the street now called Rue Oudinot) to a smaller apartment in Rue de l'Homme-Armé and plans to take her to England, away from suspicious prowlers and from strife in the streets. The letter is addressed to 'my beloved', and the endearment makes Marius's heart leap – and then plunge, for he can't follow Cosette abroad. He has no money, and even if he had he could not marry without his grandfather's permission, which would surely be refused. He writes back to his beloved, laying out the insuperable obstacles they face. Better to die on the barricades! 'I die. I love you. When you read this my soul will be with you and will smile on you.' He asks Gavroche to deliver the message to the right house, No. 7, in a street that was only half a mile from the barricade.

All kinds of connecting links could have been inserted at this point, but Hugo's inspiration was to take a step back. He returned to the prior passage describing the first day that Cosette and Valjean had spent in their new abode. The young woman, gloomy and tense, had retired to her room with a headache, and Valjean had ample time to look around. Into that still blank space he inserted an additional detail that acts as a launch-pad for the next turn in the tale. Valjean looked around the room at Rue de l'Homme-Armé *and found something*. What he found was not present in the manuscript of 1848; it was thought up and inserted in December 1860. It could not be Cosette's letter, since that was on its way to Marius; and it obviously could not be the reply, which hadn't been written yet. What struck Valjean's eye was closely related to the correspondence between the lovers, but it was something else.

Users of ballpoints may not remember that handwriting in ink applied with a quill pen stays wet for a few minutes and can easily get smudged. Drying can be accelerated with a pinch of pounce (powdered cuttlefish bone) or by dabbing the sheet with blotting paper. In the latter case the trace of what's written shows up on the blotter in left-right inversion. On a well-used piece of blotting paper different lines of mirror writing overlap and can't be deciphered at a glance. But Cosette had used her sheet only once, so the trace of her writing is clear. Even so, Valjean might not have noticed if it hadn't caught his eye in the mirror. Like blotters, mirrors invert what they reflect, so they make 'blotter writing' readable the right way round. That is the hinge. The double inversion by ink and glass of a message addressed by Cosette to her beloved triggers a moral crisis in the mind of Valjean. At the same time it is a technical trigger that sets off the continuing story told in Part V of *Les Misérables*.

There's magic in the device Hugo found to make the hinge between the old novel in front of him and the new one in his head.

He had spent nine months looking back over the manuscript. To start looking forward, he introduces something that is quite literally written backwards and then turned around thanks to a mirror on the wall. *Buvard, bavard* ('The Blathering Blotter'), the chapter title Hugo invented for this contrivance, is a play on words that makes its double function almost explicit. It joins up the story and marks the join in the writing of it.

When Gavroche arrives with Marius's reply, Valjean intercepts it and understands what it means, since he has now read the message that prompted it. He puts on his uniform as a member of the National Guard (to protect himself from arrest) and sets off for the area around Les Halles, where barricades have been set up. His intention is unstated, but his actions can only mean one thing. He aims to bring his adopted daughter's lover back home in one piece.[35]

That's where Part IV ends in the finished novel. What Hugo wrote next, in January 1861, is the start of what is now Part V, and it is completely different from all that had gone before. *Les Misères* is a conventional third-person narrative interspersed with characters' speech in dialogue form. Chapter 1 of Part V, however, is a personal essay about the 'June Days' of 1848 (see above, pp. 46–8), an event that lies entirely outside the novel's chronological frame. It is written in the voice of an 'observer of social ills' whose identity is perfectly clear. This is not the narrator. It is Victor Hugo.

The reflective analysis of the events of June 1848 that forms V.1.i has been disparaged as a digression and dismissed as the blathering of a windbag.[36] It is certainly a surprising and perhaps unprecedented intrusion of an author in a work that has the form and content of a novel. However, *Les Misérables* is not just a longer version of *Les Misères*. It is still a novel, but it is also much more.

Later on, Hugo inserted many other essays in his own voice into earlier parts of *Les Misérables*: his visit to the battlefield of Waterloo, for example, his assessment of King Louis-Philippe and so on.[37] As a result the '1848 essay' doesn't play the same role in our reading of the finished book as it did in the writing of it. However, it is retrospectively obvious that none of the dramas that arose in Hugo's life between the abandonment of *Les Misères* and the resumption of it as *Les Misérables* (the *coup d'état*, exile, political polemics, expulsion from Jersey, poetry or turning tables) affected him as profoundly as those two days in June 1848 when he helped to suppress a popular revolt. That is what he had to come to terms with to carry on with his book, and that he has to come to terms with *in* his book if it is to be the 'social and moral panorama' that he intended it to be. For the dilemma of 1848 was not his alone. As he said in the foreword to *Les Contemplations*, 'Ah! Quand je vous parle de moi, je vous parle de vous. Comment ne le sentez-vous pas?' ('Ah! When I tell you about myself, I am speaking of you. How can you not sense this?') The personal discussion of June 1848 at the start of Part V has to be about 'you' if you live in a society that has been shaken by or fears to be shaken by political violence; that is to say, if you live in France, or almost anywhere else, in the nineteenth century, and maybe even now.

Interlude: Inventing the Names

In the months of January, February and March 1861, Victor Hugo created a substantial part of *Les Misérables*, including two of its most dramatic and memorable episodes: the destruction of the barricade in Rue de la Chanvrerie, where Enjolras, Grantaire, Gavroche and many others die; and Valjean's rescue of Marius through the sewers of old Paris. There can be no greater contrast than between the ill-lit, claustrophobic scenes that he described and the vista that met his eyes when he looked up from his writing shelf: birds, rocks and sailing boats bobbing about on the never-still sea. Hugo was able to abstract himself entirely from his surroundings, for there is barely a trace of 'the view from Hauteville House' in the words of the finished text.[38] Yet there is a subterranean connection. The old coat of arms of the city of Paris shows a sailing boat, often thought of as an image derived from the elongated shape of the Ile de la Cité, the island in the Seine where Notre-Dame stands. But if the view of sailing ships indirectly brings to mind the city Hugo thought he would never see again, the motto on that old crest could also be applied of his own defiant stand. *Fluctuat nec mergitur* ('it/he floats and does not sink') could have been inscribed on the lintel of Hauteville House, to speak not of Paris but of the man upstairs.

This was also the time when Hugo finally settled the names of most of his characters. These names have become so familiar that it takes an effort to realize that they all had to be invented, for none of them was taken from the existing stock of French first and family names. The only one that wasn't changed between first draft and last is that of Thénardier, the cruel innkeeper of Montfermeil. Thénard is a genuine French family name, and it belonged to a distinguished research chemist whom the king appointed alongside Hugo to the rank of *pair de France*, but who voted against child labour reforms. But the aptness of the root name for the role its holder plays in the novel is probably unrelated to these anecdotal facts. Its second syllable, –*ard*, has the form of a suffix that casts scorn on the adjective or noun to which it is attached. A *chauffeur*, for example, is a driver, and a *chauffard* is a bad one; a *fête* is a party, and a *fêtard* is an objectionably noisy attendee. To the negative sounding –*ard* Hugo added –*ier*, a suffix that usually marks the exercise of a trade or skill. *Charpente* is a beam and *charpentier* is a carpenter, just a *pâtissier* makes pastries and a *hôtelier* runs an inn. That last is the clue, because it is as a hotel-keeper that Thénardier first appears in the novel. But what of the first syllable of his name? It has the same sound as *taenia*, the French word for tape-worm. 'Thénardier' has become part of the language and now names any rip-off artist in the hotel trade not just because Hugo's character is a memorably unpleasant example, but because the name is loaded with associations that make it fit especially well.

The Thénardiers' unloved third child, the baby we hear crying at the inn in 1823 and who reappears as the rhyming urchin at the barricade, was first called Chavroche. That name, like its final version as Gavroche, also taps into meanings contained in a suffix. In colloquial speech, especially in the dialect of Paris, –*oche* can be added to nouns and adjectives to make them smaller, less prestigious or commoner things: a battered old suitcase, *valise*, can be a *valoche*, and a run-down local cinema is a *cinoche*. The prison-fortress that was knocked down during the Revolution was popularly referred to as *La Bastoche*, and that is probably why Hugo invented the name that he did for his revolutionary scamp.

Gavroche is also the name of a kind of hat, worn by Brigitte Bardot in *Viva Maria!* in the role of an Irish bomb-maker on loan to a revolution south of the Rio Grande. Hugo's character isn't named after the hat, of course, because the hat is named after Hugo's Gavroche. However, Bardot's soft peaked cap isn't anything that Gavroche ever wore. The boy is so poor that he has 'no shirt on his body, no shoes on his feet', the only trousers he's got are adult cast-offs five sizes too big, and if he ever wears a hat, he borrows it from 'one of his other fathers' and it flops down over his ears.[39] What it resembles more or less is the headgear of a vigorous young man striding forward with a pistol in each hand in Delacroix's celebration of the 1830 Revolution, *Liberty Guiding the People*. That famous image is even taken by some to be 'a portrait of Gavroche', but as Delacroix's painting was done thirty years before *Les Misérables* was in print, that cannot possibly be right. The historical confusion is even greater than that, because the hat worn by the figure in the painting is actually a *faluche*, the standard headgear of students at the Sorbonne. It's quite bizarre. Ignorance of the clothing conventions of nineteenth-century France has led to a misunderstanding of the social meaning of a work as closely associated with the tradition of political activism as *Les Misérables*; in its turn, the misrecognition of Delacroix's militant intellectual has injected into later readings of *Les Misérables* the image of a hat that has no place in it at all. A gavroche is less of a homage to Hugo's Gavroche than an expression of the difficulty we have in understanding the past.

§

At the start of *Les Misères* the sad heroine was named Marguerite Louet, whose name becomes Fantine fairly soon. 'Fantine' was not a regular French name at that time. Hugo may have come across the word in fairy-tales from French-speaking Switzerland, where it means 'water-sprite', but it's not likely he chose it for that reason. The ending *–ine* is common enough in women's names – there's 'Léopoldine', 'Joséphine', 'Valentine' and many more. But 'Fantine' isn't made from *–ine* added on to a known stem. The best guess is that the first syllable is a contraction of *enfant*, 'child', so the name itself suggests a meaning close to that of 'kid girl'. That's just what she was: a child of the streets of Montreuil-sur-Mer, with no parents to name her and no formal identity at all.

In *Les Misères* Marguerite Louet's daughter is called Anna, and when she works as a skivvy in the Thénardiers' inn she's referred to most often as 'La Louet', in a common use of the article and surname for people of lower rank. In rural dialects (and even nowadays, south of the Loire) the final consonant was sounded out, so the girl's name was indistinguishable in speech from *l'alouette*, 'the lark'. Hugo abandoned 'Anna' for 'Cosette' later on, but kept the association of girl and bird, attributing it not to a pun but to the poetic imagination of the poor:

> the common people, who love figures of speech, had taken to naming as 'lark' this little thing no bigger than a bird who was the first in the house and the village to rise every morning and was always to be found in the streets or the field before dawn. (I.4.iii, 146)

The replacement name 'Cosette' is one of the most mysterious of Hugo's inventions. Like 'Fantine' it has a diminutive ending, and like 'Fantine' too it has no obvious stem among French names. The first syllable sounds borrowed from Italian *cosa*, or 'thing', equivalent to French *chose*, which normally has feminine gender. However, it is also used with masculine gender to mean a lad, a stripling, a puny fellow (as in Alphonse Daudet's memoir of his miserable childhood, *Le Petit Chose*). Thirdly, *chose* is also a stumble-word inserted when you don't know or can't recall the right name. When Gavroche brings Marius's letter to 7, Rue de l'Homme-Armé he finds Valjean outside the front door but as he has no idea of his name he calls him 'M. Chose', or 'Mr Thingy'. He then pretends to misremember the name of the woman to whom the letter is addressed and calls her 'Chosette', which is at the same time 'daughter of Chose', 'Miss Thingummy' and 'wee girl'. In this way Hugo uses his verbally gifted ruffian to point to the associations of the name he'd invented for the heroine of the tale. The daughter of a 'kid girl' among the most humiliated and subjected of the society she lives in, Cosette is just a 'little thingy' herself.

Cosette's beloved is called 'Thomas' in most of the first draft, but becomes 'Marius' in the scene where Éponine alerts him to danger in the garden of the house in Rue Plumet. 'Marius' sounds typically southern nowadays because of Marcel Pagnol's celebration of all that is Provence in his novel *Marius*, which he also made into a film. It had no such associations for Hugo, whose given name was Victor-Marie.[40] What he slotted in to replace 'Thomas' was simply the Latin translation of his neglected second half.

Among other names that were changed in the winter months of 1861 was that of the Thénardiers' elder daughter. Her mother had dredged up the classical 'Palmyre' from the second-rate fiction she loves to read, but Hugo replaced it with one adapted from that of a heroine of the early history of France. Epponina was the wife of a Gaulish chief, Julius Sabinus, who by claiming descent from Julius Caesar irritated the Roman Empire as much as any Astérix. In the story told by Plutarch, a Greek-speaking Roman author studied in classics classes at school, and retold in the nineteenth century by Jules Michelet and François Guizot in their accounts of the origins of the French nation, Epponina accompanied her husband to Rome, where Vespasian sentenced him to death for rebellion. The faithful wife demanded that she be allowed to die with her spouse. The wish was granted with ease, in what Plutarch thought 'the cruellest and saddest act' of that emperor's reign.[41] In Hugo's novel, Éponine dies from a bullet she deflects with her hand from the breast of Marius to her own. She earns her name.

The one name that Hugo did not finalize until he was well advanced with Part V was that of the hero of the tale. The 'Jean Tréjean' of *Les Misères* briefly became 'Jacques Sou', and turned into 'Jean Vlajean' in January or February 1861. On 20 March, during the composition of the passage on the destruction of the barricade at Rue de la Chanvrerie, Hugo inverted the order of consonant and vowel and settled for good on 'Jean Valjean'. The name is made by doubling the commonest and most basic name in the French language. Like 'Ivan' in Russian or 'John Doe' in American law, 'Jean' suggests 'somebody or other', anybody, a nobody. 'A name is a self' Valjean explains to Marius at the very end (V.7.i, 1,250, adapted), but the name that he has carries with it only an elementary level of selfhood. His father, also called Jean, was greeted by the shout 'Voilà Jean' ('There's Jean'), abbreviated in rapid speech to 'Vlà Jean', which he ran together to make into his own name.[42] It's as heartrending as a slumdog answering to the name of 'Heyou'.

There is an even lower rung than being called 'You Guy'. In a parable of Ancient Egypt, Ismail Kadare imagined that the slaves who built the pyramids had to earn enough money to buy a name, foreshadowing twentieth-century abominations that turned people into numbers to strip them of their social identities. In *Les Misérables*, the ultimate victims of social exclusion include the nephews and nieces for whom Valjean stole the loaf of bread and whose names are never given. Similarly, Gavroche never learns the names of the two lost boys he adopts on the streets and takes back with him to live in the elephant and never finds out that he is their brother. However much effort Hugo put into inventing the names of his *misérables*, he didn't forget that the greatest humiliation is to have no name at all.

PART THREE

Rooms with a View

8.

Victory at Waterloo

In 1854, a Guernseyman was found guilty of murder and sentenced to death. Hugo made a public appeal for the penalty to be commuted, since he regarded execution as a crime in itself. Dismayed when the sentence was carried out nonetheless, he dashed off a stark, black-brown watercolour of Charles Tapner hanging by the neck.

In 1859 an American abolitionist, John Brown, tried to seize an armoury at Harper's Ferry in Virginia, so as to provide slaves with the means to fight to make themselves free. The amateur coup was put down by General Robert E. Lee, and Brown was sentenced to death. Hugo penned another stirring appeal for mercy, this time to 'the United States of America'. He warned that if Brown were to be hanged there was no knowing where the campaign against slavery would end. Newspapers and cables took too long to cross the Atlantic for Hugo's thunderous humanity to have any effect: he wrote his appeal on 2 December 1859, the very day Brown was hanged. It was published all the same, in French and in translation, in newspapers around the world. It did not go down well in the United States. Hugo was told to mind his own business and stop meddling in American affairs.

A few days later, Paul Chenay, the husband of Adèle's sister Julie, came to stay at Hauteville House. Chenay was an engraver, and he offered to make a print of Hugo's image of a hanged man as part of a campaign against capital punishment – and on behalf of slaves in the United States, which was sliding towards civil war, an issue widely covered in the French press. Chenay took the watercolour with him back to Paris and set to work. The engraving was soon ready, but because it bore the date of 2 December, it was misrecognized by the political police as a hostile reference to Louis-Napoléon's seizure of power in 1851 (see above, p. 52). The plates and proofs were therefore seized and destroyed, and Chenay had to start all over again. The project had also changed. The new idea was to use Hugo's image as the frontispiece of a pamphlet consisting of Hugo's appeal to America with several other abolitionist texts he had written over the years. With that in mind, the date was erased and a new title was found. 'The Hanged Man' became 'Ecce Lex' – 'Behold the Law', intended ironically, as in 'You call that legal?' The context of the pamphlet naturally made readers see it as a picture of John Brown. Prints went round the world within weeks of publication in February 1861. As the writer in his Lookout carried on with the adventures of Valjean and Marius in the sewers of Paris, Hugo the artist, Hugo the humanitarian and Hugo the prophet loomed like a giant on the world stage. The American Civil War was about to begin.

Most of Hugo's paintings show imaginary landscapes, castles, ruins and the sea; not many show human figures, and faces are rare. In *Les Misérables*, on the other hand, pen-portraits abound, as was conventional in fiction of that time. Are any of them self-portraits? In 1832, Valjean is roughly the age Hugo was in 1861 and shares his strong constitution, but nothing more specific links the two for the eye. Marius, on the other hand, whose name is borrowed from Hugo's, is an intentional portrait of the artist as a young man.

The portrait is affectionate and serious, but it is also an ironical and self-critical one. Hugo's well-known inclination to bed women whenever he could only arose in middle age and, though it may seem surprising now, he was as chaste as his hero Marius when he was the same age. Hugo even adapted an episode from his own early life to depict Marius as a comically passionate prude. When Marius sees the wind lift Cosette's skirt in the Luxembourg Gardens, he is roused to anger and jealousy of anyone who might catch sight of her precious ankle, just as the teenage poet had berated his fiancée for lifting her skirt out of the mud when crossing Rue des

Saint-Pères. 'I cannot tell you what torture I endured,' he wrote to Adèle in 1822, 'when I saw passers-by averting their eyes. Please take note if you want to avoid the risk of my slapping the face of the first insolent man who dares look at you.'[1] However, the larger role that Marius plays in telling us what it was like to be Victor Hugo is by reproducing in broad outline the story of his political education.

Marius's father, Colonel Georges Pontmercy, was a professional soldier awarded the title of baron on the battlefield by Napoleon himself. Hugo's father held the rank of general and was made a count – several steps higher still. The fall of the Empire in 1815 was a disaster for both fathers alike. They became *demi-soldes*, that is to say, they were put on half-pay, forbidden to enter Paris and assigned to a provincial town: Vernon, halfway between Paris and Rouen, for Pontmercy, and Blois for Léopold-Sigisbert Hugo. Marius and Victor Hugo were therefore brought up in the capital by relatives who had no love for Napoleon Bonaparte. Marius's grandfather Gillenormand is an unrepentant monarchist; Hugo's mother, though not as antiquated in her person or views, was also sympathetic to the royalist cause. The political education that Marius receives at the salon of Mme de T. is a caricatural summary of the attitudes Victor Hugo absorbed in his teens;[2] and Marius's later conversion to progressive ideas compresses the path towards the left that Hugo also took in subsequent years. Adèle pointed out some of these parallels in the memoir she published just after the appearance of *Les Misérables*, and, looking back on the book a decade later, Hugo agreed without difficulty that he had 'put the whole story of his life' into the character of Marius.[3]

He does not put it all in with a completely straight face. Marius, when he first starts to learn about his father's past, takes to reading histories of the French Empire and the *Bulletins de la Grande Armée*, a military newssheet that Napoleon used to create the heroic myth of himself. Marius is enthralled by these reports of victories and derring-do and reads on late into the night:

He felt as it were a swelling tide rising within him . . . He thought he heard drums, cannon, trumpets . . . the thudding and distant gallop of cavalry . . . He was in a state of exhilaration, trembling, panting. All at once . . . he stood up, reached out of the window with both arms, stared intently into the darkness, the silence, the mysterious infinitude, and cried: *Vive l'Empereur!* (III.3.vi, 571)

Marius instantly decides to inherit the imperial barony awarded his father but not recognized in Restoration France. Hugo also called himself *vicomte* in those years, as the second son of a *comte*. What really riled the young writer as he came to understand that his father was a true hero was that for technical and political reasons the name of General Léopold-Sigisbert Hugo would not be inscribed on the Arc de Triomphe alongside the other heroes of Napoleon's wars.

Where the two fathers match most of all is in their behaviour after the defeat at Waterloo. General Hugo was not at the battle because he was an officer commanding the garrison at Thionville, in the east of France. He refused to surrender to the Prussian and Russian forces besieging the fortress-city and held out until the Peace of Vienna was signed – he was the very last French officer to yield. Colonel Pontmercy, for his part, was wounded at the battle and then fleeced by Thénardier, but instead of surrendering or returning to civilian life, he joined the rump of Napoleon's army that retreated south to the valley of the Loire, where it held out for a few weeks. That's why Gillenormand only ever refers to his son-in-law as a 'Brigand of the Loire'. But in his emulation of the real General Hugo, Pontmercy transmits to his son the same values that Hugo felt he drew from his father: do your duty, and never give in. As he'd proclaimed in *Les Châtiments* in 1853:

> Et s'il n'en reste qu'un, je serai celui-la![4]
> (And if only one remains, that man will be me!)

§

'I would like to have finished what I have begun', Hugo wrote to himself around the time he finished the discussion of 1848 and the harrowing narrative of the barricade's end. 'I pray God to order my body to hang on, and to wait until my mind is done.'[5] He also had to find a way of allowing Marius to hang on. How would he escape alive from Rue de la Chanvrerie? His ironic identification with the younger hero of the tale has to give way at this point to the central concern of the book: the trial and moral triumph of an older man, Jean Valjean.

Thirty years before, in *Notre-Dame de Paris*, Hugo had written a stunning description of medieval Paris as seen from the sky; now, he set about recreating the modern city seen from underneath. It was a similar kind of imaginative enterprise. Hugo had never visited the sewers, and he drew all his information about them from printed sources he had on his shelf. At the time of writing, there were great works in train to enlarge and extend the underground network of tunnels and pipes, and Hugo knew perfectly well that what he had to describe was a system of urban intestines that had already been swallowed up. However, the idea that the old sewers could provide escape routes for wanted men and petty crooks was not a fanciful one. What is on the brink of the impossible, of course, is that a sixty-year-old could carry a young man over his shoulders for several kilometres over alternately slippery and soggy ground, and even through a slough of shit that rises to his chin. This extraordinary feat brings Valjean close to figures from myth and legend. His escape is like one of the twelve labours of Hercules, and it echoes the visit made by Theseus to the underworld. But it is also a Calvary, for the suffering hero bears a weight on his back as heavy as any cross. When after hours of effort in the dark and foul air he reaches an outlet to the light, he finds a snarling guardian at the gate. The toll-keeper at the exit from hell turns out to be Thénardier, whose amazing ability to bob up again and again like a cork in the sea is equalled only by Valjean's repeated returns.

The two also share a frankly unbelievable immunity to the cholera bacillus, which would surely have killed anyone who spent that amount of time in the sewers of Paris in June 1832. The first case was reported on 26 March 1832; within a month, nearly 2,000 Parisians had died of the disease. The epidemic raged on through the summer, carrying off not only poor folk living in hovels, but many eminent men and women too, among them Champollion, who had deciphered Egyptian hieroglyphs, Sadi Carnot, the pioneer of thermodynamics, Casimir Périer, the prime minister, and General Lamarque, whose funeral on 5 June set off the insurrection from which Valjean now has to escape. Although nobody yet knew exactly how the disease was transmitted, it was believed that cholera was connected to water supplies and to the disposal of human waste.[6] Escaping with Marius in June 1832 was even riskier than it seems.

Book 2 of Part V begins, like Book 1, with a general essay, this one focused on the economic benefits of recycling human waste. Before the discovery of industrial methods for fixing nitrogen in the early twentieth century, only natural fertilizers were available, and these ranged from animal manure to guano (desiccated bird shit), which was imported in vast quantities from the Pacific and elsewhere. In Paris and other major cities, night soil was also used, often after processing into powder or pellets. However, Hugo had held long conversations on the foreshore of Jersey with his neighbour, Pierre Leroux, who was convinced that a more systematic reuse of human waste could bring higher agricultural yields and help to alleviate hunger among the poor. Leroux put a proposal for his system to the parliament of Jersey (it was turned down) and ran a pilot plot in his own back yard next door . . . What Hugo proposed for Paris in *Les Misérables* was no different, but it was out of date. A real engineering scheme for cleaning up the city and spreading fertilizer extracted from human waste in the market gardens of Gennevilliers was in the course of construction already – but Hugo could not possibly acknowledge anything being done in Second Empire France. His enthusiasm may seem slightly comical now, but it is powered by beliefs of greater extension and import. Hugo wants us to hear him saying that nothing is so base as to have no use or place in the world;

that the lowest may become the highest if treated the right way; that Paris is not just a ship on a coat of arms or a collection of houses and prisons, but an organic whole and a breathing monster. A Leviathan.

The escape through the belly of the beast seems designed to be put on a cinema screen. Fear of the dark, fear of getting lost, fear of drowning and of being shut in – all these 'nightmare buttons' can be operated by a solo performer in a relatively inexpensive set. It's not especially difficult to show his victory over the obstacles in his path, and his moral triumph also has a visible shape: the inert but still living body on his back belongs to a young man Valjean has reason to wish to see dead, for if he survives he will steal from him the object of his affection and care and his whole *raison d'être*. As he carries his heavy burden through stinking water that almost comes up to his eyes, Valjean turns from Hercules and Theseus into a Christ-like figure bearing his own cross. The episode in the sewers makes *Les Misérables* something grander than a novel in the nineteenth-century mode. It reaches out towards the creation of a legend and the transformation of a character into a myth.

As the weather grew milder and the days longer, *Les Misérables* emerged from under the ground. Marius started to recover, and the author's health also seemed to improve. Hugo's physician, Dr Corbin, thought his illustrious patient would benefit further from a break in such arduous work. He mentioned to Juliette that Victor was fit to travel; the idea of a trip occurred to Adèle too. For once, both wives were of one mind, that a holiday would be good for them all. Even more surprisingly, Victor agreed. He hadn't been off the islands for nine years and he would like to get away for a while. What he did not tell anyone yet was the real reason for his wish to go.

A new dock at St Peter Port had just been finished, and paddle steamers now linked Guernsey to Weymouth, Southampton and Cherbourg on a regular schedule. New railways connected the ports to London and Paris, and travel had never been easier. However, there were no passenger cabins on the *Aquila* and the *Cygnus*, which plied the Weymouth and Southampton routes, and travellers had to sit or stand on the open deck for eight to ten hours. Depending on the weather, they would be sprinkled with sea-spray, soaked by a breaking wave, or drenched by pelting rain. Damp is no greater friend to ink and paper than fire, and great precautions had to be taken by a writer with a manuscript in his bags. For the ream and a half of blue-tinted blank paper and the thousand-odd sheets of what was already written, Hugo had a custom leather case made, which was then treated by a new process to make it waterproof. Not a page of *Les Misérables* got smudged.

As she was able to enter France, Adèle left first on a two-hour crossing to Cherbourg. Two days later, on 25 March, Hugo, Juliette and Charles boarded the *Cygnus* for Weymouth. Adèle II and her aunt Julie stayed to look after the pet dogs, Sénat and Lux, and to keep company with François-Victor, who was working on the ninth volume of his translation of Shakespeare's works.

The crossing was calm. Stopping over briefly in London, Hugo called on a doctor, who gave him another clean bill of health. The trip proceeded by way of Dover and Ostend to Brussels, where the travellers joined up with Adèle. The weather was mild, and Hugo's spirits were high. He scoured antique shops – there was so much more to find in the city than in the islands. Old friends came up from Paris to see him. He went on excursions, held meetings with editors and comrades in exile . . . But he didn't forget what he'd really come to do. 'Finishing my book would please me more than all the excursions in the world,' he wrote to François-Victor.[7]

The holiday came to an end on 7 May. Leaving Adèle in Brussels with Charles, Hugo and Juliette took up residence at the Hôtel des Colonnes at Mont Saint-Jean, a village fifteen miles to the south. Their bedroom window looked directly on to the site of the Battle of Waterloo.

For the following eight weeks, Hugo wrote in his hotel room every day. For exercise, he tramped through the countryside, seeking and finding traces of the huge battle that had taken place there. But the landscape wasn't the same as it had been on 18 and 19 June

1815. Hugo's room faced the Lion of Waterloo, a monumental sculpture atop a huge conical mound. The 300,000 cubic metres of earth used to make Europe's first purpose-built war memorial had been excavated from the fields all around, radically changing the lie of the land. That was the reason that Hugo had come here: to do the fieldwork to allow him to imagine what had really happened at the Battle of Waterloo.

During these long days of writing and walking, Juliette had Victor to herself, which happened so rarely now. Hugo had inserted himself into *Les Misérables* in many ways already, and it must by now have seemed natural to use the last grand scene of the book as a homage and gift to the companion of his life. He has Marius and Cosette marry on 16 February 1833 – the night when he and Juliette had first made love. It's a touching way to say thank you to a woman who had devoted her life to serving him, but the gift was even sweeter than that. The wedding falls on Shrove Tuesday so as to allow the procession to get tangled in the festivities of Mardi Gras and to come to the notice of Thénardier, who then cooks up a plot. However, 16 February 1833 was not Shrove Tuesday, not a Tuesday at all. Had Hugo forgotten what day of the week it was when he fell head over heels in love? Certainly not. Nor had he forgotten that Mardi Gras was Juliette's favourite day of the year. Running the two days together in defiance of the calendar makes it certain that he intended to inscribe Juliette twice over in the happy ending of his greatest work in prose.

Hugo's use of dates started a real trend. James Joyce's *Ulysses* is set on 16 June 1904 to commemorate the writer's first night with Nora Barnacle. Georges Perec set the entire action of *Life A User's Manual* around 8 p.m. on 23 June 1975, because that's when his companion Catherine Binet turned up in a restaurant for their first dinner date. These classics of modernist and postmodernist fiction owe more than you might think to the allegedly old-fashioned *Misérables*.

g

At last the end of the novel was in sight. The failed skulduggery of the novel's now comical criminal-in-chief, family tensions, the great reconciliation, the death of the hero and his burial in the cemetery of Père Lachaise followed on in an uninterrupted flow. Valjean's grave is marked by a modest headstone with an epitaph now erased by rain and wind:

> He sleeps. Though fate dealt with him strangely
> He lived. Bereft of his angel, he died.
> It came about simply, of itself
> As night follows the end of day.

These last words of the book are followed in the manuscript with the time and place of their writing: 'Mont Saint-Jean, 30 June 1861, 8.30 a.m.'[8]

Hugo immediately made it a public fact by writing a letter to his disciple Auguste Vacquerie, the former suitor of Adèle II:

Dear Auguste,
This morning June 30 [1861] at half past eight, with the sun streaming through my window, I finished *Les Misérables*. I know the news will be of some interest to you and I'd like you to hear it from me. I owe you this announcement of birth . . . Rest assured, the child is doing fine.[9]

9.

The Contract of the Century

Hugo had brought the story of *Les Misérables* to its end, but it was a long way from being a finished book. As he put it in a letter to his publisher friend Pierre-Jules Hetzel:

> I have to do a proper inspection of my monster from head to toe. What I'm going to launch on the high seas is my Leviathan: it has seven masts, five funnels, paddle wheels a hundred feet across, and the lifeboats over the sides are the size of liners; it won't be able to dock anywhere and will have to ride out every storm on the high seas. There can't be a single nail missing. So I'm going to revise and reread everything; a last, major, serious incubation, and then I'll say – Go! . . .

Hugo's sea-monster was therefore bigger than the largest vessel ever built, the SS *Leviathan* (later renamed the *Great Eastern*), which had only six masts and paddle wheels fifty-six feet in diameter. It had been designed by Isambard Kingdom Brunel to steam from London to Australia without any stops for taking on fuel. Hugo must have thought that his novel had further to go.

Another letter, this one to François-Victor:

> So, the book's done. Now, when will it be published? That's a different question. I shall consider it in my own time. As you know I'm in no hurry to publish what I write . . . Meanwhile I'll lock up *Les Misérables* under six keys, *con seis llaves* as your great brother Calderón says.[10]

He locked it away for six weeks, in fact, while he took a holiday with Juliette. The couple dashed round Holland looking at medieval dungeons, renaissance churches, quaint houses and a large number of antique dealers' stores. With hardly a night in the same bed, hardly a day without a ride in the buggy rented from the owners of the Hôtel des Colonnes, Hugo threw himself into a feast of visual delights. He was overwhelmed by Rembrandt's *Night Watch* in Amsterdam, disappointed by Dutch landscapes, and ended up thinking Belgium a more interesting place. By the end of August, he was ready to get back to work. He took a steamer from Antwerp and, after changing trains and boats in England, he stepped ashore at St Peter Port on 3 September. There was a lot to do at Hauteville House. He still had to polish and complete *Les Misérables*, but he had a book to sell.

Few of Hugo's French contemporaries lived by the pen, and most of his colleagues and rivals in poetry and prose were independently wealthy men. Lamartine owned vineyards in Burgundy, Vigny had an estate near Angoulême, and Eugène Sue had inherited a fortune from his father, a famous medical man. But Hugo's father, Léopold-Sigisbert, lost almost everything in 1815. From the day he left school in 1817, Victor Hugo had to manage on what he could earn from his literary work. Georges Sand, Honoré de Balzac and Alexandre Dumas were the only other French writers of note who did the same before 1850 or thereabouts.

'Living by the pen' presupposes that authors own their own work and can receive payment for it. That may seem obvious now, but the notion of 'intellectual property' took a long time to come about. It first arose in England in 1710, in a legal statute recognizing that the content of a book could be traded in the same way as a tangible property. In France, the Declaration of the Rights of Man of 1789 established property as a fundamental right, but made intellectual property a special case. Unlike tangible assets, the contents of literary and artistic work were declared to be 'inalienable' properties. This was intended to protect writers and artists from having their work confiscated or suppressed by the state, but the formulation was also taken to mean that the underlying ownership of the content of a work could not be disposed of, even with the owner's consent. How could French writers make a living if they could not even sell their work? The walk-round solution was to sell not the work, but the right to exploit it for a stated number of years or editions. Publishers (who were often booksellers and printers too) paid up-front for these exclusive licences to make and market a given work. When the licence expired, the right to exploit the work reverted to the author, who was free to sell the rights again.

For most of Hugo's career books remained luxury items, for several reasons. Paper was made from pulped rags, and its supply was limited by the amount of cotton and silk clothing that the population of Paris cast off. Typesetting was done by hand and had a high labour cost. Printing presses were made of wood and operated by hand. They could run no more than 3,000 copies before the frame started to yield and loosen the letters in the bed, when the costly process of composition had to be undertaken again. Many important changes in the technology of printing took place in the course of Hugo's life, lowering the cost of books and making them more accessible, but even in the 1860s one volume of a new work still cost two or three times a labourer's daily wage.

Yet demand for reading matter rose consistently every year, as did literacy rates. To serve the hunger for new books that few people could afford to buy, private lending libraries were set up in the backrooms of printers' and booksellers' shops. Hugo himself acquired much of his early literary culture at the 'reading room' run by a Mme Royol, whose name Hugo uses for the only 'friend or close acquaintance' of M. Mabeuf in *Les Misérables*.[11] The number of readers a work had from being rented out by these *cabinets de lecture* made no difference to a writer's income, of course. Nor did French authors earn a penny from the pirated editions of their works printed in Belgium and smuggled back into France. Worse still: by making books available at a lower price and undercutting the market for licensed editions, Belgian trade depressed the sums that French publishers were willing to pay authors for new books.

New technology did not help at first. Steel presses raised the number of copies that could be printed from a bed of type, but as authors were paid by edition or for a set term of years, that made no difference to what they could earn. The stereotype – a thin alloy plate made from a mould of a bed of lead type – could be used to print 100,000 copies, which made logarithm tables, school texts and administrative documents far cheaper to produce, but it did nothing for new literary work. Steam power reduced the labour involved in operating a press, but it reduced costs only for works with long runs (the first proper steam press was installed by the *Times* of London to print the issue of 20 June 1815, which announced the fall of Napoleon at Waterloo). Inventors registered patents for alternative raw materials for paper and eventually hit upon esparto grass, which proved viable. Around 1860, steel, stereotype, steam and cheap paper all converged to lower the cost of reading at long last. *Les Misérables* came at the right time to foster and to take advantage of the democratization of the printed book.

Hugo was well aware of all this. He knew he had something very valuable to sell.

Fixing a value for a literary work is not easy now, and the licence system made it even harder then. In 1831, Balzac received a measly 1,150 francs for his breakthrough novel, *La Peau de chagrin* (*The Wild Ass's Skin*), and still only 3,500 for the two-volume *Père Goriot* (*Old Goriot*) in 1835.[12] At those rates, he would have needed to dash off four or five major novels a year to come close to the salary of a bishop or a judge, let alone the income of the playboys and *grandes dames* that he wrote about. At the other end of the scale, Alphonse de Lamartine earned around 250,000 francs for an eight-volume non-fiction work, *L'Histoire de Girondins*. The numbers are meaningless, of course, without taking into account the number of years the licence ran. Balzac was able to sell each of his novels many times over; Lamartine's history was sold only once. They barely suggest a range for fixing the value of *Les Misérables* in advance.

The sale of *Les Misérables* faced an additional difficulty. In 1832, Hugo's *Notre-Dame de Paris* had been a huge success, and his publishers had secured his next book by paying him a fee for a work as yet unseen. Neither party realized at the time that 12,000 francs would turn out to be far less than Hugo's next novel would be worth. That was partly why Hugo had not written a 'next novel' for thirty years. But however long he put off fulfilling its terms, the old contract remained in force. It now belonged to the bookseller Pagnerre, who had acquired the remnants of the business of Hugo's former publishers, Renduel and Gosselin. He would have to be bought out.

There was a bigger obstacle still: Louis-Napoléon Bonaparte. Censorship under the Second Empire wasn't especially stringent, but it was skittish, and that was the problem. What publisher would lay out money for a book that might have him hauled into court, like *Madame Bovary* or *Les Fleurs du mal*? Hugo's position as an irreducible opponent of the regime made it likely that his new book would be banned, or, if allowed to appear, it might then be seized and pulped. A Paris publishing house could easily consider *Les Misérables* worth nothing at all, and perhaps even less than that.

However, Paris did not have a monopoly on publishing books in French. Since French had been the near-universal language of culture in Europe for two centuries, there were French-language publishing houses in Leipzig, Amsterdam, St Petersburg, Edinburgh and elsewhere. But, they mostly issued reprints of books first published in France and paid no fees to the author of the original work, since the laws of intellectual property were for the most part national ones. But things had begun to change on that front. In 1852, France persuaded Belgium to sign the first true international copyright treaty. It put an end to the trade in pirated editions of French books by extending French copyright protection to Belgium and Belgian copyright to France. The treaty did not submit Belgian publishers to French censorship, however, as Belgium was a sovereign state. Brussels was obviously the place to look for a publisher for *Les Misérables*.

The licence fee for a new book was calculated in part by its length. That created yet another obstacle to the sale of *Les Misérables*. With a single-copy manuscript made of loose sheets not all the same size, some written on both sides and some not, Hugo could not say how many printed pages it would make overall. The work's size in pages and volumes could only be established after a neat copy had been made, but that task could not be truly started until Hugo had finalized his text. He still had things to add and some to cut, but the detail would only be worked out by the 'proper inspection' of the monster he'd told Hetzel he had yet to begin. In September 1861, he really couldn't say how big *Les Misérables* would be.

Given all those uncertainties, it might have been prudent to put off the sale. On the other hand, it was no secret that Hugo had a major new work in train, and publishers had already put in bids for the right to publish it. Pierre-Jules Hetzel came to stay at Hauteville House in June 1860, when Hugo was still gearing himself up to resume the text broken off in 1848, and offered 25,000 francs per volume for a ten-year licence of what was estimated at the time to be a six-volume novel. After he'd left on the steamer, Hugo wrote him a letter saying he could not take the offer seriously.[13] He then asked Hetzel to explore whether there were any other publishers with sufficient resources to stump up a larger sum. Hetzel reported back in January 1861 that he was not able to raise a bid at the level Hugo seemed to want. The target was not stated in writing at the time, but we do now know what it was. Hugo wanted more than had ever been paid for any book.

§

A couple of weeks after he'd written the last line at Mont Saint-Jean, Hugo was in Brussels at the start of his holiday jaunt with Juliette. He took the opportunity to have dinner with his old friend Hetzel, who thought he could now get Hugo to agree to the fee of 150,000 francs that he'd offered him the previous year. Hugo turned him down flat. Hetzel was naturally incensed when he heard a few weeks later that an upstart in the publishing trade was about to sign on with the great man at exactly the same rate. He crossed paths with Adèle at the baths of Spa in September 1861 and told her how offended he was.

What he had heard was not wrong, but it wasn't the whole story. Among the publishers contacted by Hetzel when he was trying to raise bids for Hugo's new book was a carrot-haired young business-man called Albert Lacroix. However, Lacroix had not responded to Hugo's agent. Instead, he had turned his small firm into a limited company and opened negotiations with a merchant bank. Then he wrote direct to Victor Hugo.

Hugo knew the name already. In 1855, Lacroix had sent him a copy of his doctoral dissertation on 'The Influence of Shakespeare in French Theatre', and he got a polite acknowledgement in return (Hugo was a meticulous writer of thank-you notes for books he received, few of which he ever read). Lacroix's liberal political views prevented him from obtaining an academic post, so he joined his uncle's printing firm and went into publishing instead. He turned the family press into a vehicle for left-wing propaganda and for French translations of philosophical and academic books. He pros-pered and attracted interest from the colony of French exiles in Belgium, but he had his business sights set higher than that.

Lacroix's first letter to Hugo got lost in the post, but ten days later the publisher wrote again, asking for an 'audience' with the great man. On 1 September, he tracked down Hugo's son Charles in Brussels and handed him a copy of the original letter that Hugo had never seen. No doubt primed by Charles, Lacroix wrote again to Guernsey to make it clear that if the price was right, he would not haggle and would pay cash. For the present, he needed to know: how much Hugo wanted, under different forms of sale; how long the book was; how *political* it would be; and when it would be ready to appear.[14] Reasonable questions . . . to which the answers were far from clear.

Hugo's first reply on 5 September told Lacroix to get the informa-tion from Charles, who had full powers to speak on his father's behalf; he also wrote to Charles, telling him to be 'a living letter', giving answers that would be better not written down. But he did write them down and sent them to Charles, who transcribed them for Lacroix.

> The work is not political. Its political part is purely historical, Waterloo, the reign of Louis-Philippe, the insurrection of 1832 . . . and the book, which begins in 1815, ends in 1835. So no allusion to today's regime. Moreover it is a drama: a social drama; the drama of our society and our time. It will be at least eight volumes, perhaps nine . . . The book could appear in February [1862], like *Notre-Dame de Paris*, and if it were 13 February, it would be thirty years to the day.[15]

The price Hugo set down consisted of: (1) a buy-out of the old contract with Gosselin and Renduel, at a cost of 12,000 francs; (2) 250,000 francs for an eight-year licence excluding translation rights; (3) 50,000 francs for translation rights, if wanted.[16]

That was a lot of money. It was much more than Hugo's own weight in gold – turned into twenty-franc gold pieces, it would have weighed more than 97kg. It represented twenty years of a bishop's stipend, enough money to endow a chair at the Sorbonne or to build a small railway. Taken at today's price of gold, it would come to around £3 million, but since it entitled the publisher to sell the book for only eight years, it remains the highest figure ever paid for a work of literature. Lacroix must have gulped on first reading. But he could do the sums.

Part of the deal involved translation rights, which had barely been invented.

In England and America translations were considered original works, and their ownership lay with the translator, not the author of the source text. The first international copyright treaty was signed between England and France in 1851 and under its terms authors on both sides of the Channel had the right to 'authorize' translations of their works for five years after the original had appeared. In the United States, however, copyright protection existed only for US citizens, and the country had no international agreements. The American translator of a French work required no authorization but could not publish the translation in Britain; a British translation required authorization, but it could be reprinted without penalty in the USA.[17] Step by little step, however, a broader notion of translation rights had begun to spread around Europe. Treaties similar to the Anglo-French arrangement or to the Franco-Belgian deal began to tie the major nations to the German states, to Geneva, to parts of Italy. Lacroix believed that such arrangements would soon be generalized and that a work like *Les Misérables* would generate significant income from the sale of translation rights. Hugo certainly had global ambitions for his book, but it was Lacroix who first imagined how its worldwide appeal would be monetized.

He had many doubts about the impending deal nonetheless. He thought it would be easier to sell a three- or four-volume novel than one in nine or ten (Hugo disagreed). His second concern was the degree to which its parts were linked. Were they all part of a story that reached its denouement at the end, or were they different 'takes' on the same general idea? Nowadays such questions would rarely be asked – the publisher would read the draft. But there could be no question of that. The manuscript was on Guernsey and Lacroix was not. Negotiations over the publication of *Les Misérables* had to be done entirely on trust. And in person: 'If you leave Ostend on a Tuesday you can be in London on Wednesday and Southampton by Wednesday evening and land on Guernsey on Thursday morning. The trip is nothing at all.'[18]

Lacroix was a dynamo, but he was not discreet. Soon the whole of the publishing world knew he was on his way to signing the deal of the century. That is how Hetzel learned that Hugo was planning to sell *Les Misérables* to someone else. What he had not understood was that although the nominal price per volume was roughly what he had bid, the total price offered was twice that amount.

Lacroix landed at St Peter Port on Thursday 3 October and got down to business at lightning speed. He was a small, slim, agitated man whose conversational style seemed modelled on the charge of the Light Brigade.[19] He wasted no time at all. Hugo's notebook entry for Friday 4 October read: 'Today I sold *Les Misérables* to MM A Lacroix, Verboekhoven & Cie of Brussels, for 12 years, for 240,000 francs cash and 60,000 on option. They've taken over the Gosselin Renduel contract. The agreement was signed this evening.'[20]

The biggest deal in book history was done in a day. *Les Misérables* was not finished so fast.

10.

The Five Parts of Les Misérables

Lacroix irritated everyone in the book trade by boasting he'd signed the greatest deal ever without having a cent of the cash he was committed to paying out. But he was not a crook. Members of the board of his company were friends of the head of the Brussels branch of the Oppenheim Bank, which agreed to finance the purchase of *Les Misérables*. There's some irony in a novel so firmly opposed to debt being launched on the back of a major loan – probably the first loan ever made by a merchant bank to finance a book. *Les Misérables* stands at the vanguard of the democratization of literature *and* of the use of venture capital to fund the arts.

The liquidity Lacroix needed was much more than the 300,000 francs he had promised Victor Hugo. For a book of at least eight volumes in length to appear as a single work, the printer would have to use more lead type than it would normally be prudent to stock. Subcontracting parts to other printers was out of the question for *Les Misérables*. Lacroix wanted every page crisply printed in the same face, which could not be guaranteed if other print shops were used for parts. Lacroix calculated the quantity of new-cast type he would need as a function of the size and number of the presses he had and the amount of storage he could set aside. The final order was sufficient to set thirty-five to forty printers' sheets at the same time, that's to say about one-and-a-half volumes of *Les Misérables*. It weighed 22 tons.[21]

The deal done on 4 October set a very tight deadline for both parties. Lacroix had until 2 December 1861 to come up with the first-stage payment of 125,000 francs in cash and to get it by hand to Hugo's desk at Hauteville House. Hugo for his part had the same grace period of nine weeks to come up with final copy for the first two volumes of his book. 'Fantine' had to be written out in a regular and legible hand on consecutive sheets incorporating the corrections Hugo had made on the left-hand side of his original manuscript, the changes overwritten on the right, and the many longer additions made on branch-numbered sheets – the long section on Myriel's past (I.1.i), the dinner with the senator (I.1.viii), the visit to the dying revolutionary G. (I.1.x), and much else. Only a person familiar with Hugo's handwriting and with his page-numbering scheme could cope with that, and there was only one such person around. The corrected manuscript pages went over to Juliette at La Fallue every day and came back with the fair copy when it was done.

The task was actually even more onerous than that. Hugo reread the fair copy and made more changes and insertions day by day. These additions then had to be collated with the already written sheets and in many cases copied out all over again. It was more than Juliette could manage on her own. Like Adèle and even Victor Hugo – in fact, like anyone who worked long hours in flickering light on untidy reading and writing tasks – she often had sore eyes that forced her to take time off. She needed help. Hugo first hired the teenage daughter of a visiting French family from Jersey to read out the text while Juliette wrote it down, but that did not really speed things up. François-Victor lent a hand in moments of stress, but he had his own deadlines to meet for his translation of Shakespeare's works and didn't have much time to spare. Hugo then took pity on a local woman who had been abandoned by her spouse and appointed her assistant scribe, out of charity, or so he said. But Victoire Estasse's spelling and grammar were not very good, and panic set in at Hauteville House. 'I'm in *Les Misérables* over my head, I'm sinking, drowning, on the sea floor,' Hugo wrote to a friend.[22] He begged Paul Chenay to let his wife Julie, Adèle's sister, come over to boost the output of fair copy from the Guernsey Scriptorium. She arrived on 13 November 1861 and set to work straight away. Julie was a godsend. Without her labour and skill

Hugo and his copyist could not possibly have met the deadline set by Lacroix, which was just three weeks away. Juliette was happy to see the challenge met but not overjoyed to see herself eclipsed. 'My poor adored,' she wrote in one of her twice-daily epistles to her dear great man, 'it pains and almost shames me to be unable to help you at all. I've long known that day would come but I didn't think it would be so soon'.[23]

Lacroix turned up as planned on 2 December to collect Part I of *Les Misérables*. Such was the intensity of Hugo's race against time that he almost forgot it was the tenth anniversary of the detestable *coup d'état*. But yes, the fair copy was on the table, ready to be set in type. In return, Lacroix handed over the first-stage payment of 125,000 French francs, which was converted the same day at the Old Bank of Guernsey into £5,000 sterling and placed in 3 per cent British Government stock.

Hugo's achievement in keeping to schedule seems all the more admirable when we realize what else he had on his plate in those nine weeks. On his return from the continent in September he had found his house in a pitiable state, with leaks in the roof and water seeping through the walls. He had to call in builders to strip out the mortar from the brickwork, repoint it and put on a new coat of roughcast. Meanwhile, a dozen crates of antiques acquired in Belgium and Holland had to be unpacked and their contents distributed around the house. The repairs prompted new ideas for remodelling, and Hugo decided to build his own Crystal Palace – a glass-roofed extension to his writing room, covering part of the terrace and giving him an even better view of the sea. Building the new 'Lookout' wasn't cheap, and it took much longer than planned. But Hugo did not let the hammering and the tramping of builders' feet interfere with his intense daily writing routine in the house.

The autumn months of 1861 were also gloomy ones, for Hauteville was an almost empty nest. After the summer jaunt to the continent Adèle had stayed on in Brussels and then moved to Paris to get treatment for her eyes. Charles had had enough of Guernsey's charms, and settled in Brussels to lead the life of a *littérateur*. As for Adèle II . . . She had rejected Auguste Vacquerie and every other suitor her parents had been able to drum up. She was a talented musician and a beautiful woman, but rather strange. She had set her heart on marrying a British officer, Albert Pinson, and she wandered around humming his name to herself. Hugo's stomach turned at the thought of having a British son-in-law, but in the end he had to give his blessing to his daughter's demands. She wrote to Pinson saying that if he did not come to Guernsey at Christmas to propose marriage, she would do away with herself. The atmosphere in the great house on Hauteville Street was tense and bleak.

❡

In Brussels, meanwhile, Lacroix's compositors started setting 'Fantine' in type. Each bed of type was as long and wide as the press itself and produced a single sheet of printed paper to be folded into pages to make a book. Quarto format is made by folding the printed paper four times, making eight pages out of a sheet or 'signature'. *Les Misérables* was to appear in octavo format, the standard size for new novels, calling for eight folds and giving sixteen pages of text for each one-sided proof sheet, or galley. Each sheet had to be mailed to Guernsey for Hugo's corrections, then the corrections sent back to Lacroix, who produced a second proof to send to Guernsey for Hugo's approval, signalled by the words *bon à tirer*, 'good for press' at the bottom, with the initials 'V. H.' The twelve sheets containing the first pass of the first 192 pages of *Les Misérables* reached Hauteville House on 9 January 1862. Hugo raced through four of them by midnight.

Thus began several months of hard labour that resulted in a victory of scribal effort over the nightmarish logistics of Hugo's island refuge. All the writer had by way of equipment were goose quills, paper and ink, and his only reliable means of communication with Brussels was the thrice-weekly mail boat to Southampton. This was the mad routine he adopted, because he had no choice:

146

In the morning from 7 a.m. to 11 a.m. I revise my manuscript, for I'm working on it up to the last minute, and now and again there are still things missing; in the afternoon, from 2 p.m. to 6 p.m., whilst two women, two devoted souls, copy and collate their copies without a break, I revise what they have collated, then I sort and split up the definitive copy to be used for printing; in the evening, from eight to midnight, I correct proofs, sometimes as many as six sheets a day, and I write letters. No mail boat leaves without a packet of mine.[24]

With Adèle now in residence alongside François-Victor and Julie Chenay and with Juliette at La Fallue, Hugo's household generated around 160 letters a week (excluding Juliette's twice-daily hand-delivered missives to her lover over the way). Such large use of postage stamps vindicated the recent decision of the Postmaster General, Anthony Trollope, to bring Guernsey within the ambit of the Royal Mail. Letterbox No. 1 in Saumarez Street, St Peter Port, the last remaining Victorian post box in daily use in the British Isles, must be the very one that the Hugos used for thousands of letters to Belgium, France and the world.

Les Misérables came a few years too soon for the typewriting machine and carbon paper to solve its logistical problems, and a few months too soon to make more than occasional use of the telegraph.[25] Every page was sent in hard copy by land and by sea from Brussels by way of Ostend, Dover, London and Southampton and took a minimum of three days to reach St Peter Port.

Sometimes it took longer than that, if the weather was bad or there were problems with steamers or trains. The hold-up that riled Hugo the most was what he called the 'English Sunday'. If the Saturday mail boat was delayed by weather until after the main post office closed, no postal worker would unload it before Monday at dawn. From the Lookout, Hugo could almost see his next proofs lying in the hold of the steamer in Le Havelet dock and the thirty-six-hour delay drove him wild. But at least he could grumble about it to his publisher to prove that it was not his fault if the next packet of corrections got back to Brussels days late.

Hugo marked up the proof pages with the conventional marks for 'delete', 'insert', 'replace', 'transpose' and so on, but he did not send them back. Fearful they might be lost or, worse still, stolen and leaked to a newspaper as a 'scoop', he copied over his corrections on to a list that was less costly to mail and of no use to anyone who didn't have the pages to which it referred. Like the original manuscript in Hugo's hand, the corrected proofs of *Les Misérables* never left Hauteville House.[26]

𝔤

Lacroix had the right number of steam-powered steel presses, he had the type and he had the men. Julie and Juliette worked like Trojans, and Hugo put in seven twelve-hour days every week. What could go wrong? More or less everything else.

Hugo was now correcting proofs while still changing, adding and cutting things from the chapters not yet copied over or sent out. That helps to account for the tight knitting of tiny details in different parts of the final text. For example, when going over his presentation of the generic *gamin de Paris* at the start of Part III, he slipped in a quaint example of street-speech as a clue to what lies in store: 'Ohey, Titi, oheeey! 'ere comes trouble, there's bashers about, grab your stuff and run for it, *cut through the sewer*' (III.1.viii, 528).

The disadvantage of writing on two levels at once was that adjustments in the parts of the text still being written could put them out of synch with sheets already set in type, or worse still, already corrected and passed as 'good for press'. The constraints got tighter the further Hugo went.

When the first proofs needed more than trivial correction, Hugo insisted on a second pass before approving them as 'good for press'. At the start, master and servant were courteous with each other, but it was clear who was in charge:

Hauteville House, 12 January 1862, one hour after midnight.
I cannot but request second proofs for almost all the sheets. Out of the eleven sheets corrected, I have been able to pass only four (sheets

148

1, 2, 5 and 9) and even for these I am not entirely unworried. I am happy to acknowledge the copy edits, which have been done very well and demonstrate your intelligent and meticulous attention. But despite everything, the author's eye is nearly always needed twice over.[27]

On the other hand, Lacroix conducted the business side of the project by his own lights. Contrary to the agreement made in October 1861, he did not pay cash to Pagnerre to expunge the inherited rights to Hugo's 'next novel'. Instead, he granted the bookseller exclusive rights to the first edition of *Les Misérables* inside France. The first run of final proofs would be dispatched from Brussels to Paris to provide the copy text for a separate French printing of the novel, to appear simultaneously with the Belgian 'original'. It looks like a lopsided bargain – the first French edition of *Les Misérables* was surely worth more than 12,000 francs! – but what it shows is Lacroix's common sense. If the political climate worsened in France or if Hugo made himself even more objectionable to the authorities (neither of which was unthinkable), then the book might be banned, impounded or even pulped. Lacroix didn't want his own stock to be forfeit in such an eventuality; the Brussels printing would be lapped up by the rest of Europe in any case. Lacroix pulled out all the stops to serve Victor Hugo, but he was also watching his own back.

The double printing in Brussels and Paris added an extra layer of complication through the winter and spring of 1862. As long as Hugo failed to return 'good for press' proofs in the right sequence to Brussels, Lacroix had nothing to send on to Paris, and the French printing, which was set to be the largest of all, could not even be started.

When second proofs still had blemishes (or when Hugo had further changes of his own), a third run was required. As each circuit between author and printer took from seven to ten days (and sometimes more, when the weather, or a Sunday, got in the way), some sheets took a month to go from first composition to 'good for press'; but others took a week. The page-numbers couldn't be confirmed for volume I until *all* its sheets had been passed as 'good'. As long as any sheet was still in process, the beds of type for all other parts of the volume had to stay in storage, and until they had been used to run off the final text, the letters they were made from could not be broken up and reused for the next part of the book. Storage space would soon be full to overflowing. The publisher would soon have to lay off typographers for lack of letters to use. Black clouds were gathering. As winter weather and spring tides kept mail boats in port, a storm was brewing between Hugo and Lacroix.

Lacroix had stuck his neck out in agreeing to pay a large sum for the right to license foreign-language translations of *Les Misérables* and he needed to make a start on recouping his outlay. There was no lack of foreign-language publishers who wanted to be involved, but they all needed copyright protection under the laws of their own states to stop other publishers from bringing out rival translations or pirating the ones they commissioned. That required the author of the original, whose 'intellectual property' was 'inalienable', to sign an exclusive licence for translation to this foreign publisher and that. Such documents had to be in German, English, Italian and so on to be valid in the relevant jurisdiction. Lacroix did not find it easy to get an overworked celebrity living on Guernsey who knew no languages except Latin and Spanish to bother signing papers he did not understand and to have his signature authenticated by officials of the Bailiwick who couldn't read the papers either. On 19 January, Lacroix gave his author a detailed explanation of what he had to do to navigate the waters of international rights. A month later, on 13 February, he reminded him that Leipzig was still waiting. It was still waiting on 25 February. Hugo finally got round to it and mailed the German declaration of rights on 2 March. Just in time! By then, it had been decided that Part I, 'Fantine', would go on sale on 10 April simultaneously in Brussels, Paris and Leipzig, where it was being printed, and in a dozen other cities throughout Europe and even beyond.

As French remained the language of culture of the European elite, Lacroix had an international market for the original text that was separate from the market for its translation rights. But since many European states had not yet signed copyright treaties with Belgium or France, the international status of the language of Les Misérables created its own risks. Nineteenth-century compositors not subject to proofreading and authors' corrections could work at amazing speed, and a single copy of the book in the hands of an unscrupulous Russian or Swedish printer could be turned into a spoiler edition in ten days. The best protection was to get Lacroix's own stock to the major capitals of the world in advance. As it took up to a month to get bulk freight to many of these places, all copies of the book had to be kept under embargo meanwhile. 'Do not let anyone see the manuscript, I beg you, not even your best friend!'[28] Hugo warned Lacroix, who knew why perfectly well. He was actually withholding copy-text from Pagnerre because he was not confident of the security situation in Paris. When Hugo learned from Paul Meurice that the Paris printing had not even begun, he was furious. To his mind, the way to beat pirates and cost-cutters at home and abroad was to produce cheap editions for the masses from stereotype as soon as the expensive octavo edition sold out. He could hardly wait for small-format editions to go on sale so the *people* would read Les Misérables. Lacroix didn't tell him straight out, but that was not a good business plan. To recoup the outlay of hundreds of thousands of francs and to repay the Oppenheim loan, the full-price edition had to go on providing sole means of access to the masterpiece for just as long as Lacroix could drag it out.

These realities of the jungle of books loop in and out of daily exchanges between Guernsey and Brussels that became increasingly fraught. In any case, it was insane to think the receipt and dispatch of proofs to an island in the sea could be maintained at a regular rhythm outside the summer months. Storms, high winds and fog caused foreseeable and frequent delays in the steamer service to Southampton in January, February and March. Now and again Hugo was able to get the captain of the Weymouth service (which was not supposed to carry mail) to help him out,[29] but he was basically limited to three services a week, on Mondays, Wednesdays and Saturdays. But because of the 'English' Sunday what Hugo should have been correcting in the evening of Saturday 26 January wasn't on his desk until Monday.[30] Easterly gales delayed a letter posted in Brussels on 2 February for a whole week.[31] Spring tides delayed the boat due to dock on 6 March for two days.[32] 'It would be so much easier if you weren't in St Peter Port, but in Brussels!' Lacroix protested again and again. He even rented a fine house for the writer and his team a few yards from the printing house in Rue Royale. But Hugo would not budge. He had his routine and he would stick it out, even if it meant giving up sleep. The fragile logistics that sometimes brought three separately written sets of corrections in the same post and sometimes left the printers with nothing to do for ten days drove the enterprise into a brick wall. 'We are unable to proceed at present. We have no type left, and printing is suspended. You are in possession of twenty-seven proof sheets awaiting corrections.'[33]

Hugo, who was as tense about finishing the job as Lacroix, picked a fight. The main reason for delay, he said, was clumsy typesetting and sloppy correcting. If Lacroix could get his workers to do their jobs, then he wouldn't have to send out second and third proofs. Instead of nagging him to leave his highly efficient scriptorium and waste his time packing up and settling in to a new home, Lacroix should look to his own house, and put it in order!

Then the press broke down, and two days were lost waiting for a spare part.[34]

What worried Lacroix even more was that Hugo still would not tell him how long the book was, or how it would be divided into parts. How could he trade sub-rights without telling his clients what he had to sell? It's not that Hugo was being coy. He still hadn't worked it out.

The manuscript that Hugo completed on 30 June 1861 was divided into three parts – 'Fantine', 'Cosette et Marius' and 'Jean Valjean'. A subdivision into four emerged only as he corrected the proofs of Part II in January 1862, when he divided it into II 'Cosette' and III 'Marius'. When he was going over the manuscript of 'Marius' one last time before dispatching it to Brussels in February 1862, the idea of a further subdivision occurred. 'If we have five parts [each printed in two volumes]', he wrote to Lacroix on 3 February, 'we would have only ten volumes. With four parts we would have eight. That would make for a more reasonable price and increase sales, and your profit too, which is as important to me as my own.'[35] But the five-part idea grew on him. 'I carry on thinking more and more that it will have five parts, I can see them clearly. Don't call that a promise . . . but . . . I think I am sure that there will be five parts.'[36] Two weeks later, this emergent structure was laid down in the form of an optimistic publication schedule:

Part I – 15 March
Part II – 25 March
Part III – 5 April
Part IV – 15 April
Part V – 1 May

The name of Part IV was invented when 'Fantine' was already printed and about to be dispatched to booksellers under embargo.[37] 'I think that the title of Part IV will probably be "The Idyll of Rue Plumet and the Epic of Rue Saint-Denis",' he wrote to Lacroix on 13 March. 'Make up your mind, old man,' I can hear the publisher muttering as he shuttled between his steam engines, his paper suppliers, his ink reserves, his typographers and correctors and bankers to keep everything in synch on the greatest rush job his profession would ever know.

§

The final division of *Les Misérables* into five parts may have emerged alarmingly late but it is not an arbitrary one. It gives the novel a familiar overall design – the five-act structure of a classical tragedy. In addition, each of its parts is designed in the same way: Part I begins with a step back even before the plot has begun, with a retrospective account of the life, character, ideas and actions of Bishop Myriel that 'in no way impinges on the substance of what we are about to relate (I.1.i, 5). Part II begins with a great essay on the Battle of Waterloo, Part III with a general essay on the street-children of Paris and Part IV with an essay on Louis-Philippe. The great step back at the start of Part V (or rather, the step forward, to 1848) is, by that stage, almost expected, as it confirms the pattern set up by all that precedes. Far from being digressions, the essay chapters constitute the basic rhythm of the text. They are what makes *Les Misérables* what it is: food for the heart, and food for the mind.

Interlude: The Mind of Jean Valjean

Madame Bovary takes you inside the mind of a provincial housewife; *Great Expectations* lays out the world as seen by a boy from the marshes of Kent; *Crime and Punishment* provides an exhaustive exploration of the mental turmoil of an impoverished intellectual in St Petersburg. *Les Misérables* is strikingly different from the other great novels of its age. Except at two moments of anguish, it hardly allows you to know what it was like to be Jean Valjean.

The absence of the inner man from a story in which he occupies centre stage comes in part from his taciturn nature. Valjean must surely be the least talkative protagonist of nineteenth-century fiction before Melville's Bartleby. But Hugo had several reasons to keep his hero's mouth mostly shut.

Speaking doesn't just communicate information. The words you use, the way you put them together, the pitch of your voice and the way you form the sounds also identify who you are. In written texts like novels, the converse is no less true: characters' identities are constituted by the way they speak (more correctly, by the way their speech is represented). Dickens had a knack for creating memorable and now almost proverbial characters out of the forms of language attributed to them in direct speech. You could say that Mr Micawber, Sam Weller, Miss Flyte, Magwitch and many more *are* the special languages Dickens cooked up for them. In French, Balzac is Dickens's only real rival in this domain, but Hugo performs the same act by creating the character of Gavroche out of quips, rhymes, slang, Paris dialect and puns. But he does nothing of the kind for Valjean.

A farmhand who's spent nineteen years in jail can't be expected to sound like a successful entrepreneur or a respected small-town mayor. Dickens wouldn't have left a detail of that kind unattended.

Like *Les Misérables*, *Great Expectations* is the story of a convict morally transformed by an act of kindness. When he returns from Australia, Magwitch can't show himself in public because he would give himself away on opening his mouth. 'Pint out the place!' Magwitch says on his first encounter with Pip on the marshes, with the spelling indicating a 'low' London accent. Twenty years later, floating down the Thames in a small boat, he still speaks to Pip in marked forms of lower-class speech: 'It come to be flat there [in Australia], for all I was a-growing rich. Everybody knowed Magwitch.'[38] By contrast, Valjean's enunciation of French is simply rubbed out of *Les Misérables*. The less he says, the less likely readers will notice this strange fact.

Hugo tells us how Valjean came to improve the vocabulary and syntax of his speech: 'He always took his meals alone, with a book open in front of him . . . He loved books . . . It was observed that . . . his language had grown more refined, more carefully chosen, gentler . . .' (I.5.iii, 157).

Reading can do a lot, but it doesn't change the sound of your consonants and vowels. To turn a flower girl into a lady, for example, Shaw's Professor Higgins has to train Eliza Doolittle for weeks on end to say 'Rhine in Spine' as if it rhymed with his way of saying 'pain'. Changes in the fundamental sounds of a person's speech, even those that are socially advantageous, don't come from reading books.

Valjean's accentless French is also masked by the omission of almost all reference to the accents of the other characters, which is itself masked by constant use of the word 'accent' to describe something else. 'Accents' in *Les Misérables* may be 'decisive', 'humble', 'proud' 'lugubrious', 'naive', 'natural', 'plaintive', 'pure', 'respectful', 'haughty', 'fierce', 'cold' 'measured' and 'beseeching'. In these usages, 'accent' refers not to pronunciation, but to the emotional import of the way something is said, the affect expressed in a tone of voice. It's a legitimate sense of the word in French, but its main function in *Les Misérables* is to deflect attention from one of the least plausible elements in the novel's plot.[39]

It's not that Hugo was deaf. He picked up on the foreign and regional accents of people around him and he logged curiosities in his notebooks. But as he wrote in his essay on Shakespeare, 'Everything is voluntary in a work of art'[40] – especially what's left out.

All the same, there are places in *Les Misérables* where Jean Valjean speaks out. When he is set upon by the sinister teenage criminal Montparnasse, he overpowers the younger man and gives him a piece of his mind.

> My boy, through laziness you're letting yourself in for the most arduous kind of existence. Ah! You profess to be an idler! Prepare yourself for work. Have you ever seen a machine that's to be feared? It's called a rolling-mill. You need to be wary of it, it's a crafty and ravenous thing. If it gets hold of your coat flap it'll have all the rest of you. The machine is idleness. Stop while there's still time . . .
> (IV.4.ii, 826)

A reformed convict is quite likely to disapprove of a life of crime, but this long and energetic denunciation of idleness as the source of corruption harks back directly to the ideas of Malthus – and to Hugo's own view that a decent job brings moral as well as financial improvement to the poor. In fact, this diatribe delivered on the streets within earshot of Gavroche is such a complete break with Valjean's habitual taciturnity that we are justified in thinking that the person speaking is really Victor Hugo.

With this exception, and prior to the long confession he makes to Marius, the only access that we have to the mind of Jean Valjean comes from the silent conversations he has with himself at the two crisis points in his life. The first arises when he learns that a simple-minded vagrant called Champmathieu is about to stand trial for a second offence as the former convict Valjean. He has to choose a course of action: to let the man be convicted, or to give himself up and save Champmathieu from a punishment he does not deserve. The first course will allow him to carry on being M. Madeleine, giving work and alms to a whole town. From a utilitarian perspective it is his social duty to carry on. The second course would destroy the prosperity of Montreuil-sur-Mer but it corresponds to the moral duty of saving an innocent man. It's a tough call, and it takes Valjean all night. Before dawn, he sets off for the court at Arras, but we don't know what he has decided to do – in all probability, nor does he. I don't think this is just a novelist's trick to create narrative suspense. Valjean's inner life is so hidden that we cannot know what it is really like; in addition, the balance between his duties is so fine that the out-turn of the 'storm in the mind' hangs by a thread.

The second crisis arises at the end of Part IV, when Valjean learns of Cosette's love for Marius. The second mental storm, also conducted through inner speech (including some sentences spoken aloud, heard by the narrator alone), pits the bad side of love (possessiveness, jealousy, the fear of loneliness) against a paternal wish for Cosette to find happiness with a man her own age. Here again, Hugo withholds the resolution of a conflict inside Valjean's head, but the external signs of what he's decided come sooner than in the Arras scene, because he puts on his National Guard uniform in order to go out. That can only mean he is on his way to the barricade.

The repeated retention of decisions reached through inner turmoil make Valjean into a man who can be known by what he does, not through thoughts or words. That's the way the lives of the saints used to be written. But Hugo makes it more complicated than that. When Valjean finally drops off to sleep in the course of the night spent meditating on what to do about Champmathieu, he has a dream. The novel tells us what that dream was. But how does it know? In *Les Misères*, the dream is retold in the third person, and is known to the narrator because '[Tréjean] recounted his dream many times'. That clashes with Valjean's general reluctance to open his mouth, and so, when revising the text in 1861, Hugo recast it as a first-person text put in writing by Valjean himself. It's the only piece of writing attributed to the hero in the entire novel; no explanation is given of how it came into the story-teller's possession. You could call that a continuity glitch or a novelist's sleight of hand, but the dream is so strange as to focus attention on something else: who really dreamed this dream? Does it give us access to the deep self of Jean Valjean – or to the troubled mind of Victor Hugo?

Valjean's dream is set off by a sound: midnight chimes remind him that he'd recently seen an old bell at a scrap dealer's with the inscription 'Antoine Albin de Romainville'. Around three in the morning his 'thoughts started to become confused again . . . The name of Romainville kept coming back into his mind with two lines of a song that he had once heard . . . He remembered that Romainville was a little forest near Paris where young lovers went to gather lilacs in April' (I.7.iii, 216). What is omitted – Hugo must have assumed his readers would know it – is the refrain of a popular music-hall song:

> Qu'on est heureux
> Qu'on est joyeux,
> Tranquille
> A Romainville
> Ce bois charmant
> Pour les amants
> Offre mille agréments
> (How we're happy
> How we're joyful
> And calm
> At Romainville
> This lovely forest
> offers a thousand pleasures
> for lovers)

Valjean's waking mind represses the memory, however. When he rereads the record of his dream-self entering a village that 'must be Romainville', he overwrites it with a question: *Why Romainville?* The answer may have been obvious in 1862: 'happy', 'joyful' and 'calm' is what Valjean cannot be.

The main vision in the dream is a village that turns out to be a town with no one about, yet behind every door stands a silent man with an earth-coloured face, one of whom tells the dreamer that he is already dead. The scene is close to one depicted in Stefan Grabiński's *Grey Room*, and the 'Polish Poe' may well have taken it directly from *Les Misérables*. However, Hugo's set-up of Valjean's vision of the world of the dead speaks of a walk with a brother 'that I have to say I never think about and can scarcely remember now'.

Did Valjean have a brother? What we do know is that Hugo had two. The elder, Eugène, suffered mental breakdown in 1823 and died in 1838. Many critics are therefore eager to link this part of the dream to sibling rivalry and retrospective guilt in the mind of Victor Hugo. But that is not the only way it can be understood.

Valjean didn't quite know it yet, but he had a kind of a brother he would see next day in court. When he sees Champmathieu in the defendant's box, 'He thought he saw himself, aged, with not exactly the same features, to be sure. But identical in attitude and appearance, with that bristling hair, those wary brown eyes' (I.7.ix, 242).

Champmathieu comes from Faverolles, as he does (one of the reasons he has been misidentified as Valjean), and he has the same nobody-name of Jean, pronounced *champ* in rural dialect. It's intriguing to think that what M. Madeleine sees with horror as his alter ego in the courtroom at Arras could plausibly be an actual brother of his. His nightmare would thus have been a premonition, fed by the details of the case that Javert had already given him. Other characters in *Les Misérables* meet siblings they don't know are related to them. Why not Valjean?

Seen in this light, Valjean's self-sacrifice to save Champmathieu could be understood as a fraternal act, not just metaphorically, but in a literal sense.[41] Fraternity, the too-often forgotten complement of equality and freedom in the French revolutionary creed, may be embodied in the plot of the Champmathieu affair and in the dream on which it secretly hangs.

At around the same time, in St Petersburg, a lowly clerk, a poor drudge in some obscure office of the imperial state, was constantly pestered and humiliated by his superiors. One of them had the common humanity to see that the doleful, red-rimmed eyes of the ridiculous, balding, ill-dressed Akaky Akakyevich said just one thing: 'I am your brother'.[42] Indirectly, through a premonitory dream and the shock of recognition of one *misérable* in another, the Champmathieu episode of *Les Misérables* says the same thing.

9

Near the start of Part I an unnamed traveller strides into Digne in October 1815 with a large iron-tipped walking stick and the fearsome look of a ragged and tousled giant. He has no name until he introduces himself in the next chapter but one to the priest who offers to give him a bed for the night. Instead, he is referred to in the first paragraph as a *passant*, a 'passer-by'.

In the first paragraph of Part II, another *passant* wanders along the road from Nivelles to La Hulpe, place-names known to all who have read accounts of the Battle of Waterloo. But this *passant* is 'the person telling this story', that's to say, not the narrator, but Victor Hugo. Somewhat obscured by the current English translation of the term as 'traveller', the use of the term *passant* for both Valjean and Hugo sets up a strange resonance between the author and the character in the book.[43]

The superficial similarities are trivial. Both are good walkers: Hugo once climbed up to the Mer de Glace from Chamonix, and Valjean covers thirty-six miles of hilly countryside in a day. They were about the same age: Valjean is sixty-two when he saves Marius from Rue de la Chanvrerie and Hugo fifty-nine when he wrote it. Both dress simply on purpose when they could afford finer attire, both give alms, and both stick to a plain and very light diet. (Hugo takes his distaste for rich food to an almost polemical extreme in *Les Misérables* by omitting to tell us what there is to eat on the table at Bombarda's restaurant, or even at the wedding luncheon laid out on a lavishly decorated table for Cosette and Marius. No other nineteenth century novel I know is so discreet about its characters' intake of food.) Hugo had learned what it was to be an outcast, but it doesn't make sense to compare Guernsey to the *bagne* at Toulon. Hugo had *seen* men like Valjean – at Bicêtre, on a Paris street and in Toulon – but he'd never *been* anything like one.

However, the dream he attributes to Valjean seems to have been a dream that he dreamed himself and recounted to his wife Adèle. The difficulty Valjean has in knowing where his duty really lies also matches Hugo's own split mind over what he did in June 1848. Like Hugo, Valjean doesn't follow Catholic rituals, but he believes and he prays. Obviously, it wouldn't be reasonable to think novelists could ever convincingly create characters with whom they had absolutely nothing in common. But Hugo put in a secret sign to remind himself and maybe those who knew him well that there were deep links of identity between the dutiful and persistent ex-convict and himself. Hugo was born on 26 February 1802, but because he was a slightly premature baby, he always believed he had been conceived on 24 June 1801. Valjean's prison number on his first incarceration at Toulon is 24601.

PART FOUR
War, Peace and Progress

11.
The Start of It All

Claude Lelouch's 1995 film of *Les Misérables* retells Hugo's tale as a story not of the nineteenth but of the twentieth century, and it begins with a ball on the night of 31 December 1899. As the clock hands reach midnight, they bring in a New Year that marks the calendric start of a new century. Hugo's own century did not start the same way, because at that time France used a now forgotten decimal calendar introduced in the wake of the French Revolution: 31 December 1799 coincided with the unremarkable date of 10 Nivôse, Year VIII, which can't be seen as the start of anything. However, Lelouch's invention expresses a fundamental truth about Hugo's project. *Les Misérables* aimed to be the 'novel of the nineteenth century', and so it starts at the beginning. When exactly was that? In nineteenth-century France, it was obvious that the new age had begun on 18 June 1815, on a 'drab plain' south of Brussels near a village called Waterloo.

With the exception of Lelouch, no adaptation I have seen accepts Hugo's own definition of the start of the story he tells. A recent Japanese animated serial for television, for example, starts with Fantine and Cosette walking towards Montfermeil, in 1817. Boleslawski's classic Hollywood version begins with the trial of Jean Valjean in 1796. The musical begins with a scene during Valjean's imprisonment in Toulon. The wealth of threads and loops in Hugo's narrative would permit many other plausible starts on stage or screen: a priest singled out at an imperial reception for promotion to the bishopric of D., for example, with '1805' overprinted on the screen; a raucous dinner where four boozy young men walk out on their girlfriends, with a supertitle saying

'Bombarda's Restaurant, 1817'; or a gloomily elegant salon where aged gentlemen and jewel-bedecked matrons express relief at the return of the king in front of a wide-eyed, eight-year-old Marius. It isn't absurd to use the career of Myriel (and the theme of charity), or the fall of Fantine (and the theme of poverty) or the education of Marius (and the theme of political transformation) as ways into the labyrinth of *Les Misérables*, but none of these start-points is where Hugo actually put it. Even less close to the novel's design is Tatiana Lukashevich's *Gavrosh*, a film made in the Soviet Union in 1937, which starts with a street urchin scrawling political graffiti on a wall and running away from the police. The paranoid politics of the Soviet Union at the time of the great purges meant there was probably no alternative to making 'revolution' the main theme and Gavroche the lead character in an adaptation of Hugo's book. But the fact is that *Les Misérables* really begins in 1815.

The time-line of Hugo's story maps on to historical events with great precision. Jean Valjean is arrested for the theft of a loaf, tried, sentenced and sent to Bicêtre to be chained and then transported south to the hard-labour prison at Toulon. The chaining ceremony – Hugo describes it in detail in *The Last Day of a Condemned Man* – takes place on 22 April 1796. That is to say, Valjean goes down on the same day that a young Corsican general only recently risen from the ranks won a great victory at the Battle of Montenotte. That success put Napoleon Bonaparte on track to become commander-in-chief, then first consul in 1799 and finally emperor in 1804. Throughout the nineteen years that Valjean spends in jail, Napoleon led armies of Frenchmen into battle all over Europe. They were manned initially by professionals, volunteers and enthusiasts, then increasingly by conscripts drawn from every corner of France and from the many territories incorporated into the Empire over those years. Hundreds of thousands of peasants and labourers were forced into service to fight and to die at the mass slaughters now commemorated on the Arc de Triomphe in Paris as the Battles of Lodi (1796), Rivoli (1797), the Pyramids (1798), Marengo (1800), Copenhagen

(1801), Trafalgar (1805), Austerlitz (1805), Jena (1806), Eylau (1807), Zaragoza (1808), Wagram (1809) and Borodino (1812). Many more thousands died of cold and hunger in the retreat from Moscow over the Berezina in 1813 and thousands more at Dresden before Napoleon was finally forced to abdicate in 1814.

He was exiled to the island of Elba, in the Mediterranean, under British control at that time. Amazingly, incomprehensibly, he slipped his guards on the night of 26 February and landed on the south coast of France on 1 March 1815. At the head of a constantly grow-ing band of enthusiasts, he marched north by way of Digne[1] to Lyon, where army units abandoned the hastily restored monarchy they had only just agreed to serve. Napoleon's aim was to use attack as defence, to strike the Seventh Coalition of Russia, Prussia, Holland, Austria and Britain before it could assemble in full, and by winning a military victory, extract a peace that would leave him on the throne of France. By the time he reached Belgium in early June he had almost as many men, horses and cannon at his disposal as his enemies did. The showdown came at a place he had chosen, on undulating farmland south of Brussels. Another 25,000 French sol-diers were killed or maimed in the battle that took place there on 18–19 June 1815.

Jean Valjean was not among them, because he was still in jail. Indeed, he had spent the preceding nineteen years in just about the only place in France that could have been called safe for a man of his class and physical build. His sentence may be an example of the injustice of the law, and his punishment may be seen as barbaric and cruel, but they saved his life and left Hugo with a story to tell. In fact, Valjean must have spent more than nineteen years in jail, since he emerges in the summer of 1815, a few weeks after the fall of France. Had he been released on the anniversary of his chaining, on 22 April, he would most likely have been press-ganged into military service for the last of Napoleon's battles.

One of Hugo's most hostile and conservative critics, Armand de Pontmartin, inadvertently confirmed the structural role of Valjean's imprisonment until 1815. He fished up hearsay evidence that the character of Jean Valjean was based on the real life of an ex-convict named Pierre Maurin (or Morin) who had been sentenced to five years' hard labour for stealing bread and was treated kindly by the real Bishop Miollis in Digne. Maurin was released in 1806 – and then joined the army, as he had to. He died at the Battle of Waterloo, and his bones were most likely part of the huge pile that an entrepreneur ground up to make fertilizer for Yorkshire farms.[2] This probably made-up story confirms the logic of Hugo's construction of the pre-history of the hero of *Les Misérables*. Valjean stays in jail until the nineteenth century can begin.

Twice over Hugo dated the start of his tale to that point – in *Les Misères*, which begins 'Early in the month of October 1815' (now the start of Book 2), and again at the start of the first book inserted at the head of *Les Misérables*, which begins 'In 1815 . . .' This repetition serves to remind us how special the hero of the story is. Unlike almost all of his contemporaries, Valjean is neither dead nor a war hero, nor is he a returning émigré or a traitor or a dodgy camp-follower like Thénardier. Physically intact save for a limp in his left leg from having a heavy chain attached to it all those years, he is a historical anomaly, as unburdened as a new-born by the terrible and glorious history of his land.

Another popular novel of the period begins in the same key year. Its hero, Edmond Dantès, is incarcerated in the Château d'If in 1815, just when Valjean is released from Toulon. After extraordinary adventures in an island prison and around the Mediterranean Sea, Dantès comes to Paris as the Count of Monte Cristo in the 1830s, just after the death of Valjean. The action of *Les Misérables*, from 1815 to 1835, fills the time that Monte Cristo spends in prison and on the high seas and stops at the point where the Parisian adventures of Dumas's hero begin. Valjean and Dantès book-end each other, so to speak – and for good reason. *The Count of Monte Cristo* is a story of extravagant and spectacular revenge, but *Les Misérables* asks us to be kind. Dumas's saga of daring and survival fulfils a fantasy of avenging political and financial crimes. Hugo's much more tightly wound plot is designed to promote and make manifest the possibility of

reconciliation. Though the two authors were good friends and comrades in arms in the fight against the Second Empire, their most
famous works of fiction express different moral perspectives and
different kinds of hopes for the future of France.

On a political level, Hugo sought reconciliation between the
three 'grand plans' for ruling the nation: monarchism, in the form
of loyalty to either the Bourbons or the house of Orléans; the revolutionary and republican inheritance of 1789; and the modernizing
authoritarianism of Napoleon Bonaparte. These were inherently
incompatible models of government, and much blood had been
spilled over the preceding half-century to make one or the other
prevail. But for Hugo as for most people of his generation, the key
event that allowed even a glimmer of hope to arise was what happened in June 1815 at Waterloo. A novel of the nineteenth century
could not but take it within its view.

However, Hugo did not even think about writing a chapter on
the battle when he drafted *Les Misères* in 1845–8. It does not seem to
have occurred to him in 1860 either, since there's no mention of it
on the 'to-do' list he made after rereading *Les Misères* from end to
end. He certainly did not draft it in the extraordinarily fertile winter
months of 1860–61, and he didn't write a word on the battle even
when he was staying at the Hôtel des Colonnes with a grand view
of the battle site itself. On the other hand, we have to presume that
he chose to complete *Les Misérables* at that special place because he
had Waterloo in his mind. He certainly told Lacroix that there
would be such a chapter when he signed the contract in October
1861, and by December, when Lacroix collected Part I 'Fantine' to
set in type, it was clearly understood that the next section of fair
copy would begin with a chapter on Waterloo. Except that it wasn't
written yet. The great essay on the battle that launched the great
peace of the nineteenth century turns out to have been the *last* piece
of *Les Misérables* that Hugo wrote – and only just in time. Even
essay-writers know that introductions are best written at the end.

Waterloo matters first of all because it was a national humiliation. It brought to a stop the great project of bringing the surviving

values of the French Revolution to all of Europe (an end to the privileges of the aristocracy, social promotion given to merit rather than birth, the rational organization of laws and institutions, and submission of the church to the power of the state). It also matters because from then on France was under the tutelage of foreign powers – it was occupied by British, German and Russian troops, and had a constitution based on the British model imposed on it. But it also matters in a different way. The Peace that settled the outcome ushered in a 'concert of nations' based on a balance of powers that protected Europe from major continental wars for ninety-nine years. Waterloo was the inglorious end of a glorious adventure, but also the start of a less bloody and vastly more prosperous age.

Making sense of Waterloo was therefore in Hugo's mind the only way to make sense of the century his novel aimed to portray and understand, and the only way to explain why despite its defeat France remained the moral and intellectual centre of the world. At a more visceral level, Waterloo had to be chewed over so as to settle Hugo's account with his father, General Léopold-Sigisbert, a blindly obedient hero whose rise and fall were by-products of Napoleon's reign.

However, it isn't easy to say what really happened at Waterloo, even today. As soon as the smoke cleared on 19 June 1815, historians, military analysts and political commentators started disagreeing about the event and its significance, and have gone on arguing ever since. By 1861, books about Waterloo in French and English already filled many library shelves, and that is no doubt why Hugo declares, in the plural of majesty he uses from time to time, 'We have no intention of writing the history of Waterloo' (II.1.iii, 285). Perhaps not; but 'we' certainly aimed to rewrite it, and to work out what it meant.

For the facts and for analysis Hugo used four main resources: Napoleon's own account of how and why he lost, dictated to his scribe Las Cases and published as *Le Mémorial de Sainte-Hélène* (the favourite reading of Julien Sorel, in Stendhal's *Red and Black*); a respected historical work, *Histoire de la Campagne de 1815*, by Jean-Baptiste Charras, a retired military officer with republican views; Hugo's own inspection of the battle site in May and June 1861; and his imaginative reconstruction of the way it had been in June 1815. His aim was to bring the argument about what really happened to a definitive end.[3]

The section Hugo wrote between December 1861 and mid-January 1862 consists of both a dramatic recitation of stirring events full of noise and bravery beyond belief and a reflective essay designed to answer questions that mattered deeply to French readers. But it also does much more than that. Waterloo is where Thénardier first appears in chronological sequence and encounters the father of Marius, which ties a major thread of Part I to characters and events that will come together much later on in the book. Even more: it brings to the fore the theme of excrement that Hugo had already elaborated in the chapters written the previous spring but which aren't broached in the novel until several hundred pages further on. To call these battle chapters a digression – or, even worse, to cut them out or to place them in an appendix, as some old British editions do – is not only to miss the personal, historical and political points Hugo wanted to make, but to ignore the full integration of the Waterloo episode in the finely wrought narrative of *Les Misérables*.

The 'national' question that Waterloo raised was this: could France have won the battle? Like Napoleon himself and his still numerous fans in nineteenth-century France, Hugo liked to believe that it could, and had been thwarted by mere chance. He therefore explains that overnight rain on 17 June bogged down French artillery and prevented it from being moved into position for several hours. Had the shelling started as planned at dawn, he surmises, then the outcome would have been very different. The second random blow of fate was that local guides gave misleading information to French troops, but accurate tips to the Prussian avant-garde. Wellington did not win the battle, Hugo argues, but chance lost it for France. This is now a familiar argument about military conflicts of all kinds: the 'fog of war' makes the outcome of conflict unpredictable, and momentous events may hang on trivially small causes. Hugo sums it up by saying that any battle is *'un quine'* – a lottery, a throw of the dice (II.1.xvi, 315). This echoes the point made by Stendhal in his portrait of the Battle of Waterloo at the start of *La Chartreuse de Parme* (*The Charterhouse of Parma*), where the confusion of mud and smoke is so great that no general was really in charge or in a position to determine the outcome. Tolstoy, who read Stendhal and Hugo with care, gives an even grander portrayal of random chaos in his chapters on the Battle of Borodino in *War and Peace*. This element in Hugo's analysis also provides a pragmatic basis for his pacifist convictions. If the outcome of mass violence is entirely unpredictable, then military action has no point.

So should France have won? Hugo maintains that Napoleon had sufficient cannon, horses, men and morale to beat Wellington, especially since the Iron Duke's strategy was unimaginative and old-fashioned. Without the rain, the delay and the misinformation, France *ought* to have won.

Then why did it lose? An altogether different type of argument comes in at this point. France lost because it had to, because the time had come, because it was written in the stars. In a nutshell: 'God intervened' (II.1.xiii, 310).

This looks like a retrospective illusion, but it's not entirely silly. What would have happened if the French had scored a technical victory at Waterloo? Would the assembled armies of Britain, Austria, Prussia, Holland and Russia have said, OK, you win, we'll go home? Surely not. They would have regrouped and then hammered the depleted armies of an outlaw nation with little money left and a diminished commander-in-chief who couldn't sit in a saddle for more than a few minutes at a time. Napoleon's hope that the Coalition would allow him to remain on the throne if he gave them just one more bloody nose wasn't rational. It was madness.

Hugo does not resolve history's mysterious equation of chance and necessity. He leaves it open. His chapters give equal support to the view that it might have turned out differently and to the view that it had to turn out the way it did.

But to do this, he has to say why the invincible French cavalry made no impact on Wellington's line. Chance or necessity? This is where Hugo slightly alters the weight of the dice. He inserts a hidden ravine into the landscape, the 'hollow road' of Ohain. Wider and deeper in Hugo's dramatic reconstruction of the past than it seems to have been in reality, the pit was invisible to advancing horsemen and so became their grave. That's why Napoleon did not really lose the Battle of Waterloo and why Wellington certainly did not win it. This was the view of the ex-emperor himself, of course – but even he stopped short of inventing obstacles that weren't there. Hugo's reimagination of the battlefield may owe something to literary models such as the *Song of Roland*, in which Charlemagne's rearguard was slaughtered in a similarly steep-sided cleft at Roncevaux, or a famous battle story by Balzac, *Le Colonel Chabert*, where the hero is buried alive beneath a huge pile of other corpses. Prior to mechanized warfare of the modern age, all battle writing seems to offer permutations of a limited number of themes. There are ravines at Thermopylae and Killiecrankie; pits full of corpses are as old as the stories of Tamerlane and Genghis Khan.

Who, then, did win the battle? Hugo gives two answers, one strategic and the other ideological. At Waterloo, the 'old monarchies' of Europe defeated the heir of the French Revolution, and in so doing turned back the clock. They condemned British, Russian, Austrian and Prussian citizens to the straitjacket of feudal rule, which means that the notional victors were the real losers of the fight. (By that argument, the French were losers too, since they had a restored monarchy imposed on them.)

But the law of unintended consequences produced the opposite result as well. The tens of thousands of Russian, German, Austrian and Dutch soldiers who poured into France after Waterloo came into prolonged contact with the most advanced civilization in the world. (The last detachment of Cossacks didn't evacuate France until 1821.) By osmosis, those foreign soldiers absorbed ideas of progress, human rights and democracy that were native to France and took the seeds of these delicate plants back home. In 1825, they first sprouted in Russia with the Decembrist uprising. In 1830, when France swept away the Bourbons, the Belgians also revolted and established their own free state. And so on . . . Austrians and Hungarians in 1848, then Italians in the 1850s, all bore forward ideals first forged in France, on the long march towards a universal republic that could not have begun without Waterloo. It's a national-subjective view of history that allows Hugo to believe that, despite its short-term reactionary effect, the humiliation of Waterloo was a chapter in the longer-term narrative of progress.

The more ideological answer that Hugo gives to the question of who really won in 1815 is that nobody did – at least no emperor, duke or nation. The only victor that day was a French officer who blurted out a rude word. General Cambronne, commanding the last surviving squad of Napoleon's Old Guard, was surrounded by British troops and ordered to surrender or be killed on the spot. Instead of laying down his arms he bawled 'Merde!' at the top of his voice. The valiant vulgarity of the old soldier isn't a product of Hugo's fertile imagination. It was an urban legend already.

The real Cambronne survived the barrage of fire that killed all but a few of his comrades in arms. He was wounded, taken prisoner and moved to England, where he was cared for by a Scottish nurse who became his wife. During his convalescence in London in 1816, Cambronne wrote a letter to *The Times* about the reports it had published on two declarations he was said to have made at Waterloo: 'La garde meurt et ne se rend pas!' ('The Guard dies and does not surrender!') and 'Merde!' He wished to assure readers he had never said either of these things. The stories were calumnies and lies.

Where did they come from? Why did Cambronne need to deny them? I don't know. But thanks to the letter to *The Times*, they became known to all and part of the folk history of the Battle of Waterloo until Hugo picked up one of them and turned it into a nutshell expression of the linguistic, historical and human message of *Les Misérables*.

Hugo had always been keen to loosen the rules on what kinds of words could be spoken on stage or put into print. When he congratulated himself in a poem published in 1856 for having 'put a red cap on the dictionary', he was claiming retrospectively that he'd revolutionized the lexicon of drama and verse.[4] The culmination of his essay on Waterloo in *Les Misérables* takes his 'ordinary language' campaign several steps further on. *Merde* belongs not to the register of familiar or even vulgar French, but to the set of words that are counted as taboo. It had certainly never been seen in print in a literary work before Hugo put it into *Les Misérables*.

The historical sense of 'Cambronne's word' is to bring great events down to the actions of individuals. Cambronne faces an abstract choice between the force of history, backed by overwhelming might, and fidelity to his oath of allegiance. The choice manifests itself on the ground in directly personal terms: surrender or death. It's the choices of individual men and women that make history, and the stand of Cambronne at the Battle of Waterloo is just one illustration that, in the end, it's people, not abstractions, that count.

Cambronne does not comply with an order from the enemy, but does his duty as a soldier by carrying on the fight, even when the only weapon he has left is a rude word. Writers have a natural tendency to believe that the word is mightier than the sword, and no one ever had a greater stake in the adage than Victor Hugo. By 1861, he knew that pamphlets and poems would not unseat the petty dictator who had usurped the throne and the mantle of Napoleonic France, but his own long resistance had a meaning to itself, and it was the same as the meaning of Cambronne's 'Merde!': don't give in; don't be polite; be like General Léopold-Sigisbert Hugo; best of all, be like me.

∮

In view of the importance of what Hugo has to say in the first book of Part II and of the shabby way it has been treated up to now by critics, adapters, translators and editors, I propose a new film version that would begin at the real beginning, and go something like this.

EXT. DUSK. LONG SHOT
Golden-orange sunset.
OVERPRINT: 18 JUNE 1815

EXT. DUSK. LONG SHOT PAN
Rolling fields, some with grass, some with ripening wheat, small woods. Forty-eight thousand infantry and fourteen thousand cavalry in French uniforms. Fifty thousand British infantry, eleven thousand British cavalry. Units of Hanoverian and other German troops, with small detachments of Belgians and Dutch, all in distinctive uniforms. Two hundred and fifty artillery pieces on the French lines, one hundred and fifty big guns facing them.
Sounds off: shells exploding, muskets firing, horses neighing, men screaming; bagpipes and drums.

EXT. DUSK. ZOOM IN
Small group of French soldiers standing their ground in centre field, shoulder to shoulder, armed with sabres. Surrounded by men in British uniforms on slightly higher ground.
Sounds on: clashing ironware, huffing and puffing, shouts and obscenities.

EXT. RAKING LIGHT OF SETTING SUN FROM LEFT. CLOSE UP
Face of MAITLAND, a sweaty, moustachioed British officer.

MAITLAND (*bawling*): French Soldiers! Brave Men! You are surrounded! Surrender now or face your end!

EXT. ALMOST NIGHT. MEDIUM SHOT
Group of French soldiers, including many dead and wounded, with
a small number standing. A tall, stout man steps towards camera.

EXT. NIGHT. CLOSE UP
Face of CAMBRONNE, streaked with sweat and blood.

CAMBRONNE (*at top of voice*): Fuck you!

BLACK SCREEN
Sound off: deafening blast, then complete silence.

EXT. NIGHT. MEDIUM SHOT
Limbs and debris flying randomly through black smoke.
Sounds off: groans.

BLACK SCREEN
VOICE OFF: Napoleon lost the Battle of Waterloo. But Wellington
did not win it; and Blücher did not even fight in it. The man who
gave such a magnificent reply to mortal thunder was the true victor
of the Battle of Waterloo.

EXT. NIGHT. LONG SHOT
Raking moonlight.
Corpses arrayed on top of each other in a long, narrow pit. One
crouching, black-cloaked and black-hooded figure moving along the
line like a scavenging ape or a ghoul.

EXT. NIGHT. ZOOM IN
On the figure poking about among limbs and torn uniforms.

EXT. NIGHT. CLOSE SHOT
The scavenger raises the hand of a corpse and pulls a ring off its
finger. As it falls back the hand quivers, then shows more signs of

life. The corpse-robber grasps it, pulls the arm, and raises a blood-stained man into the moonlight.

The robber fumbles inside his victim's pockets, extracting a watch and a purse. As he stashes them inside his capacious greatcoat, the dead man opens his eyes and wakes up.

EXT. NIGHT. MIDDLE SHOT

BARON GEORGES PONTMERCY (*staring blankly*): Thank you kindly, good sir.

THÉNARDIER: I'm glad to help an officer of the guard.

PONTMERCY: You have saved my life. Let me give you my purse and my watch.

THÉNARDIER (*grinning to camera*): You're most generous, captain.

PONTMERCY: May I know your name?

THÉNARDIER: I'm called Thénardier.

PONTMERCY (*enunciating with difficulty*): . . . mercy, at your service for ever more. (*He then passes out.*)

EXT. NIGHT. CLOSE UP. SIDE.

Thénardier's long, dirty, angular face with darting eyes and a fixed grin.

BLACK SCREEN
TITLE CAPTION
Les Misérables
Start Here

12.

The Paris of Les Misérables

In January 1862, Hugo and his helpers at Hauteville House worked at a frantic pace on four fronts at the same time. He wrote and they copied out the chapters urgently needed to permit Lacroix to start typesetting the first volume of Part II, beginning with the great essay on the Battle of Waterloo. Concurrently, Hugo had to decide on and then draft the matter that would figure at the head of Part I to allow the page-numbering of the first volume to be fixed. Meanwhile, after dinner every day there were galleys to be corrected and lists of corrections to be copied out and rushed down to the boat before it left, three times a week. But the main front was the final revision, collation and copying out of all the rest of Part II, where the action of the novel moves to Paris. Hats off to Hugo, Juliette and Julie, who completed all these equally huge and delicate tasks by the end of the month. By early February, Lacroix's compositors had the whole of Part II to set in type.

A large part of the matter of Part II comes out of *Les Misères*, written more than fifteen years before. Hugo needed to check his own memory of the layout of the streets and buildings he mentions, but he could not do that directly, as he refused to set foot in France. He therefore sent a scout to do this necessary work for him. Théophile Guérin, a journalist and fellow exile in Guernsey who was able to take advantage of the 1859 amnesty, sent back a meticulous topographical study of the main Paris locations of *Les Misérables*: Rue de l'Homme–Armé, the last residence of Valjean, the Rousseau restaurant, where Marius eats in his years of poverty, the wastelands north of the Pont d'Austerlitz, where Valjean and Cosette flee when Javert is on their tail, and Boulevard de l'Hôpital, alongside the present-day Gare d'Austerlitz, where the Gorbeau tenement is located. Hugo needed this information not solely in order to get his urban geography right. He needed to be sure of the real city in order to get it wrong.

Hugo's attachment to the Paris of old was deep and sincere. He lets it show at the start of Book 5 of Part II, where he steps forward and talks about his feelings directly, in the third person. Since the author of this book left the city, he writes, Paris has been transformed. 'A new city has grown up that is as it were unknown to him . . . the Paris of his youth is now a Paris of the past' (II.5.i, 404). As in the essay on the 1848 Revolution written the previous spring and at the opening of the Waterloo chapters that describe Hugo's visit to the battlefield in May 1861, 'now' means not the 'now' of the fiction, but the 'now' of writing. It is therefore easy to see nostalgia for the old city that Hugo expresses in *Les Misérables* as a barely veiled criticism of the urban renewal being carried out at a great pace by Baron Haussmann, in charge of the rebuilding of Paris at that time. However, Hugo's attachment to the fabric of Paris and his experience of rebuilding and change go back much further than that.

In his youth, Hugo the royalist had been among the first to raise alarm at the dilapidation of the city's medieval heritage by profiteers and crooks known as the *bande noire* or 'Black Gang'. His campaign to save old buildings was crowned by *Notre-Dame de Paris*, which represents the great cathedral in the form that it had at the height of its glory in the late fifteenth century. The novel had a spectacular impact not just on the history of the novel in France, but on the physical shape of the city. Largely inspired by Hugo's lavish descriptions (based on extensive research and a strong visual imagination), the architect Viollet-le-Duc drew up plans to clear away later constructions that hid Notre-Dame from view, to reconstruct its two main towers and to add a spire (as well as adding a new wing linked to the nave by those supposedly medieval flying buttresses that now adorn the south wall). The project was approved by the city council, and work began in 1845, at the time when Hugo began writing *Les Misères*. Seventeen years later, the new-old cathedral was about to emerge from the scaffolding and protective shrouds that had hidden the building site for so long. The Notre-Dame we now know was unveiled in 1862, a few weeks after the publication of *Les Misérables*. Ironically, a rather large feature of the new and unseen Paris that Hugo half-laments at the opening of Book 5 of Part II was the direct result of his own architectural imagination.

Haussmann's reinvention of the layout of the Left Bank (to which we owe the Boulevard Saint-Michel and the Boulevard Saint-Germain) and his construction of a new residential area along avenues radiating from the Arc de Triomphe were neither the first nor the largest of the changes made to Paris between the fictional time of *Les Misérables* and the time of its completion. In the course of the 1830s, while Hugo was ensconced in his apartment in Place Royale, the east–west axis of Rue de Rivoli was completed, and Place de la Bastille was remodelled around a new column commemorating the July Revolution of 1830. The greatest change came from the introduction of railways, starting in 1837 with a line to Versailles. Over the following decade, long before Hugo's exile, whole neighbourhoods were swept away to allow rail lines to bring steam trains into central Paris. Large new termini sprang up almost year by year: Gare Saint-Lazare (called the Embarcadère des Batignolles at the start) was opened in 1837; Gare d'Orléans (now Gare d'Austerlitz), in 1840; Gare du Nord, in 1846; Gare de Lyon, in 1847; Gare de l'Est, in 1849. These huge public works altered the relation of one quarter to another, just as the slow but steady spread of street lighting by gas and the metalling of main roads that began around 1835 transformed the appearance of the old city of Hugo's youth. The implicit criticism of the vandalism of the Second Empire in Hugo's resurrection from exile of a Paris that can no longer be seen is really a diversion. It serves mainly to camouflage the unreal cityscape of *Les Misérables*.

One of the sites checked out by Guérin was the address of the Gorbeau tenement – the lodgings of Valjean in the 1820s, and of Marius and Thénardier later on. The loyal scout confirmed that house-numbers in Boulevard de l'Hôpital jumped on the even side from 46 to 54, with nothing in between. That left a 'real' space for Hugo's imaginary address of '50–52'. But why those numbers in particular? Ingenious readers have suggested that Hugo wanted to make it clear by a kind of strident silence that '51' did not exist – that the year of Louis-Napoléon's detestable putsch had been expunged from the sequence of integers. Given the many other number-games played in the novel, that does not seem far-fetched.

The location of the students' barricade, on the other hand, could not be checked out, because Rue de la Chanvrerie had been demolished long before (and not by Baron Haussmann). What happens there in Parts IV and V of *Les Misérables* is, however, calqued on real events that took place somewhere else, in the Cloître Saint-Merri, about a kilometre to the east, roughly where the decorative fountain by Niki de Saint-Phalle now stands in the courtyard of the Pompidou Centre. But the most outrageous change that Hugo made to the geography of Paris can't be explained by nostalgia or resentment, or by a need to fictionalize a historical event.

When Valjean believes (quite correctly) that he has been recognized by Javert, he makes the decision to leave his lodgings in Boulevard de l'Hôpital. He takes Cosette on a zigzag walk through the real streets of the Latin Quarter to throw his pursuer off the trail, then crosses the Seine by the Austerlitz bridge. Javert and his squad are closing in on him but haven't caught up yet. Valjean plunges into a labyrinth of streets whose names can't be found on any map, in an area that has since disappeared and that Hugo calls 'Petit-Picpus'. Because of all the rebuilding of Paris in the 1830s and 1840s, including the construction of the Gare de Lyon, Hugo's readers of 1862 could easily believe that thirty years before the area had been completely different. In any case, there weren't many people left who could remember 1823 – at the age of sixty, Hugo was an old man by the standards of his day. He was also a first-rate liar when he needed to be. 'Petit-Picpus, of which no present map has retained any trace, is quite clearly marked on the 1727 map published in Paris by Denis Thierry' (II.5.iii, 410). Well, it isn't; the map is a fiction, and a far from innocent one. No area of Paris was called 'Petit-Picpus', but the one Hugo invented slots into a quite specific corner which had been mostly waste ground in the 1820s. If we plot Valjean's escape route on a real map of Paris by the left and right turns he takes after crossing the Seine and by the distances Hugo specifies between each turn, then our pencil moves inexorably towards the centre of a small rectangle bounded nowadays by Avenue Ledru-Rollin, Avenue Daumesnil, Boulevard Diderot and Rue de Lyon. It is therefore possible to say almost exactly where he was when Javert's dragnet trapped him at the tip of a Y, and what wall it was that he climbed over to get away. For there was a wall at that location – not in the 1820s, but in 1862. It was not the perimeter of a convent, but the grim face of the Maison centrale de détention, better known as the Mazas Prison, the infamous penitentiary where Louis-Napoléon Bonaparte put republicans and democrats who had not fled France.[5]

Les Misérables is very short on describing Valjean's years in a real jail. His time in a convent stands in lieu in an almost literal sense, since it is built on the site of a prison more fearful even than the *bagne* at Toulon.

Hugo's long chapters on convent life draw on the notes he had Juliette and Léonie make for him in 1847. Their reminiscences concern convent schools located in the Latin Quarter, but Hugo felt that he could not use their real location without giving offence to the nuns who still lived there and to readers who might object to a novel invading such an inherently private space. In his to-do list of May 1860 Hugo noted that he would have to 'shift the convent', and in January 1861 he got around to doing it as he revised Part II. His reprise in prose at the start of Book 5 of Baudelaire's lament that 'the shape of a city changes faster, alas, than the heart of a man' diverts attention from the unreal city he is about to describe.[6]

Why did Hugo put his characters in a convent in the first place? Why is a substantial section of a novel about the contemporary poor devoted to the description and analysis of distinctly unmodern monastic life? Albert Lacroix was the first to read the Petit-Picpus episode of *Les Misérables* but not the last to be puzzled and slightly alarmed by it. His disappointment must have been great to give him the courage to write to Hugo – with appropriate humility – to ask him to cut it out.

> After the escape into the convent, the action stops, and two admirable chapters, one descriptive, the other philosophical, interrupt and maybe even diminish the reader's impatient curiosity. I mean the common reader, the general public, not readers with a refined literary taste . . . so I ask you whether in your opinion it would not be better . . . to set aside 'Petit-Picpus' and 'Parenthesis' until the second or third edition.[7]

Lacroix was a free-thinker with no high opinion of the Catholic church, and he found it incomprehensible that Victor Hugo, the figurehead of all that was liberal and forward-looking in Europe, should have given such respectful and lengthy attention to a group of self-incarcerated fanatics. Many modern readers feel something of the same bewilderment, and almost all the adapters of *Les Misérables* for stage and screen either omit the convent episode entirely or skim over it at great speed. Is this a part of Hugo's long novel that really could be cut?

With the figure of the un-Catholic Bishop Myriel, Hugo outraged the conservatives and the devout. With the Convent of the Perpetual Adoration, he upset 'blinkered republicans' who spoke to him through his son Charles. *Les Misérables* is intentionally designed to be equally irritating to both sides. How else could it seriously promote the great reconciliation between factions and classes whose lamentable and often bloody disputes were contingent and not necessary parts of social life?

In narrative terms, the convent episode is a 'stop-the-clock' device that allows Cosette to pupate from victim in Part I to the leading lady of Parts III, IV and V. In that respect it mirrors Valjean's prison sentence, which is a kind of time machine allowing the entirety of the reign of Napoleon I to be left out. But that doesn't explain why

Hugo inserts the historical and reflective chapter that even he calls a parenthesis.

Nuns have nothing, not even their real names. Coming for the most part from aristocratic backgrounds, their self-imposed poverty is a complement or counterpoint to the humiliation of all the Fantines of the world. The convent is also an 'ideal community', offering women an escape from the contradictions of civilian life. As Hugo put it in his brief note in May: 'Describe the absurd monastic regime and say: as long as women are legal minors, as long as the problem of women remains unsolved, the convent is only a secondary crime.' Hugo did his best to make his portrayal of convent life as accurate as possible because he wanted to grant appropriate respect to autonomous, self-governing communities of women. An unlikely beginning for feminist ideas – but that is what it is.

Lacroix's disappointment with the slow narrative pace of the convent chapters reveals a surprising disregard for one of the most suspense-laden parts of the whole book. When he climbs over the wall, Valjean is accepted with open arms by the convent gardener, Fauchelevent, the man that Mayor Madeleine had rescued from under his overturned cart years before. However, Fauchelevent cannot present Valjean to the nuns and ask for him to be taken on as his assistant unless the fugitive enters by the front door, not over the back wall. The scheme to get Valjean out and then back in involves burying a deceased nun illegally in the convent's crypt and substituting Valjean for her corpse when her coffin is taken to the Vaugirard cemetery. Fauchelevent expects to be able to bribe the gravedigger to look the other way when he lets Valjean out, but alas, there's a new man on the job, who turns out to be a particularly rule-bound bore. Fauchelevent has to expend all his guile to get the man to leave, by which time Valjean has been buried alive for quite a while. He could have died. But he rises again.

This is a mockery of the resurrection, though the humour is deeply hidden. In a different vein, it begins the transformation of Valjean from the Hercules of Montfermeil and the Batman of the *Orion* into the Christ-like figure of suffering and redemption that he becomes in the sewers later on. The convent chapters provide an appropriate background to this key turn in the significance of the novel's main character and soul.

Overall, however, Hugo is respectful but not kind to the monastic life. He turns the nuns into jokey mementoes by inventing civilian names for them that inscribe details of his own life: Mother Sainte-Mechtilde is 'Mlle Gauvain', the maiden name of Juliette Drouet; Mother des Anges is 'Mlle Drouet' directly. Mothers Saint-Joseph, Miséricorde and Présentation are respectively 'Mlles de Cogolludo', 'de Cifuentes' and 'de Siguenza', named for battles won in Spain by General Léopold-Sigisbert Hugo; Mother Compassion is 'Mlle de la Militière', the name of a property that Hugo's father owned in Sologne, as was 'Laudinière', the civil name attributed to Mother Providence. These nods aside, Hugo makes it clear that monasticism is set on an irreversible decline. Whatever admirable functions convents may have played in the past, they have no future in France. Similar to his critique of King Louis-Philippe – a decent man trying to do a job that is not needed any more – Hugo's investigation of monasticism broadens the sweep of this novel of the poor in a bid to make it the all-embracing portrait of nineteenth-century life.

Albert Lacroix did not see the point. The convent chapters could be made to work, the publisher wrote, if they were tied up with 'an action that is part of the tale', or with a description or a philosophical argument that would give them life. 'Ah! how I would love to talk about all that with you . . . Could you not come [to Brussels]? Please come, please come, dear Master.'[8] Perhaps surprisingly, Hugo didn't simply tell Lacroix to get on with printing the book, but asked him to mark up the sheets of 'Picpus' and 'Parenthesis' – in pencil, not in ink! – with suggestions for cuts, as if he too were worried that these chapters weren't yet quite right. Lacroix didn't dare or didn't know how to mark up a manuscript like a modern line-editor, so instead he sent back a list of the sections and topics where he thought changes could be made. To implement them while still working on proofs and on revisions of the next part of the book, Hugo needed to have the fair copy manuscript sent back to Hauteville House. 'Brutal cuts are impossible, there have to be transitions. I can only enter the transitions on the manuscript. Send it to me in haste. It is not possible to simply cut the whole of 'Parenthesis'.[9] However, the wary publisher did not trust the post for returning something as precious as the single fair copy of Part II of *Les Misérables* – not so much because it might be lost, but because it might be stolen, leaked to the press and pirated before his own edition was out. A logistical stalemate ensued, and the argument over the convent passages petered out. They stayed as they were because there was no way to make them different, even if Hugo had been willing to take (some) of his (somewhat blinkered) editor's advice.

13.
The Politics of Les Misérables

In the long Cold War that pitted the West against the communist empire from 1945 to 1991, *Les Misérables* had the unique distinction among literary works of being cherished equally in Moscow and New York. While Victor Hugo remained without contest the most widely read French author in the Soviet Union,[10] Cameron Mackintosh adapted a French musical version for the London stage and took it to Broadway in 1987, where it broke all records in popularity and in the length of its run. The opposite outturn is just as imaginable, however, since Hugo's novel contains much that ought to be quite unacceptable to communists, and even more prominent material that their opponents ought to reject outright. On one side, it states quite clearly that 'the bourgeoisie' does not exist and that 'class warfare' is a nefarious idea; on the other, it makes heroes out of young men who want to change society by violent means. Where, then, does the novel really hang on the great washing-line of political convictions stretching from the far left to the far right?

The character of M. Mabeuf, the ruined botanist-cum-bookseller who dies on the barricade, provides a keyhole example of the double-jointed politics of *Les Misérables*. 'Get to the bottom of Mabeuf' was number 10 in the list of points Hugo made after his first rereading of *Les Misères* in May 1860 (see p. 105 above), and for good reason. 'Mabeuf' is the same bar one letter as 'Babeuf', the name of the most extreme egalitarian among the political leaders of the French Revolution of 1789, yet Hugo's Mabeuf has an almost comically non-political view of the world. He's more interested in flowers and old books than in women, and he never understood 'how men could get involved in hating each other over such nonsense as the Charter, democracy, legitimacy, the Republic and the like' (III.5.iv, 621–2). What could possibly link Gracchus Babeuf, the emblematic figure of steadfast and violent opposition, with a kindly old botanist who doesn't give a fig for politics of any kind? Perhaps only this, the song that first made Babeuf a popular figure in revolutionary France:

> Mourant de faim, mourant de froid.
> Peuple! dépouillé de tout droit.
> Tout bas tu te désoles.
> (Dying of hunger, dying of cold.
> O People! Deprived of all rights,
> You whisper your sad plight.)

This revolutionary anthem of protest describes the state of poor M. Mabeuf on the eve of the uprising of June 1832. He's lost his last cent and has nothing but starvation to look forward to in his old age, which can hardly last very long. That's what makes sense of his otherwise senseless decision to join the revolutionary students and to die on the barricade. His trajectory in the novel seems to say that poverty can turn a mouse into a lion – that *la misère* is the fundamental cause of social strife.

In the 1930s, a student society in Prague held a practice debate pitting the 'communist' against the 'socialist' interpretation of *Les Misérables*. No transcript of it survives, but I can see how Mabeuf might have provided the debaters with a suitably two-faced coin to toss. On the one side, the old man can be seen as a walking plea for retirement pensions and, more generally, for measures to relieve the victims of economic distress. That would be a 'socialist' interpretation of his case. A 'communist' interpretation, on the other hand, would see Mabeuf as Hugo's vision of the vanguard of the coming revolution, to be fuelled by the anger of the dispossessed. For one side, the flag-wielding geriatric on the barricades serves to scare the bourgeois establishment into meaningful social reforms. For the other, he glorifies revolution led by those who have nothing to lose. Whatever the result of the debate in Prague may have been, the truth is that *Les Misérables* doesn't come down on either side.

Hugo was accustomed to being asked to say which side he was on, since so many factions wanted his prestige for themselves, and he became very adept at keeping his foot out of traps of that kind. However, *Les Misérables* was due to appear in volumes at dates spread out over months, and its initial reception would hang not on the whole, but only the first part. 'The trouble with this book for people trying to review it,' Hugo wrote to Lacroix, 'is its size.'

> If it could be published in one go, I think its effect would be decisive; but since at the present time it can only be read in pieces, its overall design can't be seen; but the whole is everything . . . This book is a mountain; you can only measure or even see it properly from a distance. That's to say, all in one.[11]

Unfortunately, the reception of just the first part would most likely determine the outcome of a literary and financial enterprise like no other. So it seemed reasonable – if not essential – to give the book's first readers a steer at the start as to what its overall meaning was. The philosophical introduction Hugo had written in summer 1860 had already been set aside. Something snappier was needed, and needed very soon, since Volume 1, now in second proof, couldn't be paginated until the front matter was in place. On 1 January 1862, he drafted a single sentence to say what he thought *Les Misérables* meant. He didn't send it to Lacroix for five weeks (perhaps he didn't really write it on New Year's Day, just backdated it to give it the appearance of a new start). At any rate, what he did send in must be one of the grandest deployments of ancient rhetoric in modern dress and among the most quoted and least understood long sentences in literary history. Here it is, in a version slightly adapted from Christine Donougher's English translation:

> As long as through the workings of laws and customs there exists a damnation by society artificially creating hells in the very midst of civilization

and complicating destiny, which is divine, with a man-made fate; as long as the three problems of the century are not resolved, the debasement of men by the *prolétariat*, the moral degradation of women through hunger and the stunting of children by keeping them in darkness; as long as in certain strata social suffocation is possible; in other words, and from an even broader perspective, as long as there are ignorance and *misère* on earth, books such as this one may not be without utility.

Stripped of rhetoric and put into bullet-points, this is what it says:

- While some people still live in a hell on earth artificially created by laws (Valjean's yellow passport, for example);
- and while customs complicate the blows of fate (those that affect Fantine, for example);
- while the three main problems of this century remain unsolved;
- and, more generally, while there is still ignorance and poverty on earth;
- *Les Misérables* will always be a useful book.

The preface does not say how the 'problems of this century' should be solved, nor does it even hint at a political programme to bring about the happy day when *Les Misérables* would become a useless book. It lists what the problems are, but not their solutions. Obviously, even the most objective-seeming analysis of 'the problems of our age' is a political act, but to assess the political colour that Hugo gives to his book in this brief preface we need to understand what he means in the phrases that identify what those problems are.

Those phrases are not easy to translate into any language, including contemporary French. Let us look first at what Hugo wrote in the original before trying to decode them for today. The three problems are:

- 'la dégradation de l'homme par le prolétariat'
- 'la déchéance de la femme par la faim'
- 'l'atrophie de l'enfant par la nuit'

The third phrase has the literal meaning 'the atrophy of the child by night'. 'Night' is used here as the opposite of 'light', which, though unstated, must be understood as the conventional metaphor for 'education' or 'enlightenment'. In other words, the lack of education for the children of the poor is a 'problem of the century' because it 'dries them out', stunts their moral growth. It's hard to disagree that mass education held the prospect for a great improvement in the lives of the poor. But it does not match the lessons you could just as easily draw from the stories of uneducated Éponine and Gavroche. Their resources of generosity, passion, intelligence and good cheer make them heroes as well as victims of the society they illustrate.

The middle phrase can be represented word for word as 'the fall of woman from hunger', but in this context *déchéance*, 'fall', means prostitution and nothing else. Nineteenth-century translators give 'the ruin of women', and they were right for their own time, since that was the regular English euphemism for commercial sex.

The first of 'the problems of our age' is the hardest to crack. Literally translated, it says: 'the degradation of man by the proletariat'. But whatever can that mean?

'Proletariat' is not a real word of classical Latin. It was invented at some point in the nineteenth century from *proletarius*, a term that designated a member of the sixth and lowest class of citizens in Ancient Rome. *Proletarii* were not slaves, and only incidentally tradesmen or workers. What made them *proletarii* was that they had no property and paid no tax, and consequently did not have a vote and were not eligible for public office. Their principal function in society was to produce the next generation of citizens – and that is what the word *proletarius* actually lays down, since it is derived from *proles*, meaning 'genitor'.

Hugo, whose knowledge of Ancient Rome was beyond reproach, took the abstract noun *proletariat* to mean the 'state of being a *proletarius*', that is to say, deprived of civil rights. If I had to coin a term to translate it, 'outcastness' would come to mind. Indeed, the conventional translation of *Les Misérables* into Russian, *Otverzhennie*, means just that: 'The Outcast'.

That is not what 'proletariat' means now, in English, German, Russian or in French. 'Workers of the World, Unite', the rousing last sentence of the *Communist Manifesto* of 1848, translates Marx's German appeal to 'Proletärier aller Länder', and in the body of the text he uses *Proletärier* (proletarians) and *Proletariat* interchangeably. Friedrich Engels was aware his friend had taken a liberty with Latin roots and explained what he meant in a clever footnote to later editions of the *Manifesto*: 'By proletariat [is meant] the class of modern wage labourers, who having no means of production of their own, are reduced to selling their labour power in order to live'.[12] The Roman sense of 'having no property' is switched to 'having no means of production'. The substitution has worked very well and has obscured the meaning that Hugo thought *prolétariat* had.

Some translations of the foreword try to compromise between the now obviously meaningless 'degradation of men by the proletariat' and the suspicion that Hugo must have meant something by his strange formulation. The result is to make Hugo march under a banner that was not his. 'The debasement of men through proletarianization' is a defensible interpretation of the main thrust of Dickens's *Hard Times* and Zola's *Germinal*, but it doesn't express the message of *Les Misérables*. Waged labour in Madeleine's model factory in Montreuil is the *solution* to Fantine's woes, not their cause. As we've seen on p. 157, Valjean heartily recommends Montparnasse to 'sell his labour power in order to live' instead of living off crime. Thanks to Karl Marx's approximate Latin and to the long-lasting impact of the political movement he founded, a single word at the head of *Les Misérables* has had Hugo's masterpiece labelled a left-wing book. It is certainly a progressive one and it surely expresses moral outrage at the plight of the poor, but it does not come close to recommending any of the economic principles to which the European left has long adhered. It is a much more even-handed work than that.

All the same, it puts an act of revolutionary violence at its core. The barricade episode of *Les Misérables* is closely based on historical events, but the book's meaning is hard to assess without knowing what changes Hugo made to the events themselves.

According to official reports, the June uprising of 1832 pitted about 3,000 rioters against 30,000 government troops and National Guards. Some sources say that seventy-three soldiers and ninety-three civilians died, with around 300 wounded on either side; a more recent study reckons there were about 300 dead overall.[13] Measured against other moments of turbulence in the history of France, the barricade Hugo describes was the merest squall.

What set it off were circumstances that Hugo acknowledges but does not make much of in the text. On 16 May 1832, cholera carried off the prime minister, Casimir Périer, leaving the government leaderless. A group of deputies headed by Laffitte seized the moment to draw up a hostile assessment of the policies followed up to that point. They paid lip service to the monarchy, but their unrelenting critique of the government's actions amounted to a call to overthrow the king. To what purpose? There was no agreement about that. Supporters of the Bourbon monarchy that had disappeared in 1830 were waiting for a chance to stage a comeback; a network of supporters of Bonaparte were still on the lookout for an opportunity to stage a 'liberal-imperial' putsch; and republicans, still smarting from what they saw as the confiscation of the 1830 Revolution by King Louis-Philippe, were just as eager to head off a reactionary *coup d'état* as to seize power for themselves.

On 30 May, Évariste Galois, the mathematical genius of his era, died in a duel, fought for reasons still unknown. Galois was a militant republican, and sketchy plans were made to use his funeral as the pretext for an uprising. But before his corpse could even be loaded on a hearse came news that a better-known republican hero, General Lamarque, had died of cholera. Galois's funeral was postponed until 2 June and Lamarque's was scheduled for 5 June.

A masked executioner was stalking Paris with an invisible portable guillotine. 'We'll all be put in the sack one after the other,' my servant said with a sigh every morning when he told me how many had died . . . 'Put in the sack' was no figure of speech: coffins ran short and most of the dead were buried in bags.[14]

With people of all classes dying like fleas, disgust at Louis-Philippe's foreign policies threw more oil on the fire. The 'bourgeois monarch' had too easily given up the northern parts of France to allow the creation of the new state of Belgium and had lost an area enjoying rapid industrial growth. The king had also refused to come to the aid of the Poles when the Warsaw uprising was put down by the tsar's troops the previous year. Despairing of their land, tens of thousands of Poles migrated to the West. By 1832, many of these mostly high-status migrants had found sanctuary in Paris, where they were seen as living reproaches to the cowardly refusal of Louis-Philippe to assert France's role as the defender of freedom and civilization. (Wenceslas Steinbock, the weak-kneed sculptor in Balzac's *Cousine Bette*, was one of them; Adam Mickiewicz, Poland's national poet, was another, alongside the wealthy Prince Adam Czartoryski, who bought one of the finest houses in Paris.) That's why 'Long Live Poland' is the battle cry of Feuilly, the only worker member of the 'Friends of the ABC'.[15]

On 5 June 1832, a large crowd paid last respects to Lamarque as his coffin was paraded from Madeleine to Bastille, where General Lafayette was due to deliver the funeral oration. Organized agitators directed the crowd to attack the police, and running fights broke out in the streets. Barricades were thrown up in working-class areas but were quickly overcome, except for one. Lafayette sensed that the uprising was doomed, and he decamped to the countryside overnight. The suppression of the last enclave in the morning of 6 June was a bloody affair, but it did not last long. By three in the afternoon, the king could tell his ministers that there was nothing more to do.

Hugo fictionalized the last hold-out by moving it to Rue de la Chanvrerie and changed its nature by having it led not by the angry poor, but by a loosely organized group of intellectuals, the 'Friends of the ABC', supplemented by the desperate Mabeuf and a 'revolutionary urchin' whose main interest in it is the chance of using a gun. The myth of student involvement in the vanguard of the revolution has a root in the quite different events of July 1830, when members of the elite military academy called Polytechnique manned some of the Latin Quarter barricades. However, the main source of the enduring myth of students leading the crowd against the forces of reaction is actually *Les Misérables* itself, where it serves several different dramatic and pedagogic ends. Hugo enlisted them because educated fighters for a cause they know is lost can plausibly be made to give speeches to each other to explain what they are doing and to help us understand. All believe in 'Progress' and consider themselves the children of the French Revolution, but there are important distinctions between them. Feuilly is motivated most of all by his opposition to empires (Austrian, Ottoman, Russian . . .); Prouvaire puts his mind to understanding economic and social questions; and Combeferre represents a rational and gradualist alternative to Enjolras's rigid insistence on 'all or nothing'. But the 'Friends of the ABC' is also a bunch of (male) friends. Some of its members – notably Courfeyrac – have more of a social than a political role; alcoholic Grantaire is sceptical of politics altogether, but indefectibly loyal to his hero Enjolras.

If there is something we could call the politics of *Les Misérables*, then it would have to embrace and reconcile all these positions. But there is something else at work beyond the ideas and energies of a band of young men.

Before dawn on 6 June, the defenders of the barricade know their cause is lost because all other parts of Paris are quiet. 'Nothing to expect, nothing to hope for . . . You've been abandoned,' Enjolras tells them (V.i.iii, 1,061). Why do they decide to fight on? Because 'a voice from the group's obscurest depths' cried out and called on his comrades to carry on. Hugo elaborates on this interchange between the leadership and the masses:

> No one ever knew the name of the man who had spoken [those words]. He was some unacknowledged worker, unidentified, forgotten, a heroic *passant*, that nameless champion . . . who says the decisive word . . . and then disappears into the shadows. (V.i.iii, 1,061, adapted)

This is the legendary 'voice of people'. Heinrich Heine could hear it too: 'We appear to have passed out of that period of world history in which the deeds of individual men mark them out. The heroes of the new age are peoples, parties and the masses in themselves.'[16] Thirty years apart, the German reporter and the French novelist both think the bloody endgame arose not from the suicidal impulse of a hothead or two, but from a general will. Or from even higher up: 'the decisive word . . . disappears into the shadows, having momentarily, in a flash of lightning, represented the people of God' (1061).[17] Here, Hugo quotes and translates a Latin tag without telling you what it is: *vox populi, vox dei*, 'the voice of the people is the voice of God'. However, the one he does give in Latin in the text without translating suggests the opposite view of historical events: *Fex urbis, lex orbis* (V.i.i, 1,052), 'Shit of city, law of world', meaning that it's not God but the rabble who have the last word.

The two proverbs with their opposite meanings, one explicit, the other hardly hidden, sum up the political problem of nineteenth-century France (and of Victor Hugo) very well: the people must be in charge, except when they are wrong.

Later that night, when a National Guard challenges the insurgents to identify themselves with the conventional words 'Who goes there?', the baby-faced leader of the group shouts out 'Révolution française!' 'in a proud ringing tone', prompting a barrage of fire that brings down the red flag (IV.14.i, 1,016). You could take this as a call for a new or continuing revolution, and read it as the dramatization of the political meaning of *Les Misérables*. But that is not what Enjolras means, let alone Victor Hugo. He is declaring his allegiance to the spirit of the French Revolution of 1789 – the only one that really happened and still deserves its name, which makes it 'the greatest step forward taken by the human race since the advent of Christ' (I.1.x, 39).

Part of the essay chapter on 1848 that launches Part V of *Les Misérables* is devoted to making the distinction between 'revolution' and 'riot'. English and French both have many more words to refer to civil strife, and they express not so much distinct forms of upheaval as what you wish them to signify. If you need or wish to dismiss violence as politically and socially insignificant, you refer to the 'disturbances' (*troubles*) or 'the events'. For example, the war in Algeria was referred to throughout the 1950s by the French government as *les évènements d'Algérie*; and the barricades and tear-gas in the Latin Quarter in 1968 have always been called *les évènements de mai*.

More worthy of attention are riots, *émeutes*, cast by the word used into the role of unjustifiable attacks on law and order. That's why the barricade of June 1848 'had to be combatted, as a matter of duty' by 'the man of probity' who 'out of his very love for the mob . . . fights against it' (V.1.i, 1,052).

More significance is attached to 'a revolt', *une révolte*, a term that presupposes a genuine cause beyond the people's inclination for mayhem, but, as it lacks political legitimacy, it must also be squashed. That's the sense of it in the famous (but probably invented) story of how the news of the fall of the Bastille was received by the monarch in 1789. 'Est-ce une révolte?' ('Is it a revolt?') Louis XVI is supposed to have asked of his courtier. The reply: 'Non, Sire, c'est une révolution.'

But a 'revolution' is the turn of a wheel, of a planet around the sun, of a crank around its axis. Something that is more than a revolt but leaves things in the same place can't be called a revolution. The word Hugo used for the events of 5 June 1832, is *insurrection*.

Acts of violence committed in 'disturbances', 'events', 'riots' and 'revolts' are crimes punishable by ordinary laws. Acts of violence committed in revolutions are seen retrospectively as heroic steps on the path of progress. They are, of course, the same acts, or the same kinds of acts, just as the barricades of Rue de la Chanvrerie in 1832 looked much the same as the barricade at Rue du Temple in 1848 or the one in Rue Le Goff in May 1968. The difficulty is to know whether the acts of violence committed on both sides in an *insurrection* are to be understood as a problem of order, or as part of humanity's stumbling forward march.

The question of violence is the crux of the great debate on the barricades. All the young men accept that in the situation they have created they have to fight, to save their dignity and to leave a message to the future. For Combeferre and Courfeyrac, this is a temporary necessity, but not a principle. Enjolras insists that violence is the *only* way. 'In that, he never varied' (V.i.v, 1,067).

He does not speak for the novel, or for Hugo. The hero, Jean Valjean, has arrived from Rue de l'Homme-Armé and shows the hotheads how guns ought to be used. His past as an occasional poacher has made him a marksman, and he uses his skill to save lives, not to take them – first, by shooting through a rope that was holding a mattress aloft, to be used to bullet-proof part of the barricade (V.i.ix, 1,078); then by forcing a sniper to move out of range with a shot that knocks his helmet off.

> 'Why didn't you kill the man?' Bossuet asked Jean Valjean.
>
> Jean Valjean did not reply.
>
> Bossuet muttered in Combeferre's ear, 'He didn't answer my question.'
>
> 'He's a man who does good deeds with a gun,' said Combeferre.
>
> (V.i.xi-xii, 1,083)

When he is detailed to finish off a government spy – Javert, again – Valjean refrains from putting a bullet in his head and lets him go. His actions, implausible as they may be, give the lie to Enjolras's certainty that progress can only come from the barrel of a gun. Moral progress is *not* shooting people, the novel seems to say.

What then was Hugo's point in creating an attractive and varied group of young heroes with a range of topical ideas if they are to fall on a minor barricade while still failing to understand that the means they use are wrong? Shelley's Ozymandias laments the futility of even the grandest historical achievements, which time wipes out: 'Round the decay / Of that colossal Wreck, boundless and bare / The lone and level sands stretch far away'. Hugo takes the opposite view of his heroes in Rue de la Chanvrerie.

> It is impossible for us not to admire . . . the advocates of Utopia whether or not they succeed.
> Even when they come to grief, they are to be revered, and it is perhaps in failure that they have the greater majesty. (V.i.xx, 1,109)

> Even when fallen, especially when fallen, they fight for the great enterprise . . . They do a sacred deed . . . to bring to glorious and universal fulfilment the magnificent and irresistibly human movement begun on the fourteenth of July, 1789. (1,110)

What would such fulfilment consist of? In a high-flown peroration, Enjolras lays out what he can see on the far horizon, from 'the top of the barricade': the end of history itself, when 'you might almost say there will be no more incidents' (V.i.v, 1,070). That day, when *Les Misérables* will no longer be a useful book if the foreword is to be taken literally, would see freedom of speech, freedom of expression, freedom of belief, penal reform going as far as the abolition of prisons, full employment, pacifism and political union. To a great extent those are the founding principles of today's European Union. 'Civilization will hold its conclaves at Europe's summit, and later the centre of continents, in a great assembly of intelligence' (V.i.v, 1,068). Enjolras seems to be gifted with prophetic visions of the Berlaymont in Brussels, where 'conclaves at Europe's summit' are held, and of the United Nations and its agencies in Geneva and New York, which it is fair to call 'a great assembly of intelligence'. These pillars of stability and peace in the modern world were built by men and women, of whom a great number must have read *Les Misérables*. There's a sense in which we are all Hugolians now.

§

Enjolras also tackles the question of how a country racked by inner conflict and mass poverty will move towards such a future and drag the rest of Europe along with it. 'We have tamed the Hydra and it is called the steamer. We have tamed the dragon and it is called the locomotive. We are on the verge of taming the griffin and it is called the balloon.' (1,068)

He's right again. Science and technology have contributed massively to the eradication of poverty in the West over the 150 years since *Les Misérables* appeared. What Enjolras sets out here as the ultimate point of the insurrection of June 1832 is a broad sketch of the better side of European and world history since then.

The worse side, he cannot imagine. He's part of it already. The blond hair, fair skin and fine profile that Hugo gives him suggest he is a Greek or Roman demigod bearing values from the cradle of democracy or from the first republic of all. But his exclusive devotion to a political cause, the charisma he exercises over others more sensible than he is, his gifts for public speaking and for military action and his unshakeable faith in the purifying virtue of violence speak to us now of the kind of men who turned the twentieth century not into utopia but into sheer hell.

People doing Javert's job in the modern world might see Hugo's Enjolras as an excellent reason for keeping a close watch on intellectuals, but that does not make *Les Misérables* a 'right-wing' book. Its incompatibility with the ideas of the mainstream left lies principally in what it says about social class. Hugo does not agree that 'class' is a viable concept to account for the existence of rich and poor people. In fact, he doesn't really distinguish between 'class' and the much older term of 'caste'. He slips from one to the other:

> Some people have wanted wrongly to identify the bourgeoisie as a
> class. The bourgeoisie is simply the contented section of the people.
> The bourgeois is the man who now has time to sit down. A chair is
> not a caste . . . (IV.1.ii, 745)

Hugo had not read Marx (in any case *Capital* had not been published in French – nor yet in German, in 1862), but the idea of 'class
conflict' was in the air and no doubt reached Hugo's ears from the
more advanced political activists in exile in the Channel Islands. But
whatever 'some people' said, he, who was obviously 'bourgeois',
could not believe he was 'in conflict' with the 'people'. He was writing a novel precisely in order to show and to provoke solidarity with
those left out, pushed aside and thrust down. He was a prosperous
bourgeois, but he was generous and gave alms, like his hero, Jean
Valjean. But even if 'bourgeois' were the name of a group of people
who exploit and oppress workers, the bourgeoisie would still not be
a 'class'. 'A class is not made up of those with a failing. Selfishness is
not one of the divisions of the social order' (IV.1.ii, 745).

It is not likely that any other book would have been allowed to
say such things in the Soviet Union, but even in the darkest years of
rigid literary censorship, *Les Misérables* continued to be published in
Russian translation without cuts.[18] Hugo was the most widely read
French author in the USSR, 'and anyone who knows Russia . . . also
knows that every Russian cherishes two writers above all others,
Pushkin and Victor Hugo'.[19] One result of Hugo's unassailable
prestige was that Soviet readers had a better idea what *Les Misérables*
said about history and politics than British ones did for many years.

Les Misérables does not lay out any particular political creed, but a
limited if still ambitious programme of social action can be drawn
up from the implications of the story Hugo tells. One of these policies is stated explicitly, but the others are no less incontestable parts
of the message Hugo wished to pass on:

  1. Allow offenders to re-enter society after they have done their
      time. For example, abolish the 'yellow passport' that makes

it so difficult for Valjean to find food, lodging and work in 1815.

2. Amend the penal code, so that justice may be tempered with mercy. For example, do not send poor peasants to do hard labour because they steal bread to feed children.

3. Create more jobs for the uneducated masses. Imitate M. Madeleine, for example, whose profitable glass bead factory gave dignity to Fantine.

4. Build schools for the poor and make elementary education universal and obligatory. (This is the one policy that is proposed in eloquent and strident terms; it was also put into effect in Hugo's lifetime by the 'Jules Ferry Law', passed in 1877.)

These four aims don't add up to a 'politics', but they do lay out a pathway we can easily agree to be right because all these measures have been put into practice by governments of the left and the right over the last 150 years. We should not dismiss Hugo's blustering confidence in the future improvement of society. Nor should we underestimate the degree to which *Les Misérables* encouraged and maybe even accelerated its coming about.

14.
The Stumbling Block

Many obstacles stand in the way of the kind of progress of which Enjolras, Combeferre, Courfeyrac and Victor Hugo dreamed: the institution of monarchy, dysfunctional laws and punishments that foster instead of correcting the criminal tendencies of men, the disenfranchisement of women, human vanity and impatience, the scarcity of work and food . . . But even if all these moral and social maladies were to be cured by wise government and collective harmony, there would still be angry holdouts in the 'third floor below'. The deserving poor can certainly be helped in a thousand ways. But what can be done about the *mauvais pauvres*, the 'bad poor' who resent and undermine what others may gain?

In the musical and in the film that has been made from it, the Thénardiers provide light relief from the mostly sombre subjects of *Les Misérables*. In this book, too, I've pointed out how comically clumsy are their repeated attempts to launch business ventures that come apart. In the novel, however, they are not funny characters at all. Hugo treats them very seriously indeed, because they complicate and threaten to unravel all the values for which he stands.

Thénardier is not a victim of any misfortunes, except those he brings on himself through debt and crime. Nor is he particularly ill equipped to make something of his life: he can read and write and do his accounts, and he has quite enough intelligence to run a business and to organize fairly elaborate plots. He's not a drunk or a skirt-chaser – indeed, the Thénardiers provide the only model in the whole of *Les Misérables* of a conventional family that stays together and looks after (some of) its own. But they make poor use of their assets and gifts. Mme Thénardier reads the wrong kinds of books, addling her brain with trashy romances even more than Flaubert's Emma Bovary. Thénardier uses his not-quite-perfect literacy to write mis-spelt begging letters that give themselves away. The two of them use parental bonds to exploit their daughters on the streets (Azelma sells her charms to bring cash into the home), but ignore their male children unnaturally. What is it that turns these half-poor, half-professional people into the ultimate villains of the book?

Thénardier first appears as a camp-following corpse-robber at the Battle of Waterloo, then as an innkeeper at Montfermeil, then as the head of the Patron-Minette gang in Paris. He is imprisoned, escapes in a feat as daring as Valjean's high dive from the *Orion* in Toulon, crops up once more as the unofficial gatekeeper of the sewers of Paris, reappears in fancy dress in a float in the Mardi Gras parade before disguising himself once again in order to black-mail Marius. He's a remarkable fellow indeed, as persistent as Javert and as resourceful as Valjean, whose changes of status and identity are not more numerous than his.

But he's not entirely human. A vulture at Waterloo, a ghoul in the sewers, Thénardier is compared in each of his roles to a beast or a bird of the night: an owl, a wolf, a cat or a tiger.[20] He is also not entirely French, unlike all the other characters: 'a mongrel [who was] most likely a Fleming from Lille when in Flanders, a Frenchman in Paris, a Belgian in Brussels, conveniently astride two frontiers' (II.3.ii, 345). But he was also on the frontier between two social and moral identities: 'Thénardier had everything it takes to live as . . . an honest tradesman, a solid citizen . . . [and] he had everything it takes to be a villain . . . [he was] a shopkeeper with an element of the monster within him' (II.3.x, 384). In this respect, Hugo's 'bad guy' is much more like a character in a conventional modern novel than any of the other leading figures. Myriel, Valjean, Fantine, Cosette or Javert are all drawn in singular terms, whereas Thénardier, despite all his animal attachments, is mixed, contradictory and complicated, like human life itself.

What keeps him going, moreover, is not just greed, but passion. 'He bore a grudge against the entire human race, since he had a deep furnace of hate burning within him' (II.3.ii, 346), and his wife also harbours a 'hatred of the human race' (IV.6.i, 845). He keeps it covered up most of the time – he was a 'restrained sort of villain' who rarely let his anger show (II.3.ii, 346) – but when at last he has a supposedly wealthy man tied to a chair in front of him, he lets fly.

> Villain! Yes, I know that's what you call us, you rich folk! Well, it's true I'm a bankrupt, I'm in hiding, I've no food, I've no money, I'm a villain! I've not eaten for three days, I'm a villain! Ah! You lot keep your feet warm, you have shoes made by Sakoski, you have padded overcoats like archbishops, you live on the first floor in houses with caretakers, you eat truffles, you eat asparagus at forty francs a bunch in the month of January, and green peas, you gorge yourselves, and when you want to know whether it's cold you look in the newspaper to see what Engineer Chevalier's thermometer says. We're our own thermometers, we are! . . . We feel the blood freezing in our veins, and the ice reaching into our hearts and we say 'There is no God!' And you come into our dens, yes, our dens, and call us villains! But we will eat you! We will devour you, you poor things! (III.8.xx, 717)

Thénardier's angry diatribe against the privilege and comfort of others is a stunning act of imaginative sympathy on Hugo's part with the suffering of the dispossessed, but it is also very frightening. People as angry as that aren't going to be 'improved' by acts of kindness from a 'visitor of the poor'. Why should Thénardier starve when others do not? What barriers can stop such resentment and greed from undermining and eventually overwhelming the social order? The figure of Thénardier is a warning that Satan may make his own use of the legitimate grievances of the poor.

Les Misérables cannot answer the fundamental problem it raises in this scene. The devil himself may not exist, but evil does, in the form of resentment and greed. Thénardier sails off to the New World at the end but leaves behind the unsolved problem of the destructive potential of hate. There was nothing Hugo could do about that.

Interlude: High Style, Low Style, Latin and Slang

The rules of propriety that governed literary expression in the seventeenth century put strict limits on the vocabulary that could be used, and as a result the exquisitely crafted tragedies of Racine were made out of barely more than 2,000 different words. Hugo thought much more highly of Shakespeare, with his allegedly unparalleled lexical breadth. *Les Misérables*, with its large cast of characters, many-layered plot and multiple settings, gave him a marvellous opportunity to rival the English master and to extend the word-set of literary French beyond all previous bounds. There are around 20,000 different words in the 630,000 words of the text[21] – maybe as many as in all of Shakespeare, in fact, who was working in a language with a much larger vocabulary.[22]

Some of the words few readers of *Les Misérables* have come across before or will ever see again were literally rescued from old dictionaries that Hugo had to hand. *Chiragre*, 'suffering gout in the wrist or hand', had hardly been used for 200 years until Hugo put it back into circulation in *Les Misérable*s in his description of Luc-Esprit Gillenormand. Some of them have become obscure because they refer to things that have disappeared, such as *berlingot*, 'a rickety one-seat horse-drawn carriage', *cacolet*, 'a chair fitted to the back of a mule for carrying travellers in mountainous districts', and *maringotte*, 'a small horse-drawn vehicle used by travelling clowns and players'. Other difficult words name trades that are no longer plied, like *taillandier*, 'a maker of spades, hoes, and axes', and *tabellion*, 'a copyist in a law office' – which is where Picard-speaking Fauchelevent picked up his knowledge of standard French. Other rare words used by Hugo seem to have simply vanished of their own accord, such as *fayousse* and *pigoche*, both referring to outdoor versions of tiddlywinks played by Gavroche and his pals on the streets.

A large contingent of the special words used in *Les Misérables* refer to birds, flowers, vines, creepers, weeds and herbs. Hugo's mother had been a keen gardener and handed on to her son not only daily watering and weeding duties in the lush back yard of Les Feuillantines, the house where they lived in the Latin Quarter (recreated in the garden of Rue Plumet), but a keen eye and a correspondingly precise vocabulary for everything that grew, cheeped, crawled and fluttered around. That is why Hugo refers without difficulty or approximation to a particular kind of bean called *gourgane*, a variety of potato called *viquelotte*, bladderwort (*cotylédon*), navelwort (*utricule*), Aaron's Rod (*bouillon-blanc*), wagtails (*hoche-queue*), yellow buntings (*verdier*) and so on.

Valjean inherits the Hugos' botanical expertise, as seems reasonable for a peasant who first earned his living pruning trees. When he has become mayor of Montreuil-sur-Mer, he occasionally breaks his rule of saying as little as possible to pass on his knowledge to locals, particularly about how to make best use of nettles and weeds – *mauvaises herbes*, or 'bad grasses' in French. It is in this context that he comes out with one of the major theme statements of the novel, one which was surely intended and was often taken by Hugo's conservative critics to be an inflammatory assertion of society's overall responsibility for crime. 'There are no "bad grasses" or "bad men",' he says. 'There are only bad gardeners' (I.5.iii, 152, adapted).

Elsewhere, Hugo recycles recondite legal, ecclesiastical and political terms such as *apanagiste* (the beneficiary of a provision made for the younger children of kings), *viduité* (the state of widowhood), *psallant* ('singer of psalms'), *caloyer* ('monk of the order of St Basil') and *ochlocratie* ('rule of the mob'); historical curiosities such as *miquelet*, meaning 'a Catalan insurgent', and quaint expressions like *écoute-s'il-pleut* (literally, 'listen-if-it-rains') to mean 'eyewash' or 'wishful thinking'.[23] However, not all the words in *Les Misérables* can be found in even the largest dictionaries of French: *zinzelière*, used to describe the screen protecting Gavroche's bed from the rats, is found nowhere else in French;[24] and no dictionary lists *gargoine*, which must mean something like 'throat' or 'gullet'.[25] There's a suspicion Hugo invented some of the words of *Les Misérables* from scratch for the

impish pleasure of making his own mark on the tongue.²⁶ The lexical richness of *Les Misérables* creates a nice paradox: it is one of the
most-translated texts in world literature, yet nobody knows or has
ever known for sure what *all* the words in it mean.

Hugo pushes back the edges of what counts as French in more
ways than this. Breaking with a centuries-old tradition of scorn for
regional and rural forms of speech, he treats the dialects of France
with respect and writes them into his novel. Bishop Myriel learns to
greet his parishioners in their local tongues, Catalan and Provençal;
and Valjean's housekeeper, Toussaint, speaks in the Norman dialect
of Barneville (the nearest point to Guernsey on the mainland of
France), equally impenetrable to speakers of standard French.²⁷ He
even incorporates a Jerseyese word that he picked up from one of
the maids at Hauteville House: *scrobage*, 'floor-scrubbing', that he
might well have cut had he known it was only English in Franco-
Norman disguise.²⁸

However, the main way *Les Misérables* redefines what is French is
by introducing popular forms of speech that had rarely been put in
writing before. Hugo does not do this by sounding out the
pronunciation of 'lower' kinds of speech in the manner of Dickens,
of course, since for the sake of the plot he has to deceive us into
believing that Valjean can get away with opening his mouth. He
makes barely an exception to his iron rule of accent-free French,
and phonetic spellings arise only in Hugo's exposition of the speech
of Gavroche.²⁹ Instead of sounding out the absurdly long string
required in standard French to say 'what's that?' *qu'est-ce que c'est que
cela?* (literally, 'what is it that it is that that?'), the uneducated urchin
blurts out the contracted *keksékça*. Although it looks decidedly
un-French, the expression is one that Hugo insists all French
speakers know and use. He is certainly right that outside of 'pulpit
diction' used in church and classroom settings nobody utters the
full set of sounds of *keserkersékersa*. What Gavroche does, however,
in addition to swallowing the weak vowels indicated by *–er* in this
transcription, is to invert the order of the first *s* and *k*. This is a
genuine feature of popular Parisian French. It's likely, for example,

that Fantine would have pronounced the name of her lover as *Félisque* rather than *Félix* Tholomyès and called her dinner at Bombarda's restaurant *un lusque*, instead of *luxe*, 'a treat'.[30] Equally typical of popular Parisian is Gavroche's way of asking more general questions. Instead of inverting verb and subject, as is normal in high-register and written French, Gavroche adds the interrogative particle *ti* to the end of his verb, saying *j'ai ti* instead of *ai-je* for 'do I have . . . .'.[31] Both these dialectal features can be heard on the streets of Paris today.

Hugo does not make a clear distinction between those aspects of the language of the poor that are particular to a place or region, such as the inversion of *s* and *k* and interrogative *ti*, and those that mark a speaker as a member of a particular social class. In addition, he bundles together the vocabulary of popular, familiar and 'rough' French with the special set of words used by thieves. These technical distinctions are ignored in *Les Misérables* so as to introduce a new register of French that Hugo calls *argot*, or slang. In a sense, he is right to muddle them up, because the boundaries between 'rough' and 'proper' French are always shifting. The words Gavroche uses for 'bed' and 'sleep', for example, *piaule* and *pioncer*, which for Hugo belonged to the exotic language of the streets, are now part of the lexicon of conversational French, just as English 'snooze' and 'snitch' come from the secret language of convicts transported to Australia in the first decade of the nineteenth century.[32]

Hugo most certainly heard popular French in the speech of the servants, tradesmen and prostitutes who came across his path, and his inclusion of elements of their vernacular in a literary novel – especially his use of the taboo word *merde*, in the story of Cambronne's defiance at Waterloo – was part of his long campaign to stretch the boundaries of what could be written down. On the other hand, it is unlikely that a member of the underworld ever taught him how to operate in genuine *argot*, the secret language of crime. That's because the whole point of 'flash' or 'cant' language was to keep outsiders in the dark. The strange and exotic vocabulary of the criminal underclass was first made public in England by a convict who bought his freedom by providing the governor of the colony of New South Wales with a decoding device for spying on the plans of the prisoners in his charge,[33] and in France by the extraordinary Eugène-François Vidocq, a convict who became chief of Paris police and on his retirement published memoirs to which he appended a vocabulary of prisoners' *argot*.[34] Novelists seized upon this quaint and superficially impenetrable set of words as a resource for adventure stories set in the world of crime. Sue plundered it for *Les Mystères de Paris* in 1842, and Balzac used the same vocabulary in the prison scenes of *Splendeurs et misères des courtisanes* (*A Harlot High and Low*, 1847). Hugo used the same repeated set of terms, but also found a less well-known source for them. In the 1840s, he had Léonie Biard check Sue's slang against the anonymous *Mémoires d'un forban philosophe* (*Memoirs of a Philosopher Crook*), and in *Les Misérables* he always uses her spellings rather than Sue's for words that originally figured in the list compiled by Vidocq.[35]

However, Vidocq's list of slang words is not very long. A popular French novelist of the twentieth century, Frédéric Dard, complained in an interview that there are only about a hundred words and expressions recorded in all the dictionaries of French slang published since then. 'It's always the same ones that crop up again and again, so that led me to invent my own.'[36] He probably didn't know it, but he was following the example of Victor Hugo. The *argot* passages in *Les Misérables* are literary exercises that certainly use words found in written sources, but they also do more than that. The conversations among the members of Patron-Minette are imaginations of a heightened and richer form of the vocabulary listed by Vidocq.

Hugo also has much more to say than other novelists and linguists of his age about the significance of the 'anti-language' of the 'third floor down'.[37] At first, he defends it as a language like any other. As the professional jargon of a business called crime, he says, slang is no more exceptional than the special terms used by lawyers, sailors, cloth merchants and so on. What's more, like language in general, it is both partly archaic, retaining old words from an earlier state of French, and constantly self-renewing, inventing new words to replace those that have become overused, or known to the world at large; and it is highly dialectal, having distinct forms for the four main groups who rule the city's underworld of crime. Like other languages too, it is partly borrowed from abroad, with traces of Romany, Spanish, Italian and English in it. Above all, slang is full of metaphors and colourful figures of speech: *dévisser le coco*, 'to unscrew the coconut', for example, means 'to wring someone's neck'. In these formal respects French *argot* has the features of a regular language and deserves to be treated as an authentic form of speech.

Hugo then complicates the issue. He points out that the only thing that distinguishes *argot* from French is its vocabulary, because its grammar and morphology conform to the standard. That makes it not a language at all, but a growth, a cancer, an ugly deformation of proper French. More than that: its ugliness mirrors the lives of the people who speak it. Anticipating much later theories about the link between language, culture and thought, Hugo declares *argot* to be the natural and necessary expression of *la misère*, and that abolishing the one will rid society of the other. What began as an apparent defence of the richness and dignity of a special vernacular turns into an argument to banish it by teaching the ragged how to speak proper French.

Hugo's incoherence is no different from the internal contradiction that challenges language teachers of our own time. Respect for the linguistic dignity of vernacular forms of speech – the variety of English spoken in Singapore, for example, or Afro-American Vernacular English – conflicts with the indisputable advantages of learning to use a standard form of the language. Hugo calls for universal primary education as the solution to the 'problem' of *argot* quite explicitly. However, what his novel actually shows makes it unclear whether *argot* is in fact a problem for those who speak it, and whether formal schooling would be a solution to their plight. Éponine, Gavroche and their parents the Thénardiers are already literate without any schooling. They are also bilingual between 'slang' and standard French. 'Functional diglossia' is the norm in *Les Misérables*, just as it is in most circumstances in the world. Like Myriel, who picks up Catalan, and Fauchelevent, who drops Picard, the *misérables* of Paris learn the forms of language they need to get on in the world. Far from being imprisoned in poverty and crime because of the language they speak, Hugo's poor, spearheaded by Gavroche, play with the different registers of language they possess.

ſ

Les Misérables is a showcase not just of the vocabulary and regional and popular varieties of French, but of all the devices traditionally used to heighten the impact of spoken and written prose. Hugo's familiarity with Latin authors allowed him to transfer the ancient machinery of rhetoric to French, and he puts almost every part of it on display in *Les Misérables*. This produces an opulent, overblown style that is the opposite of how composition teachers think English should be written nowadays. Where an instructor would recommend a single illustration to support a point, Hugo goes for two or four or maybe nine. Where a plain-English style model would dictate a descriptive adjective, Hugo puts in a simile or three. Instead of just saying what happened next, the sentences of *Les Misérables* build a scaffolding of concessive and conditional and relative clauses, like a rickety pyramid of chairs in a circus act. But Hugo's foot rarely slips. His towering accumulations of words are performances of an ancient craft, and part of the point of his book is to show you how it is done. Even if you don't ever want to write this way, it is worth knowing how to name the main acts in Hugo's long show.

- 'The door on the left leads from the courtyard into the orchard. The orchard is dreadful' (II.1.ii, 282). To start a sentence with the last word of the preceding one for emphasis or suspense is called *anadiplosis*. Anadiplosis is commoner than you think.
- 'But slang! What is the good of preserving slang? What is the good of keeping slang alive? To this we have only one thing to say . . .' (IV.7.i, 884). Pretending to question something that is already decided in order to introduce the reasons for it constitutes the rhetorical device of *deliberation*. Hugo uses it frequently in the essay chapters. Is it a

pedagogical device? That question would be an instance of deliberation if the answer were laid out below.

- 'Stunning to look at, with a delicate profile, eyes of deep blue, fleshy eyelids, small arched feet, beautifully turned wrists and ankles, a white complexion showing here and there the azure-tinted branching of the veins, fresh young cheeks, the sturdy neck of Aeginetan Junos . . .' (I.3.iii, 118). This initial description of Fantine, listing 'all the parts, ways and means' of her beauty in sequence, is an application of the figure called *enumeration.*

- '. . . in his tone, in his gestures, in his eyes that set every word ablaze, in this eruption of an evil nature revealing all, in this mixture of swagger and abjectness, pride and pettiness, rage and stupidity, in this chaos of real grievances and false sentiment, in this malicious man's shameless relish of the pleasure of violence, in this brazen nakedness of an ugly soul, in this conflagration of every suffering combined with every hatred, there was something hideously evil and heart-breakingly true' (III.8.xx, 718). Here, *enumeration* is combined with *gradation*, which consists of listing ideas or objects in an order that makes each one say either slightly more or slightly less than the preceding one.

- Locked into this gradated enumeration is Hugo's most characteristic figure of speech, *antithesis,* or the arrangement of things in balancing pairs: 'swagger and abjectness, pride and pettiness, rage and stupidity . . . real grievances and false sentiment . . .'

- 'It is just about acceptable for a reader to be taken into a bridal chamber but not into a young virgin's room . . . It is the retreat of a still-unopened flower . . . it is quite improper for any of this to be recounted . . . We shall therefore show none of all that' (V.1.x, 1,080–81). This is top and tail of a paragraph that describes Cosette in her room before her wedding. The device of pretending not to be saying what you are saying is *preterition.* A stand-by of evasive politicians, *preterition* was easily recognized by nineteenth-century readers from the Latin authors studied at school.

- '. . . as long as there are ignorance and poverty on earth, books such as this one may not be useless' (from the Foreword, adapted). Herman Melville often uses double negation (Captain Delano in *Benito Cereno* is said to be 'not unbewildered'), but Hugo's spectacular use of *litotes* in this famous declaration isn't just a quirk of style. It expresses modesty and confidence at the same time, and it leaves suspended the question of the way in which *Les Misérables* might be a useful book.

- 'Up above the other speakers, on top of a pile of paving stones, Bossuet, rifle in hand, cried out, "O Cydathenaeum, O Myrrhinus, O Probalinthus, O graces of the Aeantis! Oh, who will grant that I may deliver Homer's verses like a Greek of Laurium or Aedapteon?"' (V.1.ii, 1,060). Bossuet's direct and spoken appeal to long-dead figures from classical history and myth is an *apostrophe* (direct address to another person) and an example of *prosopopeia*, treating the dead, the absent and the mythical as capable of intervening in the present world. Bossuet also learned how to do it from Greek and Latin lessons at school.

- Widow Hucheloup, who runs the Café Corinthe, claims to recall the bucolic sounds of her rural youth, where *loups-de-gorge* sang among the *ogrépines* (IV.12.i, 977). Far from being dialectal, these words are mishearings of *rouge-gorges* (robin redbreasts) and *aubépines* (hawthorn). As they incorporate the typically Parisian interchange of /l/ for /r/ these *malapropisms* give away the fact that she's a city girl. These kinds of word-distortion are a favourite resource of French humourists. In the film adaptation of the novel by Claude Lelouch, Darry Cowl, a master of the form, stammers out a three-minute plot summary of *Les Misérables* in which almost every word is 'wrong' in this way.

- Gavroche encounters a quartet of old gossips in Rue de Thorigny, and their conversation hops around like this: 'Cat's fleas don't go after people.' 'Remember the king of Rome?' 'It was the Duc de Bordeaux I liked.' 'Meat's so dear these days.' 'Mesdames, business is bad' (IV.11.ii, 965). Taking elements that make sense on their own but add up to nothing when put together is an ancient rhetorical trick called *verbigeration*.

Hugo's publisher Albert Lacroix, entranced and overwhelmed by the manuscript he had to set in type, slipped from regular business French in his correspondence with Hauteville House into increasingly Hugonic mode. By the time he acknowledged receipt of the last set of corrected galleys from St Peter Port, he was piling up accumulation, enumeration, gradation, simile, metaphor and antithesis like the great man himself:

> Your work, dear master, is that great and magnificent forest where everything exists, merges and combines. Like the song of birds, the call of the eagle, the ray of the divine, you show us all that is there: the ecstasy of hearts, the ulcers on souls, the darkness of minds, joy and suffering . . . Your book is the forest of human life and of our nineteenth century. It leaves us captivated, penetrated, moved, transfigured, renewed, improved and pensive.[38]

Lacroix's gushing praise was undoubtedly sincere, but as a pastiche it is not entirely fair, for Hugo always knew when to abandon the rhetorical devices of expansion for short sentences that deliver a sharp shock. Hugo was a master, not a prisoner of rhetoric. In fact, the alternation between lavishly long sentences and memorable one-liners creates the underlying rhythm and much of the meaning of the whole book. 'The poor girl went on the streets' (I.5.x, 172, adapted) seals the fate of Fantine. 'He must be the best of them all' (III.8.xxi, 734, adapted) sums up Jean Valjean. 'There is no other pearl to be found in the dark folds of life' (V.6.ii, 1,235, adapted) says what there is to say about love.

g

M. Madeleine pays the salary of the primary teachers in the school at Montreuil-sur-Mer, but his charitable act would surely backfire if the masters resembled the Creakles, Squeers and Blimbers who bore and torture small boys in *David Copperfield*, *Nicholas Nickleby* and *Dombey and Son*. Hugo believed in education in principle, but he says almost nothing about its practice in *Les Misérables*. We learn only that Valjean was taught to read by prison visitors, and that Cosette learned to read from him. Teaching is not a topic in Hugo's novel – because the teacher is the novel itself.

What *Les Misérables* invites you to learn first of all is more French, through a virtuoso display of the language in all its forms. Not quite everything that looks like French is worth learning, however: the circumlocutions of provincial lawyers, for example, derided as pale imitations of the already pale Racine, or the pretentious formulae of Thénardier's begging letters, where even the names of famous victories aren't spelled correctly.[39] But almost every other variety of what Hugo calls without blushing 'la grande langue humaine' ('the great language of the human race') (IV.7.i, 886, adapted) is worthy of interest, and the range is joyously wide: the administrative prose of Javert, the jolly puns of Grantaire, the clever couplets of Gavroche, the baroque expletives of Gillenormand, the language games of children and convent girls, the antique pronunciation of King Louis-Philippe,[40] and above all the stylistic tours de force of Victor Hugo, who can bring a hovel, a palace, a battle, a barricade, a meadow or an inn to life by the force of words alone. His strings of epithets and near-synonymous verbs may strike modern readers as too heavy, but they were written to delight readers of a verbally more capacious age with a five-star display of the art of writing itself.

But writing French is not enough. When a character needs to be made more black or more white, when a plot-turn is worthy of high admiration or low scorn, Hugo brings up his ultimate resource, and Latin is its name.

Modern editions usually provide translations of the numerous Latin phrases in *Les Misérables* in footnotes, but in nineteenth-century printings the only footnotes are those that translate expressions in *argot*, Catalan and Provençal. Latin you are supposed to know – or to learn.

Hugo could assume his readers would be familiar with the first words of Psalm 22, 'vermis sum' ('I am a worm') (I.1.x, 42), and the first words of the catechism, 'credo in patrem' ('I believe in the father') (I.1.xiii) because the church still used Latin, and most French people continued to go to church at least once in a while. It was just as fair to expect comprehension of Latin phrases widely used in everyday French (some are also part of English today), such as 'finis' ('end'), 'casus belli' ('cause of war'), 'currit rota' ('time moves on'), 'carpe horas' ('mark the hour'), 'quia nominor Leo' ('for my name is Lion', that's to say, 'because I'm bigger than you').[41] To be true to the Latin Quarter culture of the student members of the 'Friends of the ABC' Hugo lends them a couple of comical Franco-Latin mash-ups, such as 'Non licet omnibus adire Corinthum' (IV.12.iii, 988), literally 'Not all may approach Corinth', punning on 'the omnibus cannot reach Café Corinthe' because the street is too narrow. But that is only a small slice of the Latin inserted into the French of *Les Misérables*.

Some Latin phrases are intended to be dismissed as supercilious nonsense – when Tholomyès says 'Glory be to wine', for instance, then says it again in Latin, claiming it's Spanish. Others are glossed in the text itself, which ends up teaching you what a learned Latin tag means. For example, when Tholomyès declares that 'there's nothing new. Nothing we haven't already seen in the Creator's creation', he is translating 'nil sub sole novum' (literally, 'nothing new under the sun'), which is given in the original in the following sentence.[42] Some Latin phrases are so close to French (and to English, on occasions) that context makes them easy to guess: 'quid obscurum, quid divinum' ('something obscure, something divine'), just glosses the statement that all battles contain 'a certain amount of storm', that's to say, are subject to the fog of war. *Les Misérables* almost teaches you how to read Latin.

Why should a novel about the poor and the downtrodden try to do that? The answer was much more obvious 150 years ago than it is now.

Learning Latin helped its first readers take a step 'towards the light'. Knowledge of the language of Rome had been the distinguishing feature of the educated classes for more than 1,000 years. The mass schooling that Hugo wanted would teach people to read and write first of all, but from mass literacy would come an elite able to enjoy the cultural riches he himself had lapped up as a boy. The Latin of *Les Misérables* is a step-by-step progression from those familiar words that even the poorest would hear in church, through jokes and proverbial expressions to quotations from Virgil and Tacitus which, through careful glossing and implicit translation, make Latin comprehension achievable to those who only read French.

Teaching Latin grammar has been repeatedly defended as an aid to writing French, since French schoolbook grammar is based on Latin models. For Hugo and for generations of educationalists in France, however, the real value of Latin was higher than that. It was the foundation of the humanities, and the best thing an education could hand on. The school system that was reinvented in the 1870s with the same progressive and democratic ideals in mind as those that motivate *Les Misérables* made Latin and Greek prestige subjects in school and the principal passports to advancement.

'Elitism for all' sounds like a sour joke now, but it was a rainbow on the horizon for Victor Hugo. The splotches of Latin all over *Les Misérables* aren't there to impress you, but to help you on your way.

§

In 1817, the innkeeper's wife at The Sergeant of Waterloo in Montfermeil agrees to foster Fantine's infant child Cosette, but treats her as a skivvy since her capacity for maternal affection is fully occupied by her own daughters, Azelma and Éponine. She is just as heartless towards the baby boy she has in 1823, whom we are supposed to have heard bawling in the background when Valjean rescued Cosette on Christmas Eve.[43] Later on, while the story moves to Paris and then to the convent of Petit-Picpus, Mme Thénardier has two more sons she does not care to keep. She rents them out to an underworld acquaintance, La Magnon, who had once worked for Marius's grandfather Gillenormand. The boys are used to blackmail the old man, who is too proud of his virility to deny that he had fathered them himself. After the Thénardiers and their accomplices have been jailed for extortion in the hold-up at the Gorbeau tenement, the police round up many other members of the 'third floor down', including La Magnon, whose infant charges are left to fend for themselves with only a scrap of paper giving them the address of Gillenormand's agent to call on. But the scrap is blown away by the wind, and the two boys, who have been brought up as little gentlemen, are on the streets. Gavroche comes across the waifs and takes them under his wing. He teaches them how to filch bread from a pastry shop and how to use the language of the streets, and he takes them back to live in his secret hide-away inside the life-size plasterboard elephant that was still standing in Place de la Bastille. (It was a demonstration model for a piece of giant statuary commissioned by Napoleon, but never built.) Gavroche turns out to be the best natural teacher in the whole book. The two boys quickly internalize the new vocabulary he's given them for talking about policemen, food, clothes and the rest. Alas, Gavroche, who never knows that he's been looking after his own brothers, loses track of them on 5 June 1832, when riots break out and capture his whole attention. The starving boys find themselves at the pond in the Luxembourg Gardens, where they watch a middle-class boy throw bread to the already well-fed ducks. When the coast is clear, the older one manages to fish a soggy crust out of the pond to give to his little brother. He doesn't say, 'Here, eat that,' in the language he'd spoken up to then. In memory of the kindly urchin who'd taken them in, he uses lower-class Parisian slang: 'Colle-toi-ça dans le fusil' ('Stuff that in yer gob'). I think it's the most moving moment in the whole book. Yes, you can use the novel to learn the rudiments of Latin, but what was learned by these two boys shows the opposite direction of travel. The register of their language keeps in step with their social position. Like the nieces and nephews for whom Valjean stole a loaf in 1796, the nameless boys have now joined the ranks of the *misérables*.

PART FIVE

Great Expectations

15.
Publication Day: 4 April 1862

In the spring of 1862, Adèle went to Paris to get more treatment for her eyes, but also to serve as the publicity manager for the launch of the first two volumes of *Les Misérables*. She did not have to create public interest from scratch, of course, since there was long-standing excitement about a new novel by the most famous man not in France. Rather, she had to raise it to a pitch so high it would discourage the authorities from banning or seizing the book. But she also had to let not a scrap of it be seen in advance. The requirement to boost the book while keeping it secret made the publicity manager's job a work of art.

Adèle turned out to be very good at it. She enlisted two talented copy-writers as her aides: Paul Meurice, a playwright who was an old friend of the family and a fervent disciple of Victor Hugo, and Noël Parfait, a journalist and poet who was one of the few other people to have written about the uprising of 5 June 1832.[1] They kept in constant touch with Charles in Brussels, whose job was to oversee Belgian publicity and to liaise with Lacroix.

In the absence of electronic media, new books were promoted through advertisements, reviews and editorial comment in the printed press. It was customary to send two signed copies to regular newspaper reviewers (the extra copy was for resale) with a covering letter. This also could not be done for *Les Misérables*.

Adèle's first solution was to promote the novel through a bill-board campaign. Twenty-five illustrations of the characters of the novel commissioned for the illustrated edition that would appear a year later were printed on posters and plastered all over Paris. It was not illegal, and it made the novel's imminent appearance known to the whole world without releasing any part of its text. Nothing like it had ever been done for a book. But there never had been a book like *Les Misérables*.

Her second innovation was to create materials for newspapers to use without letting them print a word until the chosen day. Adèle called on newspaper offices with drafts of announcements penned by Charles Hugo and by Paul Meurice, perhaps even by herself, with the unprecedented request that they be held back until a signal was given by the mistress of works. *Les Misérables* was probably the first work ever launched under embargo, a system that has become commonplace nowadays. The prestige of Hugo was such that editors complied with the unusual requirements laid down by the poet's wife. No notices for Part I of *Les Misérables* appeared before the ring of the bell, meaning all appeared at once, starting on 2 April 1862.

g

Meanwhile, Hugo took time out from his heavy schedule to do something of a completely different kind. The people of Guernsey were not rich, and on the streets in town and even on the beach there were many ill-nourished children and beggars to be seen. Adèle had held a charity bazaar to raise funds for a poor school in 1861, but now Hugo decided on a new form of charitable action on the island to which he owed his precious sanctuary. On 10 March 1862, with no proofs to correct until the next steamboat came in, he invited ten children he had picked up in town to come and have a meal at Hauteville House. Mary Sixty was asked to prepare a healthy feast, which meant meat and wine, even for children. The first *dîner des pauvres*, or 'poor dinner', was a great success. Hugo decided to repeat it every other Tuesday, and the group of youngsters at table beneath the benign smile of the whiskery patriarch more than doubled in size. News of the initiative spread, and the idea was taken up first in London, then almost everywhere else. By 1867, according to Graham Robb, '60,000 urchins were being fed in the

Parish of Marylebone alone along lines set out by Victor Hugo'.[2] The tradition of bringing poor children from school to eat lunch in a middle-class household ultimately led to the introduction of canteens in publicly funded schools. Free school lunches, which became a universal right in Britain and France only two generations ago, can be traced back directly to the initiative Hugo took at St Peter Port in the brief respite the mail boat schedule gave him from the unending task of correcting proofs for Part III of *Les Misérables*.

Some of the Guernsey children who had lunches at Hauteville House were still living when the French government shipped over a striking monument to the author of *Les Misérables* in 1914.

> The statue was put up in Candie Grounds, and there was a lot of talk about it. Up to the last minute some people was saying it didn't ought to have been allowed. I like the statue myself. He is standing on the edge of a rock with his coat-tails flying in the wind, and looks as if he was alive. The trouble was that at the top of the gardens there was a statue of Queen Victoria, and all she could see of Victor Hugo was his backside . . . It's alright now, because they have built a pavilion between the Queen and Old Victor, so she doesn't have to look at his behind for the rest of her life.[3]

However, not quite everyone appreciated Hugo's invention of the *dîner des pauvres* in 1862. Charles was the first to raise objections to his father's idea of how to be good. He accused him of wanting to reinstate the role of a feudal lord, and, worse still, of turning his house into a church because the children were required to say 'Blessed be God' at the start and 'Thanks be to God' at the end.[4] Charles was outraged even more by the fact that Hugo had had photographs taken of the group of poor children gathered around him, and that these Father Christmas scenes were on sale at bookstores in St Peter Port. Charity should not be used as advertising, he thundered. Hugo agreed that the giving of alms should always be discreet, but he insisted that 'expressions of fraternity' could only serve as models for others to follow if they are seen. The whole dispute made Charles think that Bishop Myriel in *Les Misérables* was less a version of the real-life Bishop Miollis than an attempt by his father to portray himself as he wanted to be seen. Charles was not a bad judge of his father, though a harsh one. His understanding of Hugo's work and life could not but be entangled in emotions ranging from filial pride to resentment, jealousy and even hate.

§

Printing of the Paris edition proceeded at a feverish pace at Claye's works on behalf of the bookseller Pagnerre, who received the corrected proofs direct from Brussels only after Hugo had approved them as 'good for press'. The plan was to have copies go on sale in Paris the same day they were released in Brussels, Leipzig, London, St Petersburg and other major cities in Europe. Stock was dispatched in advance under guard from Brussels and Leipzig to booksellers outside of France, but it was the Paris edition – the largest printing of all – that was the most fraught with political risk. A last-minute push by Claye meant that the launch date could now be set for 7 April 1862.

Then came a foreseeable disaster: copies of an unauthorized printing of volumes 1 and 2 turned up in Belgium, presumably sold on by a worker in the printing house. There was no time to find the culprit or to use the law, and in any case, no sanction would put the clock back. If the story was out, then out it had to come. Printing was accelerated to a record-breaking rush, and publication brought forward to 4 April.

On 2 April, the editor of the Paris daily *Le Temps* inserted an announcement over his own name on the imminent appearance of a work that would 'combine the splendour of *Notre-Dame de Paris* and the analytical power of *Le Dernier Jour d'un condamné* [*The Last Day of a Condemned Man*]' and its rival *La Presse* boasted:

the chief work of the greatest creator and greatest writer of the age.
All the painful problems, all the raw issues of the nineteenth

century are compressed into these ten volumes in the living and dramatic form of characters who will enter universal memory and never leave it.[5]

These and other papers were also given short extracts to print on their front pages on publication day. Less widely distributed literary and regional periodicals took puffery to even greater heights, referring to Victor Hugo as 'illustrious master', 'the master of masters' or even 'the MASTER' in upper-case oversize font. Such a monument, such a mountain, such a masterpiece simply could not be criticized by the mortals, by the dwarves that we are, wrote Alfred Delvau in *Le Junius* a few days later. This synchronized hallelujah had two main effects. It raised the hackles of critics, even of friends; and it sold a lot of books. Old allies of Hugo found transparently weak excuses not to attend the launch dinner that Paul Meurice organized for 4 April: George Sand said she was on a diet, Théophile Gautier claimed to have the flu, Jules Janin an attack of gout . . . But the dinner went ahead. Lacroix came down from Brussels and sat next to Pagnerre. The businessmen were all smiles. Adèle reported to Victor:

'*Les Misérables* seems to be doing well?' I inquired.
'Madame', Pagnerre replied, puffing out his fleshy cheeks, 'by four this afternoon there were 3,500 copies in readers' hands.'[6]

By the next afternoon, in fact, the first Paris printing of 6,000 copies was sold out (at six francs per volume, it generated receipts of 72,000 francs). The next day, second-hand volumes (already) were fetching twelve or even twenty francs. A thousand copies from Brussels were relabelled 'second edition' and shipped to Paris overnight; the second Paris printing, misleadingly called 'third edition', went on sale on 17 April. Lacroix calculated the ratio of direct exports of 'Fantine' to the size of national populations, producing a rank order of Hugonic fandom and a map of the distribution of literacy in French: 1 Belgium, 2 France, 3 Portugal, 4 Italy, 5 England, 6 Germany,

7 Spain (though there were rumours that the shipment had been confiscated), 8 Russia.[7]

Superlatives really are in order. Lacroix had invented at Hugo's behest the first truly international book launch with an infrastructure that was barely ready for it: paddle steamers, a rail network that still had more gaps than connections, four-horse *diligences* and maybe, on the approaches to St Petersburg, a jingling three-horse sleigh. Thanks to Adèle and her helpers, the book had been trumpeted in all the media then available in a country that the author refused to enter. Despite the obstacles and the political cloud hanging over their heads, the first two volumes of *Les Misérables* sold out in two days.

☙

So 'Fantine' was out, and sold out, but the fair copy of Parts IV and V wasn't even finished, let alone set, corrected and good for press. As Juliette and Julie carried on making the fair copy, Hugo had a mass of proofs for Parts II and III on his hands. He rapped Lacroix on the knuckles repeatedly about paragraphing and punctuation, and his nightly responses to first, second and sometimes third proofs aren't much fun to read:

p. 85	line 1	after *chassait*	insert	semi-colon
	line 2	after *accroissait*	insert	semi-colon
p. 86	line 16	for *coupable*	read *criminel*[8]	

and so on, page after page. Hugo avoided colons, and considered suspension points and long dashes beneath contempt; but as rules about the use of commas in French were not yet set in stone, he was often 'corrected' by compositors, who had to be brought back into line.[9] On occasions, he picked up mistakes of gender made by Belgian compositors (*pendule*, for example, which is masculine in the sense of 'pendulum' and feminine in the sense of 'grandfather clock') and had to negotiate disagreements about the use of the subjunctive.[10]

Now that Lacroix knew how the story would unfold on the barricades, he got increasingly nervous about the political backlash the novel might unleash. Rumours that the French government was planning to impound the book arose immediately on the release of 'Fantine'. Lacroix didn't dare talk openly about a possible ban or seizure of stock, for which he used the code of *l'éventualité*, 'the potentiality' or 'the maybe'. There were warning shots: on 11 April, a student was sentenced to a month in prison for having read aloud Hugo's incendiary poem 'L'Expiation' in a café; and a newspaper that had printed a picture of Hugo had its run of 6,000 copies pulped.[11] Lacroix's anxiety increased when, after a suspicious delay of three weeks, the *Journal des débats* published an outright attack on the political meaning of 'Fantine' over the signature not of its editor Bertin or its regular literary columnist, but of a member of the imperial establishment, Armand Cuvillier-Fleury, the brother-in-law of the foreign minister, Thouvenel. It looked like a signal. Adèle went to remonstrate with the editor, and Hugo wrote a courteous but very firm letter to the critic, protesting that *Les Misérables* was not a pamphlet but a work of literature.[12] Cuvillier was swayed by the letter or perhaps pushed by higher authority, and published a follow-up piece giving Hugo credit for his story-telling gifts, but no further articles appeared in the main national daily on publication of the following volumes of *Les Misérables*. Hugo himself didn't think the authorities would dare take action against him and tried both to reassure Lacroix and to urge him to even greater haste: 'As for the *éventualité*, you have to exploit the book's dazzling success, which cloaks it in a degree of literary inviolability.'[13]

Hugo was not directly exposed to venomous gossip in Paris and Brussels, so perhaps it was easier for him to take the Olympian view. His distanced judgement of the risks turned out to be right and indirectly set a standard for how France handles its troublesome giants. When Sartre broke the law in 1960 by signing a public appeal to French soldiers to disobey orders in Algeria, de Gaulle let him be on the grounds that 'You can't jail Voltaire.' Actually, the *ancien régime* might well have flung Voltaire into a dungeon. De Gaulle would have been closer to the mark if he'd said, 'You can't ban *Les Misérables.*' Napoleon III and his ministers realized that they would only reap the whirlwind if they took action against a book with such powerful mass appeal.

ʃ

Les Misérables was received with enthusiasm by readers, but it took a beating in the press. Right-wing papers slated it, as they had to, but democratic journals responded with a noticeable lack of enthusiasm. Most of the leading critics of the day didn't review the book, and major dailies ranked it lower than *Notre-Dame de Paris* and *Les Mystères de Paris*. Hugo could afford to disregard the critics, but they hurt him nonetheless.

> There is a strange misapprehension about this book. It is a work of love and pity; it is a cry for reconciliation; I stretch out a hand from below on behalf of those who suffer to those who think and are my brothers too.
>
> Why is it that some of the people I thought I could count on to cooperate in this useful work of concord greet me with a kind of hatred? The needs of our age will emerge and time will wash this away, but I am sad to see cold shoulders where I hoped to see helping hands.[14]

One objection raised by a hostile critic was that the basic plot of 'Fantine' was impossible. According to him, a hard-labour convict like Valjean would have letters branded on his shoulder. Javert could therefore have resolved any doubt about the identity of M. Madeleine by having the mayor take off his shirt. As a result, the Champmathieu affair and the court case in Arras were artificial episodes, cooked up without regard for historical truth to make a false plea for socialistic penal reform.

But this is wrong. It is true that in the eighteenth century convicts sentenced to hard labour were branded with the letters *GAL* before being chained and dispatched to Toulon – but no less true that this humiliating ritual was one among many of the barbarous practices of the old regime that was abolished by the revolutionary government in 1789. Valjean was convicted in 1796. He did not have a brand. And as Javert knew this full well, he had no reason to ask the mayor to take off his shirt.

However, the idea that Valjean was branded has made its way from politically motivated attacks on Hugo in 1862 to the West End musical in which the lead tenor reveals his identity by ripping open his shirt to reveal the letters *GAL* stencilled on his chest. Barbey d'Aurevilly, the writer who fished up this red herring, would have been on firmer ground if he had reviewed the show, not the book.

The bad press made not a jot of difference to the readers of *Les Misérables*. Their craze reached fever pitch by the time the four volumes of 'Cosette' and 'Marius' went on sale in May. The heat was turned up by an advertising campaign just as intense as the one heralding the launch of 'Fantine'. Engravings of Valjean, Myriel, Javert and Cosette were in every bookseller's window display, and large placards announcing the sequels were posted on walls all over town. Advance extracts – 'make sure you use the "Waterloo" chapters,' Hugo insisted – were appearing in several daily newspapers, and Pagnerre was putting his entire book stock into storage to make room for a mountain of *Misérables*. The print-run of the Paris edition of Parts II and III was twice that of Part I. The stack of 48,000 octavo volumes was big enough to build a barricade, Adèle thought. Pagnerre was worried that his floor would collapse from the strain.

Before dawn on 15 May 1862, a queue began to form in Rue de Seine. Mme Pagnerre appeared in a dressing gown on the balcony to plead for patience until opening time at 6.30 a.m. Even with a policeman keeping the shoppers in line, tempers began to fray. When the doors opened outward on to a street jam-packed with cabriolets, *fiacres*, handcarts, wheelbarrows – with every and any means of carrying off books – the crush verged on a riot.

Nothing like it had ever been seen in the history of bookselling; and no such scene had ever been presented to the people of Paris before. Other shopkeepers in the street stood gaping in wonderment, they had no clue what was going on and kept on asking what it was all about.[15]

What was going on was a sell-out. New printings followed within days, and almost by the day. It was a major annoyance to many. As no other books were being bought because *Les Misérables* was sucking the market dry, Flaubert put off publishing *Salammbô* for six months. In vaudeville theatres and satirical journals instant parodies in verse and prose mocked and also confirmed the tidal wave of popular enjoyment of *Les Misérables*. When the word *misérable* was pronounced on stage in a quite unrelated play, the audience stood up to cheer.[16]

Just as reports of the triumph of the second instalment of *Les Misérables* reached Guernsey from Paris, a no less important victory was celebrated at Hauteville House: Juliette Drouet and Julie Chenay completed the fair copy transcription of the manuscript of Parts IV and V. They could now sit back and rest their eyes. The final dispatch left Guernsey on 20 May, with a covering note to Lacroix saying that 'if this ending doesn't move people to tears, I'll give up writing for good'. Hugo, who logged anniversaries with superstitious obsession, also noted that it would get to Belgium on 22 May, exactly 365 days after he had started writing those same chapters at Mont Saint-Jean.[17] Before he had the final volumes set in type, Albert Lacroix gathered his workers together and read them the last part of *Les Misérables* aloud. There were maybe as many as fifty men standing or sitting in the strangely silent printing shop that day – steam engineers, maintenance men, cleaners and shifters, typographers and proof correctors, accountants and stock managers.

I wept. I read it aloud to my associates, and twenty, thirty times I was overcome with emotion, my voice broke, I felt I was present at the death of a dear and beloved friend and I had to stop and suspend the reading, and my associates could not restrain their emotions which brought tears to their eyes too.[18]

And yet they still had plenty of work to do, and Hugo likewise, under time constraints that had never been so tight. For months, Lacroix had been urging a move to Brussels to make the correction of proofs more secure and more speedy. Now the end was in sight, he repeated his plea to the great man to come and live next to the printing shop.[19] But Hugo would not budge. And while a move may have seemed sensible and practical to Lacroix, Hugo was surely wise to resist. He had always been a celebrity, but now that the first six volumes of *Les Misérables* were an international sensation, he would have been besieged by journalists, well-wishers and petitioners for every imaginable cause in any place less remote than St Peter Port. He kept as close a watch as he could on what was being said about him in the press, but the delay of a few days or a week in his access to diatribes and put-downs made it easier for him not to react off the cuff. It was also fortunate that the nasty gossip in the small world of French letters wasn't loud enough to reach ears on an island cliff, for some of it would have raised welts on the thickest of skins. Charles Baudelaire wrote a favourable review of 'Fantine'[20] but told his mother that it proved only that he'd mastered the art of the lie, because *Les Misérables* was 'filthy and inept'.[21] Gustave Flaubert let out his spite in several letters to friends: 'This book is written for catholico-socialist shitheads and for the philosophico-evangelical ratpack' is just one example.[22] He objected to the digressions, to the 'intolerable chattering', to the 'stupid twits of the ABC' . . . Prosper Mérimée, a gifted writer who had acquired an almost official position at court, reckoned that popular enthusiasm for *Les Misérables* only showed that humans were less smart than apes.[23] Even Alexandre Dumas groused about having to wade through *Les Misérables* – it was like 'swimming in mercury', he said, or wading through mud.[24] French writers were a quarrelsome lot, but worse was to come. Alphonse de Lamartine, Hugo's companion in literary arms since 1820, his friend and his political ally in more recent times, now a ruined man from his disastrous five-month career as president of France, was making a living from an educational enterprise, the *Cours familier de littérature*, a weekly serial that anthologized extracts from great works and suggested how they should be read. When he dealt with *Les Misérables* towards the end of 1862, he wrote a devastatingly snide put-down of the entire literary project of Victor Hugo. By that time, however, Hugo had given up trying to fight his corner in the undersize ring he was supposed to be in. He dismissed Lamartine's attack as doing him no more injury than a bite from a swan. He had already taken an opportunity to insert in the proofs of Part V a sentence that explained why his work was the object of such venomous spite: 'Genius attracts insult' (V.1.ii, 1,060).

16.
A Story without End

Translators were standing by from day one with quills at the ready to start on the monumental task of getting the book into Spanish, English, German and Italian. Hugo's use of dozens of difficult words, his heady rhetoric and frequent recourse to Latin were not the only problems they faced. *Les Misérables* gives an outsize role to the French language and to the historical, moral, political and intellectual role of France. It was not obvious how the 'Francocentrism' of *Les Misérables* could be represented in countries that viewed French assertiveness as the main cause of trouble in the world for the previous hundred years.

Hugo's confidence that France was the moral and intellectual powerhouse of the world rested on a long tradition. Medieval monarchs had seen themselves as the heirs of ancient glories through the operation of *translatio imperii*. Chrétien de Troyes gave the notion an airing in the prologue to *Cligès*, written around 1176 CE. Seven hundred years later, Enjolras blurts it out again: 'What Greece began is worthy of being completed by France' (V.i.v, 1,069). Again, in the narrator's voice: 'The torch of Europe, that is to say of civilization, was first carried by Greece. Who passed it on to Italy, who passed it on to France. Divine trail-blazing nations! *Vitai lampada tradunt!*' (V.i.xx, 1,112).

The mock-classical monuments that Napoleon erected (including the elephant that got no further than a plasterboard model in Place de la Bastille) were style-coded reminders of *translatio imperii* from Ancient Rome to the French Empire of the day. Opposed to the 'Corsican upstart' because of his suppression of civil liberties, Enjolras is even more Francocentric than Bonaparte was: 'France needs no Corsica to be great. France is great by virtue of being France. *Quia nominor Leo'* (III.4.v, 608).[25]

Hugo gives the glorification of France by genealogical descent an entirely new twist, however. As it was the only nation (apart from America, which Hugo pointedly leaves out) to have remade itself through a revolution, the Revolution of 1789 was what made France the centre of the world. 'Liberty radiates from France. It is a solar phenomenon. None but the blind can fail to se it! Bonaparte said so' (II.2.iii, 336). *Les Misérables* gives the first full formulation of this now conventional explanation of the exceptional status of France, alluded to in campaign statements and presidential speeches on all sides of the political horizon: 'France is meant to stir the soul of nations, not to stifle it. Since 1792 all revolutions in Europe have been the French Revolution' (II.2.iii, 336). That is why 'noble men who throughout the universe fight for the great enterprise . . . [have] their eyes fixed on France'. Hugo rejects and derides the Bourbon doctrine of the divine right of kings, but he comes close to adopting a similar idea on behalf of 'the magnificent and irresistibly human movement begun on the fourteenth of July 1789', stating: 'The French Revolution is an act of God' (V.1.xx, 1,110).

g

If *Les Misérables* is the 'drama of the nineteenth century', then the nineteenth century must be markedly French. Hugo was not a drum-beating nationalist, however. What put France at the forefront of modern history were not its national qualities, but the generous ideas of its revolutionary motto, Liberty, Equality and Fraternity. Fraught with unforeseen consequences and abuses as they may be, these universal values are the ones that Hugo stood by.

Diluted into a national motto, these values may now seem banal, but in 1862 they were aspirations that had yet to be realized in any stable way. No European polity existed that even attempted to balance freedom with equality and both with a fraternal or unifying social bond – certainly not the British, Russian, Ottoman, or Austrian

Empires, let alone France under Louis-Napoléon Bonaparte. If they have become self-evidently desirable aims in the developed world nowadays, it is because they have been fought for again and again and made meaningful to mass audiences through works of art like *Les Misérables*.

The problem for outsiders is that Hugo promotes these universal values as specifically *French* gifts to the world. The publisher of the first Italian translation, for example, doubted whether the lengthy essays on French history and politics were needed to make the book a success abroad. 'There are some Italians, rather a lot in fact, who say: "This book, *Les Misérables*, is a French book. It is not about us. Let the French read it as history, let us read it as a novel."' Hugo disagreed and pulled out all the rhetorical stops in his grandiose reply:

> I do not know whether [my book] will be read by all, but I wrote it for everyone. It speaks to England as much as to Spain, to Italy as much as to France, to Germany as much as to Ireland, to republics with slaves as well as to empires with serfs. Social problems go beyond borders. The sores of the human race, these running sores that cover the globe, don't stop at red or blue lines drawn on the map. Wherever men are ignorant and desperate, wherever women sell themselves for bread, wherever children suffer for want of instruction or a warm hearth, *Les Misérables* knocks on the door and says: Open up, I have come for you.
>
> . . .
>
> Speaking for myself, I write for all, with a deep love for my country, but without preoccupying myself with France more than any other nation. As I grow older I grow simpler and become increasingly a patriot of humanity.
>
> That is the trend of our times and the law of radiation of the French Revolution. To respond to the growing enlargement of civilization, books must stop being exclusively French, Italian, German, Spanish or English, and become European; more than that, human. From this follows a new logic in art, and new constraints on creation

that change everything, even conventions of taste and language, which must expand, like everything else.

Some French critics have reproached me for being outside what they call French taste. I am delighted and I hope their praise is deserved.[26]

It is hard to explain, but it is certainly true that the 'Franco-French' propaganda of *Les Misérables* and Hugo's reliance on the ancient concept of *translatio imperii*, his detailed adjustments to the geography of Paris, his thoughtful discussion of the character of King Louis-Philippe, his essays on the Battle of Waterloo and the etymologies of slang have not interfered with the appeal of *Les Misérables* to readers of all nations. What the novel did was to make France itself seem like a beacon of hope to the subjects of feudal regimes and to foster such 'galloping Francophilia'[27] among the dispossessed as to make Paris the destination of their dreams.

§

The release of the full novel took three months in all: 'Fantine' came out on 4 April, 'Cosette' and 'Marius' formed a four-volume batch six weeks later, in mid-May; and another six weeks elapsed until the final four-volume set of Parts IV and V, went on sale on 30 June 1862. Lacroix did his sums and reckoned that 100,000 copies of the first two volumes had been sold: roughly 40,000 from the legal editions printed in Paris, Brussels and Leipzig; at least 25,000 from the twenty-two pirated editions he knew about; and 30,000 in the nine different translations he had authorized, including a Spanish-language edition printed in Paris, volume by volume, with a time-lag of barely six weeks.[28] But the true dissemination of *Les Misérables* in the first few months of its public life was wider still than what these record-breaking numbers suggest.

The United States did not recognize the copyright of non-citizens, so *Les Misérables* could be reprinted in French without fear of penalty – and it was, instantly, by Lassalle, in New York (the size of his print-run is not known, but it must have been large to judge by the number of copies still available second-hand). The novel could also be translated in the USA without reference or payment to the author or publisher of the original. *Fantine: A Novel*, translated by Charles Wilbour, appeared in New York as early as June 1862; *Cosette* came out in July, *Marius* and *Saint-Denis* in November, and *Jean Valjean* in December. The five volumes had a series title, *Les Misérables*, followed by a subtitle, *The Wretched*, in parentheses, on the title page. Sales of Wilbour's translation ran into the hundreds of thousands. One retail order for 25,000 copies was reported to be the largest order ever placed for a book in America, and I would guess it was the largest in the world.[29] The extraordinary speed of publication may suggest this was a piece of hack work, but Charles Wilbour was no ordinary translator. A classicist trained at Brown University, he was a journalist, then a businessman and finally an Egyptologist of great renown who discovered the first Elephantine Papyri, which are now the greatest treasure of the Brooklyn Museum. Translating *Les Misérables* in six months was only one of his achievements.

Wilbour's translation was printed in two columns on broadsheet pages suitable for splitting into parts, and pamphlet-sized sections with coloured, comic-like illustrated cover sheets went on sale for a nickel or a dime within weeks. This is the form in which *Les Misérables* first reached the mass audience that Hugo sought – but not at all where he imagined it would be found. In Richmond, Virginia, the cultural centre of the separatist confederacy of slave-owning states, where the copyright laws of the Union were not observed, a pirate edition was launched straight away. However, it was not quite the same as the one Wilbour had produced. The preface, signed 'A. F.', makes the changes clear:

> It is proper to state here that whilst every chapter and paragraph in any way connected with the story has been scrupulously preserved, several long, and it must be confessed rather rambling disquisitions on political and other matters of a purely local character, of no

ction with the characters or inci-dents of the novel, and the absence of a few anti-slavery paragraphs
will hardly be complained of by Southern readers. [30]

Consequently, where Hugo had written and Yankees read 'I voted
for the downfall of the tyrant; that is to say, for the abolition of prostitution for woman, of slavery for man, of night for the child,'
Confederates were offered 'I voted for the annihilation of the tyrant;
that is to say, for the abolition of prostitution for woman, of degen-
eracy for man, and of night for the child'. [31]

This 'localization' of Hugo's novel to the views and sensitivities
of slave-owning states is a travesty of the author's position and of
some of the meanings of his work. What is left if you suppress
Hugo's firm opposition to capital punishment, to racial prejudice
and to slavery? Quite a lot, it turns out. An old soldier recalls:

> How we wept with Fantine and Cosette! How we loved the good
> Mayor Madeline, all the dearer to us because he had once been
> Valjean! How we hated Javert, that cold and stony pillar of 'author-
> ity'! How we starved with Marius and waxed indignant in
> contemplating his frigid grandfather! How we fought over and over
> the wonderful battle of Waterloo, and compared it with other con-
> tests of which we knew!
>
> Certainly no book ever achieved the popularity of that most mar-
> vellous picture of life. [Confederate soldiers] . . . formed groups
> around the camp-fire and the man who was deemed to have the
> greatest elocutionary development was appointed reader for the
> assembly. [32]

240

Sounding out Hugo's untranslated title in a southern drawl, those campfire readers turned *Les Misérables* not into *Lez Miz*, but into *Lees Miserables*. A tiny accident in diction – the lengthening of a vowel that is often lengthened in English in the pronunciation of 'the' – made a pun that prompted powerful self-recognition. Yes, Hugo's book was really about them, the miserable soldiers of Robert E. Lee! That is how they now thought of themselves: 'I certainly laid down that night one of Lee's miserables, as we used to term ourselves after reading Victor Hugo's great novel.'[33]

In this peculiar way, a novel appealing for sympathy with the outcast and damned became the collective nickname of doomed men who saw themselves as oppressed. Seen from the French side with politics in mind, it would be comical if it weren't so abhorrent. Yet, as we have seen, Hugo's novel explicitly overrides the distinction between the destitute, the despicable and the hapless, merging them into a single collective that reconfigures the language of nineteenth-century France. 'There is a point where the poor and the wicked become mixed up and lumped together in the one fateful word: *les misérables*' [p. 671, adapted]. Why should ragged soldiers be excluded from this new community of the downtrodden? The miserable men who fought to preserve slavery in the American South did not get the meaning of the novel entirely wrong.

¶

The international dissemination of Hugo's novel was not plain sailing on every one of the seven seas, and some countries had to wait a long time for the novel to arrive on their shores. Lacroix sold the Russian rights to a publisher in St Petersburg, but the tsar's censors banned the translation of a work seen as inimical to the imperial regime. A very short abridgment was permitted in 1870, but the whole text only became available in Russian in 1892.[34] In China, the delay was even greater. A revolutionary Buddhist monk, Su Manshu, and one of the founders of the Chinese Communist Party, Chen Duxiu, first began to retell the adventures of Jin Huajin (Jean Valjean) in classical Chinese in issues of the Shanghai *Daily National* in 1903, starting with I.2, not I.1. Between chapters I.1.v and I.1.ix (chapters vi–viii were omitted) they inserted seven episodes of their own invention, introducing Chinese characters commenting on the events in Bali (Paris) and making numerous points about the need for revolutionary change. However, when they got as far as the episode of Petit-Gervais – which they altered almost beyond recognition – the journal was shut down, and the project abandoned. Twenty years later, the husband-and-wife team of Fang Yu and Li Dan began again, translating *Les Misérables* from scratch, and Part I came out in 1932. Shortly after, the publisher's office was bombed, and much of the remainder of the book went up in flames; other parts of the manuscript had been sent to Hong Kong but disappeared in the post. It was not until 1954 that the translators were able to resume the project, or rather, to begin it all over again. A new version of Parts I and II appeared at long last in 1959 – and then the Cultural Revolution intervened. Like many Western-educated intellectuals in Mao's China, the translators of *Les Misérables* were imprisoned and all their manuscripts were burned. On their release in 1971, Li Dan and Fang Yu, now in their seventies, went back to work. Li Dan died in 1977 but Fang Yu carried on on her own, completing Parts III and IV and finally, Part V. The full Chinese translation of *Les Misérables* appeared in 1984, 122 years late.[35]

The British translation, like the American one, appeared before the end of 1862. The translator, Sir Charles Lascelles Wraxall, had been suggested to Hugo by his friend Alphonse Esquiros, an exiled French writer and politician who was teaching history at Greenwich Military Academy at that time. Wraxall, who lived mostly abroad, was a military historian who had his own views about what really happened at Waterloo. He didn't hesitate to correct Hugo on such matters, and when he came across passages he didn't approve of, he left them out. There is hardly a chapter in the book that is free of editorial interventions, ranging in length from substantial omission to dropped lines and words.[36] The version of *Les Misérables* published in London by Hurst and Blackett was a disaster on every score.

Unfortunately, the publishers had bought proper translation rights from Lacroix, so only Wraxall's hodgepodge could be sold legally in the British Isles. It came out as a conventional 'triple-decker' at half a guinea a volume, an expensive format intended mainly for the stock of circulating libraries. When the inadequacies of Wraxall's work were revealed, the publishers did not make corrections or commission an alternative version. They did not print new editions in cheaper format either. British readers would have to wait a long time to read the whole of *Les Misérables*.

The egregious amendments of Lascelles Wraxall became an insular convention that lasted until the twenty-first century. Norman Denny's 1955 translation, the standard version available in the UK for fifty years, takes the books relating to the convent of Petit-Picpus (II.7) and the long essay on slang (IV.7) out of their right places and hides them away in an appendix at the end of the book. The full text of *Les Misérables* in the right order of reading was not available to British readers until 2008, in a version by the Australian writer Julie Rose. The Chinese had beaten them to it by twenty-three years.

ℊ

As he said in his letter to his Italian publisher, Hugo wanted *Les Misérables* 'to be read by all'. The ten-volume first edition in French cost sixty francs and was far too expensive for ordinary folk to buy for themselves. Some workers' clubs pooled resources to buy one copy per twelve and then drew lots for who would get the first read.[37] And as not everyone could read, chapters from *Les Misérables* were recited every night in cafés and homes throughout the land. The passion for Hugo's story was almost universal, especially among the poor, but the work could not be got to all by these means alone.

Charles Dickens faced the same issue in England, and solved it in an original way. He drafted shortened 'reading aloud' versions of his best-loved novels and went on tour around the country,

entrancing audiences in village halls with three-hour one-man performances of *Great Expectations*, *The Old Curiosity Shop* and *Oliver
Twist*. Dickens was a gifted amateur actor and a wonderful mimic
of the accents his characters have.[38] Hugo could not follow his
example, however. For one thing, he refused to set foot in France;
and despite his long experience of writing for the stage, he did not
have a great speaking voice or theatrical ambitions for himself. All
the same, he knew that the surest way of reaching a genuinely popular audience was through the stage.

Enjoyment of theatre, magically recreated by Marcel Carné in
Les Enfants du paradis (*Children of Paradise*), was one of the few
uncontentious bonds between the social classes in nineteenth-
century France. Audiences did not consist of the well-heeled and
often grey-haired folk you find watching Broadway shows nowadays.
With the wealthy in the boxes, ordinary folk in the pit and rabble up
in the gods, theatrical crowds were noisy, irreverent and socially
diverse – in *Les Misérables*, even Gavroche goes to see the latest plays.
To reach the real-life urchins of Second Empire France, Hugo's
novel had to become a play.

Because it was accessible to all social classes, however, theatre
was subject to more stringent censorship than books, and all new
plays had to obtain official approval before they could be staged.
Given Hugo's position as an irreducible enemy of Napoleon III and
the furore in the press over the political meaning of *Les Misérables*,
approval for a stage version was not likely to be obtained as long as
the Second Empire stood.

Hugo nonetheless encouraged Charles to try to make a play from
the novel, which might serve as a launch-pad for the literary career his
son hoped to have. Charles thought he might circumvent the censors
by creating a show in two parts, to be performed on successive evenings, like Part I and Part II of Shakespeare's *Henry IV*. The first part,
presenting Myriel, Valjean and Fantine would have a chance of getting past the censors, he thought, and if it were a huge success then it
might make it difficult for the authorities to refuse approval for the
sequel containing the more politically sensitive barricade scenes.

Hugo himself did not like the two-part idea. Charles's draft script was nonetheless submitted not long after the appearance of the last volumes of the book. The censors read it straight away and decided they did not like Charles's Part I either. The Paris première of 'Fantine', originally scheduled for September 1862, was promptly cancelled. A Brussels theatre stepped in to the breach, but the director insisted on a unitary play to be performed in one sitting. Adèle nagged Charles to fall into line with his father, who demanded in no uncertain terms that his son return to Guernsey and take guidance on how to redraft the script. Charles dug in his heels. He still thought that the glory of dramatizing his father's greatest work would be the real start of his own career and he wanted to do it twice over, but he was forced to give in in the end. At Hugo's request, Paul Meurice took a month out of his own work in November 1862 to serve as script-doctor to a play that would appear over Charles's sole name. *Les Misérables. Drame* was ready just in time for its Brussels première on 3 January 1863.

It has a Prologue presenting the story of Valjean and Myriel in Digne. Part I, 'Fantine', is a sequence of tableaux taking the story from Montfermeil to Montreuil-sur-Mer and Arras for the courtroom scene, then back to Montfermeil for Valjean's rescue of Cosette and to Paris for a short convent scene. Part II, 'Valjean', contains a highly compressed version of the romance between Marius and Cosette, the ambush in the Gorbeau tenement and a more developed barricade scene. Finally, the Epilogue, jumping right over the marriage of the young lovers, brings us straight to Valjean's confession and death.

Any number of other selections of material from Hugo's over-stuffed novel can be imagined, but nearly all subsequent adapters for stage and screen have followed Charles's basic decisions about what to cut. The dramatic tradition of *Les Misérables* characteristically omits: (1) the history of Myriel before meeting Valjean; (2) the story of Fantine before she entrusts Cosette to the Thénardiers; (3) the Battle of Waterloo; (4) Valjean's second imprisonment and his dramatic escape from the *Orion*; (5) almost all of the Petit-Picpus episode, including Valjean's escape in a coffin; (6) all of the story of Marius before he meets the 'Friends of the ABC'. Indicated as 'optional' scenes in the printed version of Charles's script are the episodes of Petit-Gervais and a short scene set in the convent. As a consequence of the omission of the Waterloo section, the narrative link between Thénardier and Marius disappears, and the hold-up in the Gorbeau tenement becomes a much simpler affair. Obviously, you can't get it all in a three-hour play, but it is striking how few of the later film and stage versions of the novel significantly alter the selection made by Charles. That does not mean that he got it right first time. It means that adapters of the novel have constantly maintained and renewed a tradition of reading that is almost as old as *Les Misérables* itself.

§

Charles Hugo's version is also partly responsible for the now seemingly ineradicable confusion among illustrators and rewriters of *Les Misérables* as to which of the several French revolutions its barricades defend. The anachronisms are first introduced when Valjean is released from the grip of Thénardier and his gang in the Gorbeau tenement. As Javert moves to make his arrest, a revolutionary crowd bursts into the room, led by Feuilly, the fan-maker 'Friend of the ABC'. He orders Javert to release his prisoner.

FEUILLY (*to Valjean*): Citizen, you are free.
GAVROCHE: On behalf of Citizen Éponine . . .
FEUILLY: Liberty arrests nobody today.
GAVROCHE (*to JAVERT, who is shaking from head to toe*): Long Live the Rights of Man!

Is this 1789, 1792 or 1848? Hard to tell . . . But it is certainly not 1832, when no republic emerged to make Frenchmen into citizens or to proclaim afresh the Rights of Man. Charles made a parallel alteration to the denouement of the barricade scene. In the novel, Enjolras and Grantaire, the last two men standing, cry, 'Long Live the

Republic,' before being executed by firing squad in the back room of the Café Corinthe.[39] In Charles's dramatization (in which the character of Grantaire doesn't appear) Enjolras leans out of a window to shout, 'Long Live Liberty,' before the set is destroyed by an artillery assault.

From the acorns Charles planted through these inserted keywords so as to link the novel's historical setting to a longer tradition of revolutionary acts have grown hybrid ideas that merge Gavroche with the student in Delacroix's commemoration of July 1830 and dust-jacket designs showing his Goddess of Liberty brandishing a red flag instead of the tricolour . . . For Hugo, the uprising of 5 June 1832 was best suited to talking about the meaning of revolution in general. Confusing it with other revolutions by appropriating their icons and keywords irritates scholarly guardians of the past, but at bottom it only extends Hugo's own transformation of history into myth.

Charles's play was not a success when it opened in Brussels. There was not a single notice in the Paris press, and it had few mentions even in Belgium. The flop must have been at least half-expected at Hauteville House. Neither Hugo nor any other family member made the trip to see its opening night.

The half-title page of the published edition of *Les Misérables. Drame* states that the play had been licensed for performance in French in Liège, Antwerp, Hamburg, Berlin, Pest, Stockholm, Lisbon and Madrid, making it seem it was a European success. But it's far from sure that any of these licences were taken up. The influence of the first full dramatization of *Les Misérables* comes from the fact that it was printed and published as a book by Albert Lacroix and remained accessible to later adapters for many decades.

A far more spectacular theatrical career awaited Valjean, Fantine, Cosette and Javert outside of the French-speaking world. First of all in Italy, where dramatized scenes from the earlier parts of the novel went on tour with a travelling company in June 1862 even before the last volumes had appeared, and then, repeatedly, in England. This may be because Wraxall's translation was both awful and too expensive for most people to read, but, whatever the cause, new adaptations roll by in theatrical journals year by year: *Charity*, by Charles H. Hazlewood, 'founded on Victor Hugo's story of *Les Misérables*', London, November 1862; *Jean Valjean*, by Harry Seymour, London, 1863; *Out of Evil Cometh Good*, by Clarance Holt, Birmingham, 1867; *The Barricade*, also by Clarance Holt, London, 1869; *Atonement* by W. Muskerry, London and Manchester, 1872. These titles, like many others that can be found in various parts of the English-speaking world – *Fantine* and *Cosette* in Boston in 1869 and 1875, *The Yellow Passport*, performed in Guernsey in 1868 and then in Sydney, Australia, in 1874, then retitled *Saint or Sinner* and *A Convict Martyr*, staged in Australia and California – show that the narrative elements of Part I 'Fantine' provided most of the material for the English-language stage, and that the 'revolutionary' parts were nearly always ignored.

Les Misérables also reached audiences in other foreign languages through the stage. In Yiddish a play adapted from the novel under the title *Der Giber in Keyten*, 'The Hero in Chains', was performed in Warsaw in 1911; other versions were staged in Vilna and printed as play scripts too.[40] One of these had a musical accompaniment, but that was already nothing new. The first musical of *Les Misérables* was performed in Philadelphia within weeks of the novel's completion in American English, in January 1863: *Fantine or The Fate of a Grisette* by Albert Cassedy, with a musical score by Charles Koppitz.

§

In 1895, Louis and Auguste Lumière perfected a device for recording moving images, which they called the *cinématographe*. They used it as a documentary device and shot short reels of a train arriving in a station, a crowd leaving a factory and, soon after, street scenes in cities all over the world. In 1897, they recorded an act by a quick-change artiste from the Paris music-hall. In this historic sixty-second clip, an unknown performer uses wigs, hats, scarves, posture and expression to represent in rapid succession Victor Hugo, Jean Valjean, Thénardier, Marius and Javert.[41] It is the first entrance into the cinema not just of *Les Misérables*, but of fiction of any kind. Ever since, Hugo's novel has fed the film industries of almost every country in the world, and *Les Misérables* has become the most frequently adapted novel of all time. Some of these films are monuments in the history of cinema: Albert Capellani's 1912 version in four parts and six hours; Henri Fescourt's even longer silent film in 1925 (recently restored and performed to the original score at a gala in Toulouse); and the first sound adaptation by Raymond Bernard, in 1934. Adaptations of parts of the novel have appeared in Hollywood every few years since 1909, and the long tradition of filming of *Les Misérables* in East Asia began in Japan in 1923 (*Ah! Ah! Mujo*, by Kiyochiko Ushihara) and includes Tomu Ushida's *Jan Barujan* (1931), a multi-authored *Remizeraburu* in 1950, animated cartoon versions by Keiji Hisoaka in 1980 and Koichi Motohashi (*Shojou Cosetta*, 2007) and other movies made in Korea and India. Overall, there are now at least sixty-five screen versions of *Les Misérables* in languages as varied as Russian, Farsi, Turkish, Tamul and Arabic as well as in French, English and Japanese.[42] Though they have made all kinds of historical mistakes and often misrepresented the beliefs and attitudes of its author, film-makers have lent Victor Hugo a powerful hand in bringing his story to the global audience he sought.

ʃ

'Your great work is at an end, dear master,' Lacroix wrote to Hugo in June 1862 on receipt of the last corrected proofs from Hauteville House.

> I've got so accustomed to living with your mind and to providing my workers with their daily tasks that I find it painful to utter the word: *end*. Why does that have to be everything? Why must Valjean die, why must Cosette and Marius abandon us . . . ?[43]

He was the first but far from the last reader of Hugo's 365 chapters to wish there were many more. And there could have been, even then. In the extraordinary long burst of creative energy that kept Hugo writing throughout 1861 and the first half of 1862 all kinds of details, descriptions, analyses and loops in the plot were added, but there were some new and old inventions that were cut away at the last minute. The '*Reliquat des* Misérable*s*', a large folder of notes, materials, drafts and 'leftovers', contains alternative versions of various parts of the story, and a substantial extension of it too, in seven supplementary chapters that would have followed on from III.7.ii.

This dropped underworld episode consists of an account of the practice of 'marriage' between prisoners and women outside the walls. Every prison community has an artist, Hugo says, who draws a bouquet of flowers for a group of inmates. The flowers are numbered by each prisoner's cell. The flower-picture finds its way to the women's detention centre at Saint-Lazare, and responses come back by way of a secret mail service to inform the senders 'that Palmyra has chosen the tuberose, that Fanny has fallen for the azalea, and that Séraphine has adopted the geranium'.[44] The bandits identified by the flower and therefore by their cell-number now have wives, for the women, whose detention was usually not very long, considered themselves married to men they did not know and might well never see. All for a flower! 'You think it's funny? You are wrong. It is worthy of awe.'[45] The story of these 'flowers of evil' leads into an essay on the mysteries of the human heart and the 'black zone' at the heart of Paris, where we return to the criminal part of the plot of *Les Misérables*. Claquesous, Gueulemer and Babet, three of Thénardier's sinister accomplices in the Patron-Minette gang, are the 'flower-husbands' of Dahlia, Zéphine and Favourite, the three companions of Fantine in her life as a kept woman before 1817. In the twelve years since we last saw them, these young women have withered away, stepping down from circle to circle into the 'seventh ring of hell'.[46]

Hugo cut the 'flower chapters' during the frantic preparation of the manuscript of Part III in February 1862, considering it more suited to joining the philosophical preface he'd written the previous summer as the core of another work on 'The Soul', which was never pursued.[47] However, the existence of a vanished fragment that neatly connects two widely separated parts of the narrative invites us to wonder if other interstitial links might have been invented by Hugo – and whether we could imagine any ourselves.

Every story ever told makes the same invitation, and even the most perfectly crafted plays and novels can prompt later writers to fill in the gaps. Tom Stoppard's *Rosencrantz and Guildenstern Are Dead* offers a sidelight on the strange goings-on at Elsinore from the angle of two characters Shakespeare hardly mentions; Raymond Jean's *Mademoiselle Bovary* imagines the life of Berthe, the daughter that Emma (and her author) neglected; and Kamel Daoud's recent *Meursault Investigation* fills in the back-story of the Arab victim that Camus didn't even name in *The Outsider*. Hugo's much vaster novel may seem to fill in every detail on its oversize canvas, but the multiplicity of its characters, events, settings and topics also allows for an infinite number of connections between them that readers may wish to make up.

Victor Hugo's descendants, acting in defence of the 'moral right' of their ancestor to control the use made of his book in France even long after the end of copyright protection, refused to allow the publication of explicit continuations of the story of Marius and Cosette. They ignored Laura Kalpakian's *Cosette* in 1995 because it was published in the USA, but they took François Cérésa to court for *Cosette ou le temps des illusions* and *Marius ou le fugitif*, both published in 2001. The case went to appeal and was finally resolved in 2008 in favour of the artistic freedom of writers to reuse characters and write new stories about them even from the most sacred of literary texts. But these explicitly commercial works, like Susan Fletcher's *A Little in Love* (2014), which retells and extends the story of Éponine, aren't the best evidence of the power of *Les Misérables* to grow new branches of its plot.

Inuki Takako's 'super-deformed' manga, *Aloette na uta* ('The Song of Aloette') retells the story of Cosette under the thumb of the Thénardiers at Montfermeil, and of Fantine's expulsion from the factory in Montreuil. The artist adapts it to a Japanese perspective and also introduces an additional character, a Western-looking priest who advises Cosette to be patient and submissive, for suffering is the human lot. The drawings bring Cosette's suffering at the hands of a quite hideous Mme Thénardier close to torture, and by the end the poor girl is so badly harried and thrashed that she stops being able to speak and to hear. The final large panel has a narrator intervene to explain that late-onset autism was quite common in nineteenth-century Europe, so harshly were children treated then. This is an entirely original addition to Hugo's conception of what suffering may do to a child, but it is also more than what it seems. For a specialist in modern Japan, it is a coded protest at the way Japanese children are given excessive workloads at school nowadays, at the risk of driving them out of their minds.[48]

Nowadays, however, *Les Misérables* grows and changes not just in sequels and adaptations for radio, film, television and graphic books, but in the vast and unpoliced universe of amateur writing on the web. Fan fiction consists of short texts that modify, expand or fill in the gaps of a published work, written by mostly young readers who, like Lacroix in 1862, don't want the stories they love to have a final shape and a definitive end. The leading 'vehicles' for writing of this kind are children's and young adult novels like *Harry Potter*, *Twilight* and *Lord of the Rings*, so it is quite surprising – and gratifying – to see that *Les Misérables* is among them. Some fan fictioneers try to answer quite interesting questions. For example: what crimes did Javert solve between his arrest of Valjean in 1823 and his pursuit of him through Paris in 1829? What were the names of the nieces and nephews for whom Valjean stole the loaf in 1796, and what happened to them after that? Exactly how did Thénardier get from the prison of La Force on to the roof of a ruined house in Rue du Roi-de-Sicile? (Hugo says 'that is what no one has been able to explain or understand', IV.6.iii, 872).

Most of these 'ficlets', as they are called, pursue the idea implicit in Hugo's work that in some sense the dead live on. That is also a feature of *Shojou Cosetta*, a 52-part Japanese animated television cartoon in which an eternal Gavroche becomes Cosette's best friend.[49] Imagining that Éponine, Enjolras, Grantaire and so on survive the barricade or else return from the beyond, fan fictioneers typically reinsert their closest generational relatives in the novel into circumstances that belong to them: Café Musain may become a Starbucks where Enjolras and Grantaire discover they are gay; Marius may find himself torn between a loyal wife and a passion for Éponine; or Enjolras may pursue a romance with the undead Éponine – a formerly popular 'ship' that received its own 'smush name', 'Enjonine'. Since then, there's been a wave of 'alternative universe' rewritings that have nominally resurrected revolutionaries discussing not the political issues of the nineteenth century but questions of greater relevance to the writers themselves. Chief among them at the moment is the representation of 'marginalized groups', so the 'Friends of the ABC' now figure on sites like *An Archive of Our Own* as a rainbow of different racial, sexual and gender identities. I am told by those who navigate this underground ocean that a fictional addition to *Les Misérables* presenting a boy–girl romance between non-black youngsters with no physical handicap would now be considered by denizens of the deep as a positively reactionary political act.[50]

Indirectly, the repoliticization of the sentimental potential of Hugo's story points to a singular feature of the novel itself. Dickens's novels of the London poor ask us to respect and to love characters with physical and mental disabilities of many kinds: Amy Dorritt suffers from dwarfism, for example, Miss Flyte has a wandering mind, Tiny Tim has a crippled leg, and Jenny Wren is a wheelchair case. There is nothing of the kind in *Les Misérables*. All of Hugo's characters have all their limbs and all their faculties too. I'm not sure why this is so, for the *misérables* of Paris must have been afflicted by these kinds of misfortune just as much as the London poor. If there are some kinds of outcast that Hugo inadvertently casts out, we might think of saying thank you to amateur scribblers who have brought them back into the fold.

17.
The Meaning of Les Misérables

Despite the complexity of its plot, the crowd of characters it puts on stage and the range of topics it covers, *Les Misérables* conveys a central message that arises exclusively from the actions of its hero, Jean Valjean.

In the course of his life he overcomes many physical obstacles and copes with three personal crises: his last unnecessary act as a thug when he robs Petit-Gervais of his coin; the temptation to let his 'brother' Champmathieu take the rap for him in Montreuil; and his jealous anger in Paris when a young man arises to rob him of his beloved adoptee, Cosette. Muscular strength, acrobatic skills learned in prison and an ability to tolerate pain allow him to release Fauchelevent from under his cart, to climb the convent wall, to escape from the hold-up and to carry Marius through the sewers. But what resources does he have that allow him to overcome the moral obstacles in his path?

Hugo gives several answers, and allows readers to make a choice.

Valjean's pursuit of a moral life arises from his strange encounter with a righteous man. In a reversal of Mephistopheles' pact with Dr Faust, Myriel purchases the ex-prisoner's soul with an unsolicited and almost inconceivable gift. Valjean makes no promise in return, yet the bishop tells him he has one to keep: 'Don't forget . . . you promised to use this money to become an honest man' (I.2.xii, 99). Valjean is hardly himself when he strides away from Digne, for he is in thrall to a spirit not his own. He rebels against such possession when he comes across Petit-Gervais. He does a bad deed, so it seems, solely in order to be himself. But as soon as the mountain lad has run off in fright, the spirit of Myriel reasserts itself over him.

Around three the next morning the coach driver coming in from Grenoble 'saw a man who looked as if he was praying, kneeling on the ground in the darkness at Monseigneur Bienvenu's front door' (I.2.xiii, 106). Kneeling is recognized as a ritual of contrition in every corner of the globe. The reawakening of Valjean's moral fibre is thus presented in these early chapters of the book as a story of *possession*, in a vaguely religious light.

Taking his new name 'Madeleine' from La Madelaine-sous-Montreuil, a hamlet nestled beneath the ramparts of the town at the end of his road,[51] Valjean opens a factory and is soon rich enough to give alms and to fund education and health for the poor, in *emulation* of the charitable actions of Bishop Bienvenu. He is especially attentive to lads from Savoie, presumably because he hopes to come across Petit-Gervais and make amends for having stolen his two-franc coin.[52] From then on, Mayor Madeleine has only two aims, 'to conceal his name, and to sanctify his life' (I.7.iii, 202). However, when he has to decide what to do about the charges against Champmathieu, he cannot rely only on 'possession' and 'emulation', the two resources the novel has given him up to that point. The tussle between his commitment to the community and his obligation to rescue an innocent man can't be resolved without recourse to values that override them both. His night of doubt begins when he extinguishes the light.

> He had the feeling that someone could see him.
> Someone? Who?
> . . . What he wanted to strike blind was staring at him. His conscience.
> His conscience, that is to say God. (I.7.iii, 204)

The French-Russian-Polish novelist Romain Gary, whose entire literary project grew out of an early reading of *Les Misérables*,[53] also gives a central role to an 'inner witness' guiding his path – not the divinity, in his account, but the all-seeing eye of his mother, even from beyond the grave.[54] We too can set aside Hugo's invocation of

God if we wish and understand *conscience* as moral self-awareness. The looking eye belongs interchangeably to the bishop ('all the more present for being dead', 208) gazing steadily at him, and to himself. *Conscience* dictates his provisional decision to turn himself in, but the words Valjean utters at this point call on a different concept of what is morally right: 'Let's take this course! Let's do our duty! Let's save this man!'

Valjean goes round in circles for some time after this, and Hugo maintains narrative suspense and psychological veracity by not announcing in advance what Madeleine is going to do at the trial. But although he also brings in an 'inner voice' and allows those who wish to hear it as the voice of God, the key word laid down after 'conscience' in this dense and intricate chapter is *duty*.

Possession, emulation, conscience and duty push Valjean in the same direction, and you could say that they're just rhetorical variations on the same basic thing. But that thing – what makes right right and wrong wrong – is uncommonly hard to name for itself. Hugo's variations, moreover, are handles that open doors on to a variety of different cultures. Jewish, Muslim, Protestant and Catholic believers can relate all these terms to Hugo's own preferred source of moral discrimination, which he calls God; but in cultures where the old and the scholarly are revered, emulation (of Myriel) may seem the better guide to the righteous path; and in other frames of reference, such as Hugo's imagination of the Ancient World, duty would be the ultimate decider. It's not that Hugo was hedging his bets. By getting different value-systems to converge on the dilemma of one man, he created a story that can be grasped and applied far beyond nineteenth-century France.

These alternative value-systems converge when, near the end of the story, Valjean has to decide how he should relate to his adopted daughter she is married. As the young couple's good fortune is his creation twice over (he rescued Cosette from Montfermeil and Marius from the barricade), he would be justified in profiting from the material and emotional comfort that the two of them could provide him in old age. If he did so, however, he would bring into their happy and respectable home the memory of his unexpunged crime and thus expose a bourgeois family to the risk of being undone.[55] In a vague replay of the dilemmas of King Lear and Old Goriot (and of all kinds of real people who reach a certain age), Valjean needs to determine what role a redundant parent should play in the future life of a child. This conflict between what is convenient and what is right repeats the conundrum Valjean faced at the courthouse in Arras and again when he discovered the 'bothersome blotter' revealing that Cosette was not his alone. The problem could be translated into banal domestic terms nowadays as a decision grandparents may have to make between indulging their affection for children by moving in and crowding them out and respecting their right to get on with their lives on their own. But those are not the terms Hugo uses to analyse a crossroads dramatically exacerbated by the past and present circumstances of Jean Valjean. Accumulation and gradation structure the question: 'What would he do? Would he impose himself . . . Would he remain the kind of father he had been up to now? Would he continue to say nothing? . . . Would he be destiny's sinister mute alongside these two happy creatures?' (V.6.iv, 1,239). The first abstract formulation Hugo gives of this inner struggle is 'the fight between our selfishness and our duty'. He then casts Valjean's deliberations as a virtual fistfight between a man and 'the sacred shadow', 'the inexorable', 'the invisible', which he also calls 'conscience'. The hero lies prostrate for twelve hours (with arms outstretched, like a man taken down from a cross) grappling with the dilemma while 'his mind slithered and soared, now like the hydra, now like the eagle' (1,241). If you'd seen him lying rigid like that, you might have thought he was dead, but suddenly he shuddered convulsively, and you could see he was alive.

Hugo then takes a liberty with grammar to produce an eerie formula that sticks in every reader's mind. To express the passive voice – to say 'it could be seen' – French typically uses the active voice with an all-purpose impersonal pronoun, *on*, similar to 'one' in English: *on voit*, 'one sees', which I've translated as 'you could see' at the end of the last paragraph. French *on* isn't anybody, it's just a formal convenience, but Hugo treats it as if it referred to a real subject of the verb 'to see'. He therefore asks, almost like a child, 'Qui? On?' ('Who's that? Who is "One"?') and gives an answer that has no precedent in grown-up prose: 'Le On qui est dans les ténèbres' ('The "One" who is in the shadows'). The upper-case O leaves you in no doubt that this is a way of naming God. In that case, given the issue and the way it has been articulated up to this point, Hugo's God is an externalization of moral conscience and a guide to what duty is – unless it is the other way round. In addition, the 'seeing eye in the shadows' is a perfectly Romantic ghost, and quite possibly the ghost of Bishop Myriel. Possession, emulation, duty, conscience and the divine are all wrapped up in the new use Hugo found for the lowliest function word the French language has.

ɡ

Hollywood and Broadway have grasped *Les Misérables* in a different way, setting duty and conscience against each other, not on parallel tracks. To simplify these simplifications: where Valjean hears the voice of conscience, Javert hears duty, which leads him not to a lesser good, but to evil. For Hugo, however, the policeman was not bad, but blind.

As a child of convicts who becomes an inspector of the Paris police, Javert is an inspiring example of the 'careers based on merit' that Napoleon I's institutional reforms were designed to promote. His sense of honour is exemplary: when he realizes (incorrectly) that he has denounced Madeleine unjustly, he insists on being dismissed from his post. His devotion to duty is not what sets him against Valjean. How could it be, when Valjean justifies the most serious choices he makes by the same value, *duty*? The sleuth's tragic flaw is something else.

Javert's dogged persistence can be 'translated' into our own pet hates – bureaucratic myopia, mindless literalism, mental rigidity –

but his meaning is broader than any of these. Javert's limited vision of the social sphere is both a product and a pillar of the society he strives to uphold. For him, there are two and only two kinds of person, the well-to-do and the ne'er-do-well. Javert sees these classes as fundamentally incompatible, and his job is to keep them apart. A bourgeois lout like Bamatabois must be in the right because he belongs to the righteous class, and a streetwalker like Fantine must be in the wrong. Javert's attitudes and actions exploit and also redouble the social injustice that legal justice served to maintain under the monarchy after 1815. The figure of Javert is marginal to the philosophical and religious dimensions of Les Misérables, but near the heart of its social and political critique. Equality is mocked when laws are understood and implemented in terms of social class. Justice is only served if the misérables are treated as equal members of the human race.

Javert's too-simple understanding of duty is contradicted by the noble behaviour of Valjean, who lets the police spy go free instead of shooting him dead. A member of the underclass behaving with generosity shatters Javert's view of the world. Unable to grasp how he could reconcile himself to the existence of a man whose actions have turned his world upside down, he throws himself into the Seine. At this late stage in the narrative of Les Misérables, psychological plausibility is less vital than the symbolic meaning of the act: those who refuse reconciliation between social classes in the name of law and order are swept away. Moral progress cannot be realized as long as Javert's two-part vision of humanity persists.

The moral compass of Les Misérables thus spreads far beyond the history, geography, politics and economics of the world in which its story is set. The novel achieves the extraordinary feat of being at the same time an intricately realistic portrait of a specific place and time, a dramatic page-turner with masterful moments of theatrical suspense and surprise, an encyclopedia of facts and ideas and an easily understood demonstration of generous moral principles that we could do far worse than apply to our own lives.

Epilogue: Journey's End

On 14 June 1862 Victor Hugo corrected the last galley of the last volume of *Les Misérables* and dispatched it to Brussels. He could now switch to a less demanding routine.

He would rise at dawn and swallow two raw eggs with his coffee. In the morning he stood in his Crystal Palace, writing until eleven, then took a bath in cold water on the roof. Lunch with visitors, afternoons devoted to a variety of tasks, including home improvement and a swim in the sea, an evening meal, and long conversations into the night.

He was always doing something with his hands. One of his diversions was to rescue the last quills he'd used to write and correct *Les Misérables*. He sewed them with twine on to a stiff paper backing and had the montage framed.

Hugo had been confined to Hauteville House for nine months, and what he'd done in that time almost beggars belief. He'd turned a single-copy manuscript of a still unfinished work into the greatest publishing sensation of his age. Not single-handedly – Juliette Drouet, Julie Chenay and Victoire Estasse, Albert Lacroix and Eugène Verboekhoven, Pagnerre and the printer Claye, François-Victor and Charles had played indispensible roles, and a whole team of supporters, headed by Adèle, with Auguste Vacquerie, Paul Meurice and Noël Parfait beside her, had laboured to smooth the work's path to success. All the same, it was his book. And now it was done.

On 21 July, the feast of Saint-Victor and thus Hugo's name-day, loyal Lacroix arrived in Guernsey to pay his respects and talk business about the next books of Hugo's that he wanted to bring out. A week later, writer and publisher set off on the return journey together, accompanied by Juliette. The sea was calm, the sun was bright, and the boat ride to Southampton sheer pleasure. On to London to see the real Crystal Palace at Sydenham, and then to Brussels to stay with Lacroix before taking Juliette on another jaunt by train, riverboat and horse-drawn buggy through the Ardennes and other parts of the Low Countries that they loved so much. He got back to Brussels in mid-September for the banquet that Lacroix was going to host in his own lavish home, which sat alongside and on top of his great printing works at 2, Impasse du Parc.

The *Banquet des Misérables*, held on 16 September, from 6:30 p.m. until dawn next day, must be the biggest book bash in history. There were eighty guests, from Belgium, France, Spain, Sweden, England and Italy: friends and relatives of the publisher and author, local and foreign journalists, the speaker of the Belgian Parliament and the burgomaster of Brussels, and acquaintances who didn't yet know they were the great-uncle of Marguerite Yourcenar and the grand-father of the publisher of *Tintin*. All received a signed photograph of Victor Hugo as a souvenir and were photographed in their turn before entering the dining room.[56]

Adèle declined the invitation on health grounds, but Juliette crept into the hall and hid behind a curtain, 'like Polonius behind the arras', to watch her dear great man enjoy this moment of glory. It was still the nineteenth century.

The horseshoe table was laid with such an amount of silver and porcelain that it struck one visitor as a 'fairy palace, or the gold-room of King Charlemagne'. With eighty place settings and chairs the dining room was so crowded that the inward-opening windows had to stay shut. To make the atmosphere breathable in a room that filled up with a lot of hot air, Lacroix had some of the windows smashed, like the aristocratic host of the Vaubyessard Ball that Emma Bovary attends.

I'll skip the speeches, and readers with delicate stomachs might want to skip what follows. For the record, here are all the dishes that the author of *Les Misérables* could have picked at while well-wishers and hangers-on praised to the skies his political positions, his moral example and his art.

Soupe de queue de boeuf
(Oxtail soup)
Petites bouchées crevettes
(Shrimp vol-au-vent)
Saumon sauce genevoise
(Salmon in fish-head sauce)
Filet de boeuf béarnaise
(Beef filet with egg-and-butter sauce)
Jambon de Bayonne aux petits pois
(Gammon and peas)
Chapons de Breda à la Toulouse
(Poached chicken breasts in mushroom sauce)
Canard aux olives
(Duck with olives)
Chaud-froid de bécassines aux truffes
(Snipe in cream sauce with truffles)
Mayonnaise de homards
(Lobster mayonnaise)
Sorbet à l'ananas
(Pineapple sorbet)

*

Champignons à la provençale
(Mushrooms with garlic and parsley)
Fonds d'artichauts à l'italienne
(Artichoke hearts in lemon and vinegar)
Perdreaux truffés
(Young partridge stuffed with truffles)
Ortolans bardés
(Songbirds wrapped in bacon)
Foie gras
(Goose Liver)
Écrevisses de la Meuse
(Locally sourced crayfish)
Pêches à la Condé
(Rice cake with peaches)
Macédoine de fruits au marasquin
(Diced fruit in Maraschino)
Glaces
Fruits
Desserts

The first edition of *Les Misérables* is remarkably clean. Despite the lunatic logistics of dispatching and receiving every page by means of three trains and two ships, only a few typos got through, and the text you read today is almost identical to the one Hugo first held in his hands in July 1862. With one big exception, and it takes us back to the start.

Before dawn on 19 June 1815, a camp-following scavenger lifts the watch and the purse from what he takes to be a corpse in the gulley of Ohain. The scavenger is Thénardier, and the corpse belongs to the father of Marius. But the soldier is not quite dead. He awakes from his faint to thank a man who has the minimal decency to help him rise from the grave. In the manuscript, on the first and second proofs and in the first edition, Colonel Georges Pontmercy *tells Thénardier his name*.

Years later, at Boulevard de l'Hôpital, the man masquerading as Jondrette learns the name of his neighbour, Marius Pontmercy, but does not recognize it. Had he known it, he would certainly have tried to claim a reward for having 'rescued' the young man's father. Hugo realized that his plot was incoherent at this point a few weeks after the novel was out, and he asked Lacroix to correct a key passage in III.8.xx. Where in the first edition Thénardier says, 'I was at Waterloo, I was! I saved a general called Comte de Pontmercy,' later editions have 'Comte somebody-or-other' together with an explanatory insertion straight after: 'He told me his name but his damned voice was so weak I didn't hear. All I heard was *"merci"*' (III.8.xx, 717).

By creating asymmetry in knowledge between the crook and the spy looking through the gap in the plasterwork, Hugo fixed a huge glitch in the moral drama of the master-scene in Boulevard de l'Hôpital.

Are there other slips that he missed? A few. But I don't want to end this book with a list of minor blunders in the all-conquering novel of the nineteenth century. If you do want to know what they are, I invite you to read *Les Misérables* again rather slowly and to enter all the characters' names with the dates and locations of their actions on a chart, which will probably need to be the size of a wall. You will find far more echoes and connections that you hadn't noticed before than glitches and mistakes. *Les Misérables* is very tightly knit.

Albert Lacroix's performance as publisher and financier was flawless. He paid as he had promised: 125,000 francs on 2 December 1861; 60,000 francs on 23 February 1862; 55,000 francs on 17 June; and 60,000 francs for translation rights in a separate transaction. *Les Misérables* earned it all back in a matter of weeks, enabling Lacroix to settle his account with the Oppenheim Bank without over-running his time or his credit limit. He brought out Adèle's memoir of Victor Hugo in spring 1863 and then moved his main base of operation to Paris, with branch offices in Livorno and Leipzig. He became a big shot in international publishing whilst remaining a remarkably successful talent-spotter. He published the first full edition of Lautréamont's *Les Chants de Maldoror* (*The Songs of Maldoror*), a foundational work in the transformation of French poetry; *Thérèse Raquin*, by a still unknown novelist called Émile Zola; and *Thyl Eulenspiegel* by Charles de Coster, an instant bestseller which became the first real classic of Belgian literature in the French language. But his luck ran out within a decade. He quarrelled with Hugo and then lost most of his capital in unwise investments in French property. In the 1870s, his still famous firm was a shadow of its former self.

Hugo's daughter Adèle II absconded in 1863 in search of her fantasy lover Pinson. She wandered around the New World for several years, suffered a mental breakdown and was repatriated from Barbados in 1872. She spent the rest of her days in an institution and died in 1915. Her story was adapted for the screen by François Truffaut in *L'Histoire d'Adèle H.*

Charles Hugo left Guernsey in 1864 to settle in Brussels, where he married and started a family of his own. In January 1865, François-Victor also left Hauteville House for good. His mother accompanied him to Brussels and stayed there two years. Hugo stayed on the island with Juliette Drouet beside him. 'I had to choose between my family and my work, between happiness and duty,' Hugo said about these years of (purely relative) solitude. But I do not think he was insincere or had his tongue near his cheek when he said: 'I chose duty. That is the law of my life.'[57] It is the 'law' of *Les Misérables*.

Adèle died in Brussels in 1868. Victor accompanied her coffin to the French border but did not cross it. He had said he would not return to France while it was ruled by Louis-Napoléon and he kept his word. Juliette Drouet lived a longer life and passed away in Paris in 1883.

In 1870, Louis-Napoléon foolishly declared war on Prussia, and his armies were quickly defeated and forced to surrender at Sedan. The hated Second Empire came to an inglorious end, and Victor Hugo immediately returned to Paris via Brussels, with a retinue and baggage train that filled nine railway carriages. That winter, Paris was under siege and desperately short of food. In the spring of 1871, left-wing socialists seized power and turned the city into a commune. The reconstituted French army took six weeks to put the Commune down and exacted bloodthirsty revenge. Almost like the British royal family during the Blitz, Hugo remained steadfast in his loyalty to the city during the siege and the Commune. *L'Année Terrible*, his account of the events of 1870–71, remains a precious historical source.

Hugo never sold Hauteville House, and he took long breaks in Guernsey throughout the 1870s. His *Toilers of the Sea* is a wonderful homage to the Channel Islands. Its long introduction, though not always factually correct, remains an enchanting portrait of Normandy-in-the-Sea.

Hugo's son Charles died of a heart attack in 1871, at the age of forty-four. His brother François-Victor died two years later.

Hugo continued to write fiction and verse into old age and was never short of an opinion on national and international affairs. He became almost a tutelary deity as the Third Republic put into practice some of his key ideas – chief among them, universal male suffrage and universal primary education. In 1883, he visited the foundry works of the sculptor Bartholdi and admired the huge new statue in course of assembly, soon to be dismantled and shipped to the United States. It was called *Liberty*.

The joy of Hugo's last years were Charles's two children, Jeanne and Georges. It is for them that he wrote one of his best-loved poetry collections, *The Art of Being a Grandfather* (1877).

He died in 1885 at the age of eighty-three, having outlived his sons, his wife, his lover and almost every man of his own generation.

Around two million people took part in the procession accompanying his mortal remains to the Panthéon. Never before and never since has such a large crowd been seen in Paris. The entire city turned out to honour the playwright, the poet, the reformer and campaigner, but the vast mass of people following his hearse were paying homage to the beloved author of *Les Misérables*.

Statue of Victor Hugo (1913), by Jean Boucher. Candie Gardens,
St Peter Port, Guernsey

France in the Nineteenth Century: A Time Line

1789	Fall of the Bastille. The French Revolution begins
1791	Declaration of the Rights of Man
1792	Execution of King Louis XVI. The First Republic
1793–4	Mass public executions of real and supposed opponents of the revolutionary regime ('The Terror')
1796	Napoleon Bonaparte wins the Battle of Montenotte
1799	Napoleon Bonaparte becomes First Consul
1802	Reform of the penal code
	Birth of Victor Hugo
1803	Reform of the currency system
1804	Bonaparte crowned Emperor Napoleon I
	The First Empire
1805	Battle of Austerlitz
1812	Napoleon's 'Great Army' takes Moscow
1813	The Great Army retreats from Russia
1814	Napoleon abdicates and is exiled to Elba
	Louis XVIII becomes King
	The First Restoration
1815	Napoleon escapes from Elba and raises an army
	The One Hundred Days
	19 June: Battle of Waterloo
	France occupied by foreign troops, and Louis XVIII resumes the throne
	The Second Restoration
1823	France invades Spain
1824	Charles X succeeds Louis XVIII
1825	Charles X crowned at Rheims
1830	France seizes Algiers

The July Revolution ('the three glorious days') puts Charles X to flight

Louis-Philippe d'Orléans accedes to the throne

The July Monarchy

1832   June: a small uprising in Paris is put down in a day

1837   First railway in France

1840   Louis Daguerre makes the first photographic image

1848   February: an uprising deposes Louis-Philippe

The Second Republic

June: popular riots are put down with great violence

November: Louis-Napoléon Bonaparte, the nephew of Napoleon I, elected president of the Republic

1851   2 December: Louis-Napoléon abolishes parliament and seizes full control

1852   Louis-Napoléon crowned Emperor Napoleon III

The Second Empire

1856   Crimean War, fought by Britain and France against Russia

1861   Nice and Savoy incorporated into the French state by plebiscite

1862   Publication of *Les Misérables*

1864   Red Cross founded in Geneva

1870   Franco-Prussian War. Louis-Napoléon abdicates. Siege of Paris

1871   The Commune

1875   Formal inauguration of the Third Republic, a parliamentary democracy with universal male suffrage that survived until 1940

1877   Obligatory universal free primary education introduced in France

1885   Death of Victor Hugo

1895   Louis and Auguste Lumière capture the moving image on film

Acknowledgements

My thanks go first of all to learned scholars in France and elsewhere who have revealed so much about the composition, meaning and transmission of *Les Misérables*, chief amongst them René Journet, Bernard Leuilliot, Guy Robert and Guy Rosa. My great debt to Hugo's biographers, Graham Robb and Jean-Marc Hovasse, is apparent from the frequent appearance of their names in the notes where (barring forgetfulness on my part) I have acknowledged all the sources drawn on in this book.

I also owe many precious facts and ideas to old and new friends, to colleagues and to current and former students at Princeton and elsewhere, and I hope I have not omitted any of them from the following list: Jeffrey Angles, David Bell, Natalie Berkman, Guy de Boeck, Jessica Christy, Peter Cogman, Denis Feeney, Michaël Ferrier, Harold James, Michael Jennings, Robert Kaufman, Pierre László, Tuo Liu, Simone Marchesi, Pierre Masson, Amanda Mazur, Serguei Oushakine, Richard Register, Patrick Schwemmer, Bradley Stephens, Michael Wachtel and Liesl Yamaguchi.

Special thanks go to Ilona Morison for the hike that started me off on this journey, and to Pascale Voilley, who put up with my trudging on to the end.

I am tremendously grateful to my agent, Rebecca Carter, and to her predecessor at Janklow & Nesbitt, Claire Conrad, and also to the impressive team of copy-editors, map makers, typographers and cover designers at Penguin Books who have made this book what it is. I wish to thank most of all my editor, Helen Conford, whose wise advice and unstinting attention removed many blemishes from earlier drafts. All remaining infelicities are undoubtedly my own.

Works Cited

By Victor Hugo

Actes et Paroles. I. – Avant l'Exil, vol. 43 of *Œuvres complètes* (Paris: Hetzel, 1880–89).

Choses vues. Souvenirs, journaux, cahiers, 1830–1885, ed. Hubert Juin, revised edn (Paris: Gallimard, 2002).

Claude Gueux (1834), ed. P. Savey-Casard (Paris: Presses universitaires de France, 1956).

Les Contemplations (1856), ed. Léon Cellier (Paris: Garnier, 1969).

Correspondance (Paris: Albin Michel, 1950).

Le Dernier Jour d'un condamné (1829), ed. Roger Borderie (Paris: Folio Classique, 1970).

Lettres à Juliette Drouet, ed. Jean Gaudon (Paris: Pauvert, 1964).

Les Misérables, ed. Maurice Allem (Paris: Gallimard, 'Bibliothèque de la Pléïade', 1951).

Les Misérables, ed. Marius-François Guyard (Paris: Garnier, 1963).

Œuvres complètes (Paris: Édition de l'Imprimerie nationale, 1909).

Œuvres complètes, chronological edition, ed. Jean Massin (Paris: Club français du livre, 1967–70).

Œuvres complètes (Paris: Laffont, Collection Bouquins, 1985).

Toute la lyre (Paris: Hetzel, 1888).

By Members of Hugo's Immediate Entourage

Hugo, Adèle, *Victor Hugo raconté par Adèle Hugo*, ed. Evelyne Blewer et al. (Paris: Plon, 1985).

Hugo, Adèle (Adèle II), *Journal*, ed. Frances Vernor Guille (Paris: Minard, 1968 (vol. 1), 1971 (vol. 2), 1984 (vol. 3)).

Hugo, Charles, *Les Misérables. Drame* (Brussels: Lacroix et Verboekhoven, 1863).

Hugo, Charles, *Les Hommes de l'Exil* (Paris: Lemerre, 1875).

Parfait, Noël, *L'Aurore d'un beau jour: Épisodes des 5 et 6 juin 1832* (Paris: Bousquet, 1833).

Vacquerie, Auguste, *Profils et grimaces* (Paris: Pagnerre, 1854).

By Others

Anon. *Les Éditeurs belges de Victor Hugo et le Banquet des* Misérables, catalogue of the exhibition 'Lacroix et Verboekhoven', Musée Wellington à Waterloo, 1962 (Brussels: Crédit communal, 1962).

Bach, Max, 'Critique et politique: La Réception des *Misérables* en 1862', *PMLA* 77.5 (1962), pp. 595–608.

Balzac, Honoré de, *La Comédie humaine*, ed. Pierre-Georges Castex (Paris: Gallimard, Bibliothèque de la Pléiade, 1976).

Balzac, Honoré de, *Lettres à Madame Hanska*, ed. Roger Pierrot (Paris: Delta, 1967).

Balzac, Honoré de, *Old Goriot* (1835), trans. Marion Ayton Crawford (London: Penguin, 1972).

Baudelaire, Charles, *Correspondance*, ed. Claude Pichois (Paris: Gallimard, 1973).

Baudelaire, Charles, *Œuvres complètes*, ed. Claude Pichois (Paris: Gallimard, 1975).

Behr, Edward, *Les Misérables. History in the Making* (New York: Arcade, 1989).

Bellos, David, 'An Icon of 1830: Interpreting Delacroix's *Liberty Guiding the People*', in Martina Lauster and Günther Oesterle (eds.), *Vormärzliteratur in europäischer Perspektive* 2 (Bielefeld: Aisthesis Verlag, 1997), pp. 251–63.

Bellos, David, 'Momo et *les Misérables*', in Julien Roumette (ed.), *Les Voix de Romain Gary* (Paris: Champion, 2016).

Bellos, David, 'Sounding Out *Les Misérables*', *Dix-Neuf Journal* 20.3 (2016).

Blix, Göran, 'Le Livre des passants: l'héroïsm obscur dans *Les Misérables*', *Revue des sciences humaines* 302.2 (2011), pp. 63–75.

Bouchet, Thomas, *Le Roi et les barricades. Une histoire des 5 et 6 juin 1832* (Paris: Seli Arslan, 2000).

Brombert, Victor, *Victor Hugo and the Visionary Novel* (Cambridge, MA: Harvard University Press, 1984).

Brunet, Étienne, *Le Vocabulaire de Victor Hugo*, 3 vols. (Paris: Champion, 1988).

Chevalier, Louis, *Laboring Classes and Dangerous Classes in Paris during the First Half of the Nineteenth Century*, trans. Frank Jellinek (New York: Howard Fertig, 1973).

De Gérando, Joseph-Marie, *Le Visiteur du pauvre* (Paris: L. Colas, 1820).

Descotes, Maurice, *Victor Hugo et Waterloo*, Archives Victor Hugo 10 (Paris: Minard, 1984).

Dickens, Charles, *Letters of Charles Dickens*, vol. V, ed. Graham Storey and K. J. Fielding (Oxford: Oxford University Press, 1981).

Dickens, Charles, *The Public Readings*, ed. Philip Collins (Oxford: Clarendon Press, 1975).

Dickens, Charles, *Dealings with the Firm of Dombey and Son, Wholesale, Retail and for Exportation* (1848) (Oxford: Oxford University Press, 'The Works of Charles Dickens', 1907).

Dickens, Charles, *The Personal History of David Copperfield* (1850) (London: Dutton, 'Everyman's Library', 1907).

Dickens, Charles, *Great Expectations* (1861), ed. Kenneth Hayens (London: Collins, 1953).

Dumas, Alexandre, *Correspondances: deux cent lettres pour un bicentenaire* (Port-Marly: Société des Amis d'Alexandre Dumas, 2002).

Edwards, G. B., *The Book of Ebenezer Le Page* (1981) (New York: New York Review Classics, 2012).

Flaubert, Gustave, *Correspondance*, ed. Jean Bruneau (Paris: Gallimard, 1973).

Galbeau, Patrice, *La Vie entre les lignes*, five-part interview with Romain Gary broadcast by France-Culture between September and December 1973.

Gamel, Mireille, and Michel Serceau, *Le Victor Hugo des cinéastes* (CinémAction, issue 119) (Paris: Corlet, 2005).

Gary, Romain, *La Nuit sera calme* (1974) (Paris: Folio, 1980).

Gaudon, Jean, 'Note sur l'origine de Fantine', *Bulletin de la Faculté des Lettres de Strasbourg* (April 1964).

Gillery, Francis and François Rivière (eds.), *Je me suis raconté des histoires très tôt. Propos inédits de Frédéric Dard* (Paris: Fleuve noir, 2011).

Gogol, Nikolai, *The Overcoat* (1832), in *The Collected Tales and Plays of Nikolai Gogol*, trans. Constance Garnett (revised) (New York: Pantheon, 1964).

Grossman, Kathryn, *Figuring Transcendence in* Les Misérables: *Hugo's Romantic Sublime* (Carbondale: Southern Illinois University Press, 1994).

Grossman, Kathryn and Bradley Stephens (eds.), *Les Misérables and Its Afterlives* (Farnham: Ashgate, 2015).

Gueslin, André, *Gens pauvres, pauvres gens dans la France du XIXe siècle* (Paris: Aubier, 1998).

Hadjinicolaou, Nicos, '*La Liberté guidant le peuple* de Delacroix devant son premier public', *Actes de la recherche en sciences sociales* 28 (1979), pp. 3–26.

Halliday, M. A. K., 'Anti-Languages', *American Anthropologist* 78.3 (1976), pp. 570–84.

Heine, Heinrich, *Französische Zustände* (Leipzig, 1833); French edition, *De la France* (Paris: Renduel, 1833).

Himmelfarb, Gertrude, *Alexis de Tocqueville's Memoir on Pauperism* (London: Civitas, 1997).

Himmelfarb, Gertrude, *The Idea of Poverty. England in the Early Industrial Age* (New York: Knopf, 1984).

Hoffheimer, Michael, 'Copyright, Competition, and the First English-Language Translations of *Les Misérables*', *Marquette Intellectual Property Law Review* 17.2 (2013), pp. 163–90.

Hoffheimer, Michael, 'Jean Valjean's Nightmare: Rehabilitation and Redemption in *Les Misérables*', *McGeorge Law Review* 43 (2012), pp. 169–98.

Hoffmann, Léon-François, 'Victor Hugo, les noirs et l'esclavage', *Francofonia* 16 (1996), pp. 74–90.

Hovasse, Jean-Marc, *Victor Hugo*, vol. II: *Pendant l'exil I. 1851–1864* (Paris: Fayard, 2008).

Huard, Georges, 'Le Petit-Picpus des *Misérables* et les informatrices de Hugo', *Revue d'Histoire littéraire de la France* 60.3 (1960), pp. 345–87.

James, A. R. W., 'Waterloo sans Cambronne ou les méfaits de Lascelles Wraxall', in A. R. W. James (ed.), *Victor Hugo et la Grande-Bretagne* (Liverpool: Francis Cairns, 1986), pp. 183–201.

Jean, Raymond, *Mademoiselle Bovary* (Arles: Actes Sud, 1991).

Journet, René and Guy Robert, *Le Manuscrit des* Misérables (Paris: Les Belles Lettres, 1963).

Laforgue, Pierre, *Gavroche*. Études sur *Les Misérables* (Paris: SEDES, 1994).

Langlois, Gauthier, 'Enquête sur une lettre mystérieuse. Contribution à l'histoire d'une célèbre mystification littéraire', https://paratge.wordpress.com/2014/12/16/, accessed 18 July 2016.

László, Pierre, *Copal benjoin colophane* (Paris: Le Pommier, 2007).

Leuilliot, Bernard, 'Présentation de Jean Valjean', in *Hommage à Victor Hugo* (Strasbourg, 1962), pp. 51–67.

Leuilliot, Bernard, *Victor Hugo publie les* Misérables. *Correspondance avec Albert Lacroix, 1861–1862* (Paris: Klincksieck, 1970).

Martin-Dupont, N., *Victor Hugo anecdotique* (Paris: Storck, 1904).

Marx, Karl, *Manifesto of the Communist Party*, authorized English translation edited and annotated by Frederick Engels (London: Reeves, 1888).

Mérimée, Prosper, *Correspondance Générale*, ed. Maurice Parturier (Paris: Le Divan, 1957).

Miete, Graeme Marett, *A History of the Telegraph in Jersey, 1858–1940*, revised edn, 2009, available at http://www.marett.org/telecom/telegraph.pdf, accessed 18 July 2016.

Monod, Sylvère, 'Les Premiers Traducteurs français de Dickens', *Romantisme* 106 (1999), pp. 119–28.

Nabet, Jean-Claude and Guy Rosa, 'L'Argent des *Misérables*', *Romantisme* 40 (1983), pp. 87–114.

Neri, Antonio, Christopher Merret and Johannes Kunckel, *L'Art de la verrerie* (Paris, 1752).

Olivier, Juste, *Paris en 1830. Journal* (Paris: Mercure de France, 1951).

Paris, Gaston, '*Ti*, signe d'interrogation', in *Mélanges linguistiques* (Paris: Champion, 1909), pp. 276–85.

Parménie, A., with C. Bonnier de la Chapelle, *Histoire d'un éditeur et de ses auteurs. P.-J. Hetzel (Stahl)* (Paris: Albin Michel, 1953).

Pickett, La Salle Corbell, *Pickett and His Men* (Atlanta, GA: Foote and Davies, 1899).

Pierrot, Roger, 'Quelques contrats d'édition de Balzac', *Bulletin d'informations de l'A.B.F.* (1957), pp. 19–21.

Plutarch, *Dialogue on Love*, in *Moralia*, Loeb Classical Library (Cambridge, MA: Harvard University Press, 1961), vol. 9.

Robb, Graham, *Victor Hugo. A Biography* (New York: Norton, 1997).

Robespierre, Maximilien, *Œuvres*, ed. Marc Bouloiseau and Albert Soboul (Paris: Presses Universitaires de France, 1967).

Sainéan, Lazar, *Le Langage parisien au XIXe siècle* (Paris: Boccard, 1920).

Sartorius, Francis, 'L'Éditeur Albert Lacroix', in *Les Éditeurs belges de Victor Hugo* (Brussels: Crédit Communal, 1986).

Sokologorsky, Irène, 'Victor Hugo et le XIXe siècle russe', in *Idéologies hugoliennes*, ed. Anne-Marie Amiot (Nice: Serre, 1985), pp. 191–8.

Solntsev, N., '*Les Misérables* en Russie et en URSS', *Europe* 394 (1962), pp. 197–200.

Stapfer, Paul, *Victor Hugo à Guernesey* (Paris, 1905).

Stevens, Philip, *Victor Hugo in Jersey* (Chichester: Phillimore, 2002).

Stiles, Robert, *Four Years Under Marse Robert* (Washington, DC: Neale, 1903).

Stoppard, Tom, *Rosencrantz and Guildenstern Are Dead* (London: Faber, 1967).

Takako, Inuki, *Aolette na uta* (Tokyo: Bunkasha Comics, 2000).

Thiesse, Anne-Marie, 'Écrivain/Public: Les Mystères de la communication littéraire', *Europe* 643 (1982), pp. 36–46.

Tolstoy, Lev Nikolaevich, 'Episkop Miriel', in *Polnoe Sobranie Sochinenii* (Moscow, 1928–58), vol. 42, pp. 278–84.

Tomalin, Claire, *Charles Dickens. A Life* (London: Penguin, 2011).

Vachon, Stéphane, *Les Travaux et les jours d'Honoré de Balzac* (Paris: Presses du CNRS, 1992).

Vargas Llosa, Mario, *The Temptation of the Impossible, Victor Hugo and* Les Misérables, trans. John King (Princeton: Princeton University Press, 2007).

Works Cited

Vaux, James Hardy, 'A Vocabulary of the Flash Language' (1812), in Noel McLachlan (ed.), *The Memoirs of James Hardy Vaux* (London: Heinemann, 1964), pp. 219–80.

Vidocq, Eugène-François, *Mémoires* (Paris: Tenon, 1828).

Woollen, Geoff, 'Brand *Loyauté* in Balzac Criticism', *French Studies Bulletin* 59 (1996), pp. 11–13.

Notes

Author's Note

1 *William Shakespeare*, quoted in Leuilliot, 'Présentation', p. 57.

Introduction: The Journey of Les Misérables

1 Stevens, *Victor Hugo in Jersey*, pp. 123–5.
2 According to Langlois, 'Enquête sur une lettre mystérieuse', Hugo was one among many recipients of begging letters from a 'Ludovic Picard', who also wrote as 'Delphine de Saint-Aignan'.

Part One: Crimes and Punishments

1 *Choses vues*, pp. 114–16; Gaudon, *Bulletin*, and Adèle Hugo, *Victor Hugo raconté par Adèle Hugo*, p. 840.
2 I.5.xii, 175. See page xi above for an explanation of references to the text.
3 *Choses vues*, pp. 198–9.
4 To convert francs into *sous* and vice versa, see p. 60 below.
5 *Choses vues*, p. 413.
6 Quoted in Gueslin, *Gens pauvres*, p. 148.
7 I.1.ii, 9, 11.
8 III.8.ix, 681.
9 Himmelfarb, *Tocqueville*.
10 Himmelfarb, *Idea of Poverty*, p. 187.
11 Monod, 'Les Premiers Traducteurs', gives full details.
12 Quoted in Behr, *Les Misérables*, p. 50.
13 Tomalin, *Charles Dickens*, p. 190.

14 Thiesse, 'Ecrivain/Public'.

15 Balzac, *La Comédie humaine*, vol. 1, p. 12.

16 Balzac, *Lettres à Mme Hanska*, vol. 3, p. 216.

17 *Contemplations*, p. 567, attributed to the unpublished manuscript of the diary of Adèle II.

18 I.3.viii, 131.

19 *Contemplations*, p. 567.

20 Olivier, *Paris en 1830*, pp. 65, 123.

21 Hugo, *Le Dernier Jour*, p. 301.

22 V.3.viii, 813–20.

23 *Claude Gueux*, p. 123.

24 I.2.vii, 86–8.

25 Journet and Robert, *Le Manuscrit des* Misérables, p. 19.

26 See II.3.iv, 350.

27 See V.1.xiv, 1,088.

28 *Choses vues*, p. 247; Huard, 'Le Petit-Picpus', p. 356; II.5.v, 415.

29 Adèle Hugo, *Victor Hugo raconté par Adèle Hugo*, 283–4. The version of Adèle's memoir published in 1863 contains an abridged version of the Joly anecdote in chapter 26.

30 *Œuvres completes*, ed. Massin, vol. 11, p. 1,016.

31 An address already known to readers of Balzac: the Pension Vauquer, the main location of *Old Goriot*, is located right next door.

32 *Choses vues*, p. 516.

33 *Choses vues*, p. 517.

34 *Choses vues*, p. 522–3.

35 Hoffmann treats this as a reflection of Hugo's views, not as an ironical observation about race.

36 *Choses vues*, p. 551 (May 1848).

37 Voting tallies from Robb, *Victor Hugo*, p. 267.

38 *Choses vues*, p. 566.

39 *Choses vues*, p. 566.

40 *Choses vues*, p. 603.

41 The full transcript of Hugo's intervention is in *Actes et Paroles*, p. 204.

42 *Actes et paroles*, 17 July 1851.

43 See I.2.iii, 73.

44 Heine, *Französische Zustände*, chapter 12, dated 8 June 1832; *De la France* omits this and several other sections.

45 IV.12.v, 993.

46 IV.14.ii, 1,017, 1,019.

47 *Choses vues*, p. 536.

48 This does not include familiar or slang terms, such as those used by Éponine at III.8.iv, 670.

49 I.2.xiii, 101.

50 III.8.xix, 711; many translations mistakenly give the figure of 3,000 francs.

51 Some translators skip the complication by expressing the sum in francs twenty pages too early.

52 See III.4.vi, 612 for Hugo's explanation.

53 See II.3.vi, 357 for Louis XVIII and V.6.i, 1,221 for the wedding coach.

54 III.3.vii, 577.

55 I.1.iii, 14.

56 I.2.i, 60.

Part Two: Treasure Islands

1 I.4.i, 141.

2 Thénardier's debts are tracked at I.4.i, 142, II.3.ii, 347 and IV.6.i, 845.

3 László, *Copal benjoin colophane*.

4 Neri et al., *L'Art de la verrerie*, p. 378.

5 See I.5.i, 148.

6 V.9.v.

7 I.5.ii, 148; II.2.iii, 335.

8 Fauchelevent's souvenir is reproduced in facsimile on II.8.ix, 512; for Grantaire's *assignat*, see IV.1.vi, 770.

9 Balzac, *Old Goriot*, p. 136.

10 Hovasse, *Victor Hugo*, vol. 2, p. 611.

11 *Toute la lyre*, vol. 5, p. 16.

12 *Œuvres complètes*, ed. Massin, vol. 9, p. 1,217.

13 Séance of 15 September 1853, quoted in Hovasse, *Victor Hugo*, vol. 2, p. 244.

14 Hovasse, *Victor Hugo*, vol. 2, p. 387, quoting Hugo's diary for 2 December 1855.

15 Juliette Drouet to Victor Hugo, 25 April 1860, quoted in Hovasse, *Victor Hugo*, vol. 2, p. 614.

16 At school in Madrid his mother got him off religious observances on the fake grounds that he was Protestant. Adèle Hugo, *Victor Hugo raconté par Adèle Hugo*, p. 228.

17 Martin-Dupont, *Victor Hugo anecdotique*, p. 22.

18 Adapted from Adèle II, *Journal*, vol. 3, pp. 283–4.

19 Martin-Dupont, *Victor Hugo anecdotique*, p. 162.

20 See II.3.ii, 345.

21 Martin-Dupont, *Victor Hugo anecdotique*, p. 85.

22 Baron Francis de Miollis, *L'Union*, 28 April 1862, quoted in Leuilliot, 'Présentation', p. 53.

23 Dickens, *Dombey*, p. 949.

24 V.6.ii, 1,227.

25 Robespierre, *Œuvres*, vol. 10, p. 196.

26 *Contemplations*, VI.8, dated December 1846, but written in December 1854.

27 The medical term used in English at the time was *anthrax*; in French it was called *charbon*, or 'coal'. The bacillus was first identified in 1875 by Robert Koch.

28 III.5.iv, 623.

29 The changes in the hero's name are explained on pp. 119–20 below.

30 The handwriting can be read several ways; this is what makes best sense to me.

31 *Les Misérables*, ed. Guyard, vol. 2, pp. 837–8.

32 Ibid., p. 468.

33 Ibid., p. 534.

34 Hovasse, *Victor Hugo*, p. 635.

35 IV.15.iii, 1,043.

36 Vargas Llosa, *Temptation of the Impossible*, p. 11: 'The main character . . . is this insolent narrator who is constantly cropping up between his creation and the reader.'

37 II.1.i, IV.1.iii.

38 The interior of the barricade looking in the half-light of dawn 'like the deck of a ship in distress' (V.1.ii, 1,059) might count as an exception.

39 III.1.i, 519.

40 'Marie' was a masculine as well as a feminine name until quite recently, especially in hyphenated forms. French continues to have many ungendered first names.

41 Plutarch, *Dialogue on Love*, p. 435.

42 I.2.vi, 78.

Part Three: Rooms with a View

1 III.6.viii, 645; Hugo to Adèle Foucher, 4 March 1822, quoted in *Les Misérables*, ed. Allem, p. 1,623.

2 See 'A Salon of the Past', III.3.i, 549–52.

3 Stapfer, *Victor Hugo à Guernesey*, p. 44.

4 The concluding line of 'Ultima Verba' ('Last Words'), from *Les Châtiments*, Book VII.

5 Note dated 24 January 1861, quoted in Hovasse, *Victor Hugo*, p. 636.

6 The link between sewage and cholera was first established in England by John Snow in the 1850s. The bacillus was first identified in Germany by Robert Koch in 1883. The first vaccine was invented in Russia by Vladimir Haffkin in 1892.

7 Hovasse, *Victor Hugo*, p. 643.

8 *Œuvres complètes*, Édition de l'Imprimerie nationale, vol. 6, p. 409, is a facsimile.

9 *Correspondance*, vol. 2, p. 375.

10 *Correspondance*, vol. 2, p. 375.

11 III.5.iv, 623.

12 Vachon, *Les Travaux*, p. 152, n. 20; Pierrot, 'Quelques contrats d'édition de Balzac', p. 20.

13 Leuilliot, *Victor Hugo publie les* Misérables, p. 28 (letter dated 21 June 1860).

14 Leuilliot, *Victor Hugo publie les* Misérables, p. 98 (letter dated 2 September 1861).

15 *Notre-Dame de Paris* was published on 16 March 1831. Hugo liked numerical coincidences and anniversary dates, even if he had to invent them.

16 Leuilliot, *Victor Hugo publie les* Misérables, p. 100 (letter from Charles Hugo to Lacroix, 9 September 1861, from Spa).

17 Hoffheimer, 'Copyright', pp. 170–71.

18 Leuilliot, *Victor Hugo publie les* Misérables, p. 104 (letter from Hugo to Lacroix, 20 September 1861).

19 Description adapted from Charles Hugo, *Les Hommes de l'Exil*, quoted in Sartorius, 'L'Éditeur Albert Lacroix', p. 18.

20 Quoted in Hovasse, *Victor Hugo*, p. 669.

21 Leuilliot, *Victor Hugo publie les* Misérables, p. 350 (Lacroix to Hugo, 5 June 1862).

22 Victor Hugo to Paul Meurice, 19 December 1861, quoted in Hovasse, *Victor Hugo*, pp. 675–6.

23 Juliette Drouet to Victor Hugo, 5 December 1861, quoted in Hovasse, *Victor Hugo*, p. 676.

24 *Correspondance*, vol. 2, p. 379.

25 The first working submarine cable in the world, from Weymouth via Alderney and Guernsey to St Helier in Jersey, was opened for use on 7 September 1858. It was at the cutting edge of technology and kept on breaking down. On 24 February 1862, the Guernsey–Jersey cable failed again, and in May, the Guernsey office closed for good. During the few months when it was able to provide a reliable service, the Channel Islands Telegraph Company set prices that stunned even Victor Hugo. See Miete, *A History of the Telegraph in Jersey*.

26 Years later, Hugo gave them to Juliette in a hand-made box. They are now at the Château des Roches at Bièvres.

27 Leuilliot, *Victor Hugo publie les* Misérables, pp. 123–4 (Hugo to Lacroix, 12 January 1862).

28 Leuilliot, *Victor Hugo publie les* Misérables, p. 156 (Hugo to Lacroix, 7 February 1862).

29 Leuilliot, *Victor Hugo publie les* Misérables, p. 144 (31 January 1862), p. 155 (7 February 1862).

30 Leuilliot, *Victor Hugo publie les* Misérables, p. 139.

31 Leuilliot, *Victor Hugo publie les* Misérables, p. 159.

32 Leuilliot, *Victor Hugo publie les* Misérables, p. 208.

33 Leuilliot, *Victor Hugo publie les* Misérables, p. 147 (Lacroix to Hugo, 2 February 1862).

34 Leuilliot, *Victor Hugo publie les* Misérables, p. 308 (Lacroix to Hugo, 11 May 1862).

35 Leuilliot, *Victor Hugo publie les* Misérables, p. 149.

36 Leuilliot, *Victor Hugo publie les* Misérables, p. 165 (Hugo to Lacroix, 12 February 1862).

37 French books were sold with pages sewn but not cut and the volume not bound. This explains why *Les Misérables* could be put on sale so soon after printing.

38 Dickens, *Great Expectations*, pp. 16, 373.

39 See Bellos, 'Sounding Out', for a fuller treatment of diction in *Les Misérables*.

40 *William Shakespeare*, quoted in Leuilliot, 'Présentation', p. 57.

41 I owe these insights to Michael Hoffheimer's 'Jean Valjean's Nightmare'.

42 Gogol, *The Overcoat*, p. 565.

43 The word *passant*, often used to draw attention to heroes and especially war victims honoured in memorials and monuments, is an echo of Lamentations I.12.21, 'all ye that pass by' ('vous qui passez par le chemin').

Part Four: War, Peace and Progress

1 Myriel refused to acknowledge Napoleon when he passed through Digne, one of the very few actions that Hugo criticizes in his saintly bishop (I.1.xi, 46).

2 Leuilliot, 'Présentation', pp. 55–6.

3 On Hugo's use (and abuse) of his sources, see Descotes, *Victor Hugo et Waterloo.*

4 'Réponse à un acte d'accusation', in *Contemplations* I.7, lines 65–6: 'Je fis souffler un vent révolutionnaire / Je mis un bonnet rouge au vieux dictionnaire' ('I made a revolutionary wind blow / I put a red cap on the old dictionary').

5 Huard, 'Le Petit-Picpus des *Misérables*', p. 374.

6 'la forme d'une ville / Change plus vite, hélas! que le coeur d'un mortel', from 'Le Cygne', in *Les Fleurs du mal*, 1857.

7 Leuilliot, *Victor Hugo publie les* Misérables, p. 161 (Lacroix to Hugo, 9 February 1862).

8 Leuilliot, *Victor Hugo publie les* Misérables, pp. 161, 162 (Lacroix to Hugo, 9 February 1862).

9 Leuilliot, *Victor Hugo publie les* Misérables, p. 177 (Hugo to Lacroix, 18 February 1862).

10 Sokologorsky, 'Victor Hugo et le XIXe siècle russe', p. 197.

11 Leuilliot, *Victor Hugo publie les* Misérables, p. 155 (Hugo to Lacroix, 7 February 1862).

12 Marx, *Manifesto of the Communist Party*, footnote to the title of Section 1, 'Bourgeois and Proletarians'.

13 Bouchet, *Le Roi et les barricades*, p. 69.

14 Heine, *De la France*, p. 149.

15 IV.11.iv, 969.

16 Heine, *De la France*, p. 243.

17 See Blix, 'Le Livre des passants'; Brombert, *Victor Hugo and the Visionary Novel*, pp. 90–94.

18 Information provided by Serguei Oushakine.

19 Sokologorsky, 'Victor Hugo et le XIXe siècle russe', p. 197.

20 II.5.x, 425; II.3.x, 386; III.8.xx, 724; III.8.xx, 721; V.3.viii, 1,168.

21 No authoritative study of the vocabulary of *Les Misérables* yet exists. My figure is derived from the tables in Étienne Brunet's larger linguistic survey of a corpus of works by Victor Hugo. Computations of this kind must always be taken with a pinch of salt, since they do not usually count different words that are spelled the same way (English

'light' and 'light', for example) or distinguish between words used with radically different meanings (such as (railway) 'train' and (bridal) 'train').

22 The *American Heritage Dictionary* claims there are 29,066 distinct word-forms in Shakespeare's complete works, but that figure includes proper names. Other estimates put Shakespeare's vocabulary range between 18,000 and 25,000.

23 II.8.iii, 487; II.7.iii, 464; V.1.i, 1,051; I.1.viii, 31.

24 IV.6.ii, 866, as 'mosquito net'.

25 V.6.ii, 1,231.

26 See Brunet, *Le Vocabulaire de Victor Hugo*, for a full study of Hugo's lexical exuberance and a list of all the *hapax legomena* ('one-time-only' words) in his work. Hugo also enriched the geography of the Middle East with the fictitious location of Jérimadeth, invented because 'I have to rhyme on "dé"'('j'ai rime à "dait"'), *Booz endormi*, l. 81.

27 I.1.iv, 15; other instances of southern dialects can be found at I.1.i, 6 and I.2.i, 64; IV.15.i, 1,031 (Norman).

28 I.3.vii, 127.

29 Javert's pronunciation of 'Allons vite' ('let's get a move on') as 'allon-ouaite' (I.8.iv, 266) doesn't represent a social or regional accent so much as peremptory, harsh and contemptuous diction.

30 Sainéan, *Le Langage parisien*, p. 95.

31 Paris, '*Ti*, signe d'interrogation'.

32 Vaux, 'A Vocabulary of the Flash Language'.

33 Ibid.

34 Vidocq, *Mémoires*.

35 Huard, 'Le Petit-Picpus des *Misérables*', p. 384. There were also two older guides to 'rough language' that Hugo could have used in the 1840s: Leroux's *Dictionnaire comique* of 1718, and *Histoire et recherches des antiquités de la ville de Paris* by Henri Sauval (1724), one of the main sources for *Notre-Dame de Paris*.

36 Gillery and Rivière, *Je me suis raconté*, p. 18.

37 See Halliday, 'Anti-Languages', for a comparative study of linguistic phenomena similar to thieves' slang.

38 Leuilliot, *Victor Hugo publie les* Misérables, p. 358 (Lacroix to Hugo, 8 June 1862).

39 I.7.ix, 245; III.8.vi, 673.

40 'm'allant coucher je trouvis . . . je m'y couchis'. I.6.v, 445, not represented in the translation; IV.1.iii, 748.

41 I.1.viii, 31; I.3.vii, 125; I.3.vii, 128; III.1.iv, 522; IV.12.i, 976; III.4.v, 608.

42 I.3.vii, 126, 130.

43 III.8.xxii, 735.

Part Five: Great Expectations

1 Parfait, *L'Aurore d'un beau jour*.

2 Robb, *Victor Hugo*, p. 407.

3 Edwards, *Ebenezer Le Page*, pp. 89–90.

4 Hovasse, *Victor Hugo*, p. 693.

5 A. Nefftzer, *Le Temps* (2 April 1862); Adolphe Gaiffe, *La Presse* (2 April 1862), quoted in Bach, 'Critique et politique', p. 595.

6 Adèle Hugo to Victor Hugo, 6 April 1862; quoted in Hovasse, *Victor Hugo*, vol. 2, p. 700.

7 Leuilliot, *Victor Hugo publie les* Misérables, p. 256 (Lacroix to Hugo, 13 April 1862).

8 Adapted from Leuilliot, *Victor Hugo publie les* Misérables, p. 315 (15 May 1862).

9 Leuilliot, *Victor Hugo publie les* Misérables p. 74 gives a good summary of Hugo's views on these matters.

10 Leuilliot, *Victor Hugo publie les* Misérables, pp. 361–2 (Hugo to Lacroix, 11 June 1862).

11 Hovasse, *Victor Hugo*, p. 706–7.

12 A wit has claimed that Hugo addressed the critic as 'Villier-Fleury' so as not to write the sound of a word even more vulgar than Cambronne's *merde*, namely *cul*, meaning 'arse'.

13 Leuilliot, *Victor Hugo publie les* Misérables, p. 312 (12 May 1862).

14 Hugo to Janin, 18 May 1862, quoted in Hovasse, *Victor Hugo*, p. 712.

15 Jules Claye to Victor Hugo, 15 May 1862, quoted in Hovasse, *Victor Hugo*, p. 710.

16 Reported by Adèle in a letter to Hugo, 28 April 1862, quoted in Hovasse, *Victor Hugo*, p. 702. The play was Paul Meurice's *Jean Baudry*, performed at the Comédie française.

17 Leuilliot, *Victor Hugo publie les* Misérables, p. 323, note 9.

18 Leuilliot, *Victor Hugo publie les* Misérables, p. 331 (Lacroix to Hugo, 25 May 1862).

19 Leuilliot, *Victor Hugo publie les* Misérables, p. 286 (27 April 1862) and p. 335 (28 May 1862).

20 *Le Boulevard*, 20 April 1862, in Baudelaire, *Œuvres complètes*, vol. 2, p. 224.

21 Baudelaire, *Correspondance*, vol. 2, p. 254.

22 Flaubert to Mme Roger des Genettes, in *Correspondance*, vol. 3, p. 235.

23 Mérimée, *Correspondance Générale*, vol. 11, p. 177.

24 Dumas, *Correspondances*, p. 288.

25 The Latin tag is translated on p. 218 above.

26 Hugo, letter to Gino Daëlli, 18 October 1862. Included as an afterword in the last edition of *Les Misérables* published in Hugo's lifetime.

27 The phrase was used by Romain Gary in episode 4 of his interview with Patrice Galbeau to explain why his Litwak mother, alongside thousands of other inhabitants of Wilno and Kaunas, thought of emigrating only to France.

28 Hovasse, *Victor Hugo*, p. 720; but see also p. 1,156 n. 236, which reports that government estimates were much lower.

29 *Publishers' Weekly* (2 September, 1916), quoted in Hoffheimer, 'Copyright', p. 174, n. 47.

30 Preface signed 'A. F. Richmond, May, 1863'.

31 My thanks to Jessica Christy for finding the Richmond edition.

32 Pickett, *Pickett and His Men*, pp. 357–9.

33 Stiles, *Four Years Under Marse Robert*, p. 252.

34 Solntsev, 'Les Misérables en Russie et en URSS'.

35 My thanks to Tuo Liu for this information.

36 A. R. W. James, 'Waterloo sans Cambronne'.

37 Adèle Hugo to Victor Hugo, 11 May 1862, quoted in Hovasse, *Victor Hugo*, p. 704.

38 Dickens, *The Public Readings*, contains the transcripts.

39 V.i.xxiii, 1,123.

40 *Der Giber in Keyten*, Warsaw, 1911; a 'life drama in six tableaux' under the same title, dramatized by H. Dashevsky, Vilna, undated; and a separate stage play, *Gavrosh*, 'baarbt in Idish fun Yekhezekl Dobrishin', Moscow, undated.

41 Item 970 in the official catalogue of the Lumières' films at catalogue. lumière.com.

42 Gamel and Serceau, *Le Victor Hugo des cinéastes*, pp. 255–61, gives an exhaustive list of cinema versions of *Les Misérables* down to 2005; see Grossman and Stephens, *Les Misérables and Its Afterlives*, for more up-to-date discussions of film adaptations.

43 Leuilliot, *Victor Hugo publie les* Misérables, p. 366.

44 Laffont edition, vol. 12, p. 536.

45 Ibid, p. 537.

46 Ibid, p. 559.

47 That's why this fragment is referred to as 'The Soul' in some editions.

48 My thanks to Michael Ferrier for sending me the manga and to Patrick Schwemmer for translating and explaining it to me.

49 レ・ミゼラブル少女コゼット (*Re Mizeraburu Shōjo Kozetto*), Nippon Animation, 2007.

50 I owe much of this information to Jessica Christy.

51 'Madeleine' is also the biblical name of a sinner who repents, which makes it quite apt for Valjean in his new guise.

52 I.5.iv, 155.

53 See Bellos, 'Momo et *Les Misérables*'.

54 Gary, *La Nuit sera calme*, p. 25.

55 He can never cease to be an escaped convict and officially a member of the 'most dangerous' class of men.

56 Sartorius, 'L'Éditeur Albert Lacroix', which also reproduces the photographs of the guests and the menu.

57 *Correspondance*, vol. 3, p. 144.

Index of Names

Page numbers in **boldface** indicate longer or more significant mentions.

Index

A NOTE ABOUT THE AUTHOR

David Bellos is a well-known translator of modern French fiction and the author of several prizewinning biographies of French literary figures. His irreverent study of translation, *Is That a Fish in Your Ear?* (2011), was a runner-up for the Los Angeles Times Book Prize and has itself been translated into Korean, Spanish, German, and French. Bellos teaches French and comparative literature at Princeton University and holds the rank of Officier in France's Ordre des Arts et des Lettres.

A NOTE ABOUT THE AUTHOR